Point Man Up

One Marine's Memories of Vietnam

Walter T. Steinbacher

For Jim and Christine,
Have fun and be safe
as you travel through
lifes' adventures.

Semper Fi !
Walter "Stein" Steinbacher

To Denny Eaker, Gary Lorson,
and all whose lives
were touched by this war

Country Gentleman
for Walter T. Steinbacher

What does a seventeen-year-old know?
Daisy gone when I got home, sold
for taxes, two hundred dollars
she brought. I went wild, tearing
out to her empty stall, throwing
myself into her place. Raised
from a calf–how I loved her.
The cleanest straw, the tender
best hay. Many a time I caught
Mom and Dad mulling over her sale,
that winter hard, money scarce. Yet,
I believed that day would never come.
Daisy–the beginning and the end
of my life. Every dawn found me
milking her. Come evening, I'd
confide what happened that day.
She was the one who knew my plans
for saving our farm: I'd buy a whole
herd, heifers, a bull, one collie
to bring them in, cats for keeping
the rats down. Never got over her.
Hated my parent's guts. That spring
I signed up. The Marines. Fall,
Vietnam. When my bunkmates hunkered
inside their weed or hundred proof,
I pictured Daisy, her big, brown eyes
understanding every word I spoke,

how if I made it, I'd scout her out,
spend my days just resting my cheek
against her warm flank, breathing
in her cow breath, her fresh manure.
I'd plant a truck garden, planting
the whole plot while holding off
my fire, what did that doe-eyed kid,
that mama-san do to me or mine, what,
that water buffalo yoked to a plow?
For good and ill, I held my fire.
There'd be long, green rows of Country
Gentlemen corn, carrots, pole beans…
I'd cut the poles from that birch
growing straight out from the hill…
Wounded two days short, dumb luck, but
made it home. Not to Daisy. Married
the girl a cornfield away, work
the swing shift at Bethlehem Steel.
Mother died first. Dad caught up.
They're forgiven now. What the hell,
we had to eat. Built a new foundation
under the barn with stones from White
Deer Mountain. Second hand hinges
match her old stall door. This year,
a crop of hay. And next…
don't tell me a man can't make a good
living out of cows.

-Mary Steinbacher Tisera

Table of Contents

Preface

THE LONG AND TEDIOUS TASK to put into words the events and emotions in this book began in 1988 when I composed a rough draft equivalent to the first eight chapters. A major career change forced me to concentrate on economic survival until, in 2001, I wrote a short story about a particular event in Vietnam that I could no longer keep pent up inside my spirit. After that story, I composed another piece about a six-hour event in Vietnam. A year later, I told myself, 'It's time to start writing a memoir.'

I would not recommend composing a book using my method—pen and dictionary. Yes, the first draft and the edited finished product were handwritten. I can't begin to count the number of pens that were drained of ink. On the other hand, I must admit, while I am computer literate, I am not amused at staring at a screen and I have no patience when the screen doesn't respond because the *wrong* key is hit!

My other activities and passions also slowed my progress while writing. My favorite playground is a large lush garden. Next to the garden, red raspberries, blueberries, and grapes grow happily. To the right of the grapes, apple, pear, peach, and nectarine trees provide more fruit than two families can eat. Another passion is forestry—harvesting firewood, planting trees, and cutting logs for lumber. Simply put, the list includes any task that requires the outdoors and the use of my hands. Most of all, my soulmate and I enjoy supporting our grown children when needed.

Perhaps the single largest obstacle to writing this memoir came from within. Many years passed before I could talk freely about Vietnam. I only talked about it in answer to questions and would quickly squirm free from the subject. Likewise, another stone wall to overcome was my past desire to hide in the shadows and minimize my time in a combat zone. Finally, I looked into the mirror and demanded from myself: 'If you're to write a memoir, you'll have to slide out of the shadows and be totally honest about yourself, the people, and events captured in this book—no candy-coating anything!'

My intent was simply to tell the story of how young, gritty men survived each day confronted with horrific stress. Although I've read and studied many of the ugly policies of the war, I wanted to steer clear of revising the war. Yes, the human race should learn from historical events. However, one hard fact remains: once that steel round leaves the rifle chamber, the artillery shell blasts from the barrel, the mortar round pops from the tube, the bomb falls from the sky—*it becomes history*, because it is impossible to simply push a recall button.

Another crucial message to remember: this memoir is meant to be much larger than my personal journey. There are thousands upon thousands of accounts that could be written. Therefore, I am also writing for all the young men and women who dropped everything they were doing in the '60s and early '70s and left behind secure jobs, classrooms, families, girlfriends, boyfriends, spouses, and children to make a difference for other members of the human race. This memoir is also written for those lives that crossed the Pacific Ocean to the frozen, dangerous tundra of Korea and for those tenacious souls who left loved ones for the Second

World War. And I cannot forget those brave souls who stepped forward in Grenada, Panama, Bosnia, Somalia, who faced the blistering hot sand in the two brutal Iraq Wars, the cold barren mountains of Afghanistan, and many other dangerous locations throughout the world. I am compelled to honor the souls that did not return to their loved ones in a shower of hugs and tears.

Furthermore, this memoir is for *everyone* who, for whatever reason, did not end up in Vietnam or any other war. Not everyone goes to war. In fact, only one half of one percent of the US population are combat veterans. I would have to admit that's a good thing!

I am humbled as you, the reader, turn this page and walk with me 'on point' and then beyond, into my life after Vietnam.

* * *

At 0100 hours, 17 September 1966, in a thick, dark jungle, a few scant miles south of the DMZ that separated North and South Vietnam, Alpha Company, 1st Battalion, 26th Marines, were locked in a death grip with a large force of attacking North Vietnamese Army troopers (NVA). Hundreds of streaking AK-47 rounds filled the air space around me, while hand grenades and mortars were ripping at the red earth around me. I strained my eyes to find targets in the blackness. There were green tracers coming from my right, but there were Marines in that direction, so I had to hold my fire until the NVA attacked from my front. My heart pounded like a jackhammer smashing concrete. It felt like my beating life line would explode out of my chest. I heard continuous screams from men who were injured while rifle fire roared like a motor running at break neck speed. Then, beside me, James Pierce screamed, "Stein, if we don't stop them soon, we'll be fucking overrun!"

Chapter 1:
No Turning Back — October 1965

The Homestead, overlooked by Bald Eagle Mountain

I STEPPED OUTSIDE on a cold, crisp early October morning, as the bright sun began peeking its face over the rugged Bald Eagle Mountain—a range south of the homestead. While standing on the stone sidewalk, I heard Canadian geese squawking and noted their "V" formation as they flew south over the 1500-foot slope. A curious chill shot down my spine. That chill was a big question: 'Would I still be on the mountain when the geese flew north the following spring?'

In early September 1965, I had traveled with a bus-load of eighteen and nineteen-year-old men from nearby cities, valleys, and mountains to New Cumberland's Army Depot. There I passed my pre-induction physical and received an A-1 classification, a rating that guaranteed my ass would be drafted into the U.S. Army in about three months!

I didn't have one good reason for leaving the mountain and the scenic and safe Susquehanna valley. I had a decent job at a local silk mill, Syntex Fabrics, where I was a bobbin filler—and a damn good one! Moreover, I drove a hot 1961 Thunderbird and I thought I was bad shit racing east on Third Street and then west up Fourth Street in Williamsport, against GTOs, Corvettes, and 442 Oldsmobiles. Most of those drivers were also draft-age young men.

I was the oldest sibling left at home. My younger brother, Steve, was in southern Virginia at a seminary. My oldest sister, Mary, was married and living in Erie, Pennsylvania. My younger sisters, Bernadette, Theresa, and Pauline were still in grade school. As the oldest at home, I embraced my role, sharing a portion of my income and tending to the welfare of my younger siblings. Leaving would place a burden on the family and the thought tortured me.

Walter's 1961 Thunderbird

However, my choices in 1965 were limited; allow myself to be drafted by the Army, enroll in a two-year course at a college, flee the country, or lastly, enlist in another branch of the military. None of those choices appealed to me, but I felt a giant magnet was pulling at my spirit to leave my present lifestyle and go assist other members of the human race half-way around the world. Obviously, I had a life-changing decision to make, but I would not succumb easily to any of those poor choices!

As an example, my first day of work the week after the bus trip, I punched out at 2:00 p.m. and sped up Fourth Street as my mind worked overtime. I had decided to join a military branch, ending my misery once and for all. A bit later I pulled the shiny Thunderbird in front of the large grey post office building in Williamsport; the building's second floor housed all the recruiters.

Outside the heavy wooden doors to the main entrance were bright small signs for all branches of the military. I slammed the car door and stormed up the ten stone steps, stopped at the signs, stared and said to myself, 'Screw this.' I took the steps two at a time down and hopped back into the safety of the 'bird. I roared up Fourth Street and headed home.

The next day, Tuesday, I again drove to the post office after my shift, saying to myself, 'Today I will take the plunge and sign up.' I once again climbed those steps and went inside where I was confronted by large colorful, shiny posters displaying the Army, Marines, Navy, and Air Force. There was an arrow pointing up the long stairs to the second floor. The sharply dressed men on the posters seemed to be glaring at me. I thought, 'Enough of this shit,' turned around, and in a flash I was down the steps and back inside my beloved 'bird. As I drove home along the narrow road with the mountain on my left and the peaceful Susquehanna on my right, I pondered whether I should just allow the Army to draft me.

On October 29th, decision made, I went to the post office, briskly ascended the steps, entered the building, and made the long climb to the second floor. To the left was my destination, down a long hallway. All the perfectly dressed recruiters were standing outside their office doors staring straight at me. My heart began pumping faster, especially after climbing the stairs. As I started down the hallway, almost in unison they said, "Can we help you?"

I was speechless. I strutted right past them and stopped at a large window where I could see the crimson-colored trees on the mountain north of Williamsport. I gained my composure and calmly walked back to the tall Marine standing by his door. I asked to talk to him and he motioned for me to enter his office. Sergeant Fellows asked me to sit and got right to the point: "So you think you want to sign on with the Marines?"

I replied, "My draft date is near and I am exploring my options."

"Well," he calmly stated, "we can offer you two, three, and four-year enlistments," but, he warned, "a two-year stint most likely will land you in Vietnam."

I pondered that and then blurted out, "If I join for two years, can I sign on for more years later?" He came back with a yes. I quickly answered, "I'll take two." Upon hearing my response, he shoved some official forms across his desk and I signed for two years plus four reserve years. In one simple stroke of the pen, I had enlisted in the Marines, an institution of warriors since 1775!

Fellows stood, shook my hand, and indicated that he would call later in the month regarding my departure date. I quickly departed and sped home to announce the news. As I entered the warm kitchen, Mom was preparing buckwheat cakes and scrapple over the black combination stove (fueled by wood and coal with gas burners on the opposite side). I greeted her, "It smells heavenly in here Mom."

She smiled and asked, "How was your day today?"

"Mom, I joined the Marines today, and I'll most likely depart soon."

She was visibly shaken; however, her everlasting support for her children shined brightly on her face. "Son, you will come through your time in the Marines with flying colors."

"Maybe, Mom, but will my leaving create a hardship for the family?" She assured me the family would be fine.

The next day after my shift, I was met in the Syntex parking lot by my close childhood friend, Gary Lorson. He shouted at me, "What the hell did you do?"

I replied, "I joined the Marines!"

"You son of a bitch, you didn't even wait for me," he responded. The next day after his shift at Stroehmann's Bread plant, he enlisted! The stage was set for two friends, bonded since they were six years old, to plunge into the Marine Corps institution together. It was our destiny—we attended grade school together and competed fiercely together in baseball, football, and basketball. Despite our bond, I felt a little guilty for sucking him into the Marines.

At suppertime a week later, Mom was cooking our regular Thursday night dinner of spaghetti, meatballs, and coleslaw. Dad arrived from his shift at Pennsylvania Power and Light at Shamokin Dam, Pennsylvania. The phone rang as Dad hung up his coat, and he answered. The recruiter, Fellows, called to confirm my enlistment and give me my departure date.

Dad called up the stairs, "Walter, a Sergeant Fellows wants to talk to you."

I knew what he wanted. "The hell with the Marines!" I yelled back. "I don't want to talk to him."

He hollered again, "Walter you've got to talk to him."

I bounded down the stairs, grabbed the receiver, and coldly said hello. Sergeant Fellows asked me if I was still committed, and if so, the departure date would be November 30th at the bus station at 8:00 a.m. I managed to utter a reluctant yes, and he said he would be in touch if anything changed.

I quickly hung up the receiver and turned to Mom. "Mom, I'll be down for supper in about fifteen minutes. I am going for a short walk in the woods, past the pig pen." I ambled towards the mountain about one hundred yards and sat down on a white ash stump. Dad and I had cut it down with our sharp crosscut saw last year for firewood. The light from the setting sun bounced off the brook stream water and illuminated the brightly colored leaves of the nearby maple tree.

I pondered as I gazed toward the rugged north slope of the Bald Eagle Mountain. As a few tears trickled down my cheek, I thought to myself, 'I'll be leaving you, old girl mountain, but I'll be back someday to climb your rocky slope.' A bit later I sauntered back to the house and reassured myself that there was no turning back now—I would be a Marine.

November passed like a lightning bolt during a thunderstorm. November 29th dawned, and I holed up in the warm kitchen while talking to Mom. It was the first day of buck season in Pennsylvania; however, unlike prior years, I had zero ambition for hunting. Besides, I wanted to have some time one-on-one with Mom. The day passed quickly as she skillfully filled the kitchen with the sweet smell of home-made bread, and I kept the large coal and wood furnace in the basement burning hot.

For supper that night, Mom prepared smoked ham and boiled potatoes with Kentucky wonder beans. As usual, all the food prepared that night came from our small farm, tucked safely beside the mountain. My three sisters, Mom, Dad, and I enjoyed a luscious meal in the cozy kitchen—my last before departing the homestead for the *first* time in my life!

Tuesday morning broke with a crisp wind as the orange sun peeked over the mountain. I was to meet the Sergeant at 8:00 a.m. After watching most of the folks board the bus, I gave Mom and Mrs. Lorson a hug, and Gary and I boarded. As I looked around the bus, it appeared that most of the travelers were young men between eighteen and nineteen years of age. They were all headed south to be sworn into the military. It demonstrated that along the Susquehanna River and throughout the surrounding mountains and valleys, the West Branch Valley's parents were already giving up their sons to the military in late 1965.

The driver slammed the door shut after loading the passengers and bags, and the bus lumbered across the Market Street bridge, soon turning south to travel along the mountain. I looked up at the mountain and pondered—what the hell would happen to me during the coming great adventure?

* * *

We arrived in Philadelphia at 3:00 p.m. and quickly changed buses to take us to a large government building. Next, we entered a large room and found more civilians, all waiting to be sworn into the Army or Marines—more than seventy-five bodies standing tall.

"I swear to defend the USA and our Constitution from all foreign enemies..." That oath was a damn serious statement—it meant we were ready to die for our country! But what eighteen- or nineteen-year-old man or woman wanted to die for any cause or country? The afternoon passed quickly, and by 6:00 p.m. (now 1800 hours) Gary and I were at the Philadelphia airport seated in a large four-propeller airplane. We sped down the runway, lifted above the twinkling city lights, and headed south. Our adventure was only beginning, but it was exhilarating flying for the first time.

Two hours later the plane touched down in Charleston, South Carolina. We got off the plane and our group gathered in a room at the terminal to wait for buses to take us to Parris Island. While we waited, we stared into space and no one talked. Thoughts of that mysterious island were dancing in our heads. At midnight the wait ended as I boarded a bus. Soon there were two buses speeding south on a bumpy, two-lane road. Around 0130 hours the brakes screeched, and out of nowhere two Marines wearing broad-brimmed Smokey-bear hats burst through the open bus door. They screamed and cursed, "You fucking girls, fall out; I want this bus cleared in one second."

Following that outburst, frightened men smashed into each other, desperately attempting to get out, stumbling with their hearts racing. I thought, 'My God, this can't be real—what do I do next?' as I shoved my way past a foaming-from-the-mouth drill instructor, who yelled: "You scumbags, move!"

The mystique of Parris Island unfolded before me. To my left and right men took up positions standing on yellow footprints painted on the pavement, awaiting the next assault from the DIs. Everyone was thinking, *'What the fuck hell-hole did I stumble into this time?'*

We were marched at a race pace towards an old white building with the DI ranting, "Get into step, ladies." Absurd, since we knew zero about marching or staying in step. We tripped into the building and were told to find a rack and get some sleep. It was 0430h.

At 0530 hours the chaos resumed. The DI shouted, "Did you girls think you were going to sleep the day away? Fall in." Fall in where? "Dumb fucks, get in front of your racks and face me, now! You civilians are about to get a taste of Marine Corps chow."

We fell out into the chilled air as we half-assed marched to the mess hall with two screaming DIs on each side of the formation. We chowed down some scrambled eggs, shit on the shingle (a concoction of creamed hamburger on toast), and orange juice. The DIs roved around knocking hands off of the table, shouting, "You ladies need one arm on your lap and one to slop down the food." It immediately became apparent to me that any old habits from our past lives were taboo at Parris Island.

To erase all semblance of civilian appearance, the first order of business was the buzz haircut, and then the fitting of clothing. We looked like ragamuffins in our wrinkly greens. No starching of uniforms until a few days before graduation, they told us. The day flew by and before long it was noon, chow time, and then PT, followed by a two-mile run. There was a lot of panting and wheezing and sweating bodies. Sergeant Bradley halted us and screamed, "That was just a taste, ladies. We'll get that civilian blood out before I am done with you!"

At 2200 hours, after a breakneck day, we hit the racks. But before the lights switched off, we were ordered to recite the Lord's Prayer.

Day two at 0500 hours the DI slammed on the lights shouting, "Everyone out of those racks, I mean now!" Eighty groggy lives were scrambling and stumbling to get in front of the racks. The slow ones drew scorn from the DI, who continued to shout instructions. "And then count off one at a time down the line of bunks and back the other way as you yell your name." When it became my turn, I shouted: "Private Steinbacher at attention."

Thus, our established routine became clear. Fall out for a run, then chow, military classes, run, and more marching. Evenings from 1800h to 2200h included chow, shoe shining, uniform preparation, showering, and then writing letters. Finally, as we lay flat in our bunks, reciting the Lord's Prayer, the DI would snap off the lights. I usually fell fast asleep in minutes.

After the first week, the shock of boot camp subsided, and my confidence increased. Pride set in, knowing that if the men beside me could conquer this hefty challenge, then I could conquer it with them.

Parris Island was a world separated from ordinary people's everyday pursuits. The sights and sounds conjured up a mysterious planet. Early morning and late afternoon, hundreds of recruits were drilling on a giant parade deck; the drill instructors were barking cadence—AR, PR, left—in deep echoing voices, while the eighty-man platoons banged shoe leather to the cadence, in unison. Likewise, other orders echoed through the air—to the rear, march, left oblique, right oblique, right shoulder arms, left shoulder arms—followed by the loud clapping of rifle butts slamming down on pavement and shoulders.

In week six, our platoon moved to the new barracks at the rifle range. Our first three days were spent snapping in, which consisted of conditioning the muscles, using the rifle sling to train our arms and shoulders and upper body to hold the rifle steady while sitting, standing, and laying in the prone position. Without question, those exercises were the most painful I endured during boot camp. However, that method of madness was necessary to train us to hold the heavy M-14 super tight while firing at 200, 300, and 500 yards. Skilled instructors also taught us to hit a 20-inch bulls-eye at 500 yards in the prone position.

After another week of rifle training, Friday was qualification day and I was all over the targets on the 200 standing and 300 sitting, but my rifle instructor discovered that my rear peep was loose. He properly tightened the peep and I shot well the following eight rounds; however, not quite well enough. I needed a score of 190 to qualify as a marksman, but I shot a 186. Twelve of us recruits failed to qualify, and we were ordered to the side and stand at attention. You were considered a disgrace, a dunce, if you failed to qualify. Like everyone else I felt low, but I quickly recovered, knowing that I was deadly bringing game home for the family—always with single shot weapons. Fuck those stupid targets. I knew I could shoot.

The last week of boot camp we marched for hours on end to prepare for the final competition the day prior to graduation where the platoons competed for the top marching unit in the battalion.

That week we completed the last brutal physical fitness tests and the five-mile run, carrying fifty pounds on our back and rifle in hand.

Then, graduation day came. Somehow I held up and survived this incredible challenge. Even though I knew I was in good physical shape when I left home, doubts still persisted—would I make it?

Graduation day on Parris Island is a grand event with parents invited to sit in the grandstands. Unfortunately, Mom, Dad, and Gary's parents were unable to attend. Each platoon marched by in review and formed a battalion which consists of twelve platoons. Then we were inspected and officially declared Marines. We were now members of a proud institution that had endured since 1775. We were expected to uphold traditions that included bloody campaigns and wars since the Revolution.

After the graduation ceremony, 900 proud and sharp young men were given free time until 1700 hours. Gary and I explored the PX and ate burgers and French fries at the base cafeteria. As we returned to the barracks, the DIs were waiting. After pushing us to the edge for the past nine weeks, they did an about face, and we were treated with respect for the first time. The cursing and 'scumbags and ladies' language ceased as they welcomed us into the fraternity.

* * *

On February 2nd, a cold, windy morning, Gary and I stepped up into one of the many buses for the trip to Camp Lejeune, North Carolina. After five hours, we entered the gate at Camp Lejeune mainside. I peered out the window and before me I saw many neat barracks and other freshly painted buildings—an improvement compared to the Island, I thought. The buses drove on for a few more miles into the boonies where we stopped at a sprawling camp named Geiger—a drab looking camp dominated by grey buildings and Quonset huts.

After leaving the bus, we soon were in a cattle truck bouncing further out into the boonies. A short time later we arrived at our final destination, yet another camp dominated by Quonset huts. I jumped from the cattle truck and soon I was assigned to A Company, part of a training battalion. Gary was assigned to the same Company, but in a different platoon.

I dragged my sea bag into my new home, a grey Quonset hut, also home to a platoon of men. That night I slept well, but kept the green wool blanket pulled to my chin because I was in a bunk some distance from the little oil-fired stove—the only source of heat. The next morning the entire company marched three-quarters of a mile through a lush, loblolly pine forest to the giant mess hall at Camp Geiger.

After breakfast, we marched back to our huts and by 0900 hours the company boarded cattle trucks for a ride to the firing range where we began our intense training. Later that morning, I was introduced to a vast arsenal of weapons including: the Bazooka, a World War II-era rocket launcher; M-72 LAW, a plastic rocket launcher; and M-60 machine gun, capable of spitting out more than 500 rounds a minute. Another weapon, the M-79 40-millimeter, fired like a breach-loaded single-shot shotgun. Although we didn't fire anything that day, the instructor informed us, "By the end of the week you'll all be proficient at shooting these weapons." By Saturday afternoon I had mastered all those weapons. As soon as training ended early Saturday, we were granted time off until Monday morning. After the first week, I thought AIT at Lejeune was slack time compared to boot camp.

The next three weeks went by fast. I was busy packing exciting new skills into my brain, best illustrated in a February 24th, 1966 letter to Mom and Dad.

Dear Mom & Dad,

Time to say hello again. I am still here and training just as hard as ever. I hope both of you are fine.

We did some interesting things this week so far. I threw live hand grenades, fired the flame thrower, had an interesting two-hour orientation on Vietnam, not to mention crawling through the infiltration course which consisted of live machine gun fire going over my head & T.N.T. going off in nearby pits. These barbed-wire obstacles are quite tricky at times. Remember Mom, I told you about such a course before leaving home. Tonight I am supposed to be bivouacking, but they called it off because of rain and cold weather. What a relief. Today I ate "C" rations for the first time and it was a 'big deal' for being the first time. You get a neat little box with meat in one can, fruit in another and peanut butter and crackers or cheese spread. No one complained either because it was a change from the chow hall.

This I.T.R. training is producing 5,000 trained Marines in one month which is a 3,000 raise over last year. I read a paper where it said the Marine trainees are putting forth more towards training than ever before.

Well, I have to be going again so,

> *God bless you both always,*
>> *Wally*

P.S. Your last letter and sports was well appreciated.

About a week after sending that letter home, I was informed that I needed more advanced infantry training because my military MOS was 0311 Infantry. In short, this meant I was destined to be a 'Marine grunt,' a 'ground pounder.' Turns out that Gary also classified as 0311; thus, we would be traveling home together the third week of March.

The first Sunday of March, my cousin, Gary Steinbacher, contacted me and said he could pick me up at Camp Stone Bay. My cousin had joined the Marines right after high school in June 1964 and was now stationed at Lejeune. Quickly I contacted the NCO on duty and he gave me an afternoon leave as long as I stayed on the base.

A bit later, Gary picked me up and he drove me in to mainside Camp Lejeune in his shiny 1963 Buick LeSabre. While at mainside, he took me to the cafeteria and we had a burger and drank some coffee. Neither Gary nor I were of legal age to drink alcohol. Shooting the bull with a cousin from Pennsylvania was a diversion from my training. Later, at 1700 hours he let me out in front of my barracks and shouted, "Take care jarhead!" I did not see my cousin again until late February 1968, two years later.

The next few weeks training was fast and furious. The first week our instructors, some Vietnam veterans, gave classes about what a Marine would encounter in the paddies and jungles—booby traps, snipers, and snakes. We also walked through simulated jungle trails. The last ten days I received a taste of company-sized war games, where we chased down aggressors while shooting blanks from our M-1 rifles. I slept under the stars a few times and woke with frost on my blanket. And finally, the last day of training—the most exciting event of the past three and a half months—I was picked up by a helicopter in pitch blackness and joined by Marines in other choppers. We flew briefly over the

Atlantic Ocean and about a half-hour later we dropped into a landing zone surrounded by loblolly pines. Once the choppers lifted out of the LZ, we marched a half mile back to Camp Stone Bay.

The next morning, March 21st, I received my orders: "Leave from March 23rd until April 23rd, then report to Camp Pendleton, California, where you will be part of 1st Battalion, 26th Marines, 5th Marine Division"—which had previously been disbanded after the Second World War. It was a sobering moment, as I knew Camp Pendleton duty was only a stopover on the journey to Vietnam.

* * *

Early morning on March 22nd, Gary Lorson and I boarded a Greyhound bus at Lejeune for the long trip to Williamsport, Pennsylvania. When we pulled into the Washington, D.C., terminal, the driver announced, "Those people traveling north have a six-hour layover." Gary and I promptly found a small local bar a few steps from the terminal to celebrate the hard work of the last four months. We sloshed down some beer, smoked a few cigarettes, and enjoyed our new freedom from military discipline. When the bus pulled out of the terminal, I was fully relaxed and slept some of the time before we arrived in Williamsport at 7:00 a.m.

The next few days I enjoyed life back at the homestead, the nightly meals with Mom, Dad, Bernadette, Theresa, and the youngest, Pauline. After that first week, I visited friends, cousins, aunts, uncles, and most importantly, my sister Mary and brother Steve.

I traveled to Lyndora, Pennsylvania, to visit Mary, her husband Horacio, and nine-month-old John. I had a delightful visit, interacting with the little guy and talking with Mary and Horacio about old times. When I drove out of Lyndora, a thought streaked through my mind: 'Will I ever see her, the new baby she's carrying, and Horacio again?'

Two days later I sped south with Mom and Dad to visit Steve at Father Judge Seminary, 390 miles south of the homestead. We spent two joy-filled days at the Seminary; however, when I waved goodbye and drove away, tears streamed down my cheeks. I wondered if I would ever see my brother again. Throughout my leave, that recurring thought hit me every time I said goodbye.

About ten days before my departure date, I became increasingly stir crazy, and felt the need to perform a task using my hands. The next day I started hand spading the large garden in the back of the homestead. Dad did not own a tractor; thus, he had to hire neighbors to plow the deep, fertile soil each spring. That spring I was the tractor, turning over spade after spade of soil, row by row. I was joined each morning by doves cooing out by the spring house. In the apple trees, bright red cardinals sang their happy songs of spring, as they had done my entire lifetime.

I hated leaving that sweet-smelling soil and the birds behind, but I knew I had a job to do. I was leaving on a long journey to help some people living 11,000 miles from these hills. Four days before my departure date, I had plowed an area one hundred feet by sixty feet. It was about three quarters of the ground where we planted tomatoes, cabbage, corn, beets, carrots, melons, peppers, squash, and other food-stuff needed to feed our family during the cold and snowy winters of northern Pennsylvania. I was extremely pleased—maybe it was the last deed I would give the family.

Three days before leaving, I took my dear next-door neighbor and girlfriend, Diane, up the road to the fire tower on White Deer Mountain—the very site that Dad and Mom visited before they married. Dad took our family to the tower atop a 2,000-foot mountain in the fall when the leaves turned crimson. To me it was a spiritual site. It was peaceful and tranquil. From the top of the tower, blue mountains were visible for twenty-five miles in every direction. I needed to experience that mystical place one last time with Diane by my side. That morning, we climbed half way up the tower and I held her tight as we looked north towards the many mountains. Just above us, vultures floated in the wind as tears slid gently down my cheeks.

Diane and Walter, April 1966

Sunday afternoon Diane and I had our picture taken by the lush blue spruce tree in front of the homestead. Diane was radiant, dressed in a cute, green wool dress. I had my dress green Marine uniform on for the occasion. Although we were both teary-eyed when the picture was taken, I considered the tree a good luck charm since our family had used that tree as a backdrop for many pictures over the years.

On Monday morning I was already out of bed when the sky showed crimson from the east. I wanted to say goodbye to Dad, who left daily at 5:45 a.m. Dad was a maintenance man and welder at Pennsylvania Power and Light, located 35 miles south of our home. Although he had not served in the military, Dad worked as a welder during the Second World War at Sparrows Point Yard in Baltimore, Maryland, where he helped build ships.

After drinking a cup of coffee together, Dad grabbed his steel lunch box and started towards the kitchen door. He stopped abruptly, turned sharply around and he hugged me—we had never hugged before. I knew he was being brave as he walked down the mountain-stone steps, crossed the bridge over the brook, opened the door of his 1957 Chrysler, and drove out of the driveway, never looking back. In that moment he had given up both his sons—this one to the military, his other son to the Seminary some three years earlier.

Around 7:30 that morning I drank a cup of freshly perked coffee as The Mamas & the Papas sang 'Monday, Monday' on the little radio in the warm kitchen. I heard the train whistle blow on a train passing the house on tracks 100 yards away. By 10:00 a.m. I would be on a train traveling west.

I dragged my heavy sea bag out the door at 9:30, looked up at the mountain one last time, and got behind the wheel of my Thunderbird. Diane, who faked illness and skipped school to see me off, sat beside me in the front seat. Mom and Bernadette also came to say goodbye. When we arrived at the train station, Gary was waiting with his mother, June. A short while later, the train whistle blew, and we shared hugs, kisses, and tears, and then Gary and I boarded the train. Minutes later we both waved through the closed window to all those loved ones standing on the platform as the train smoked west. The same scenario played out at scores of train stations, bus stations, and airports across the country on that Monday morning in late April 1966.

Chapter 2:
Vietnam, at Last

Walter in front of barracks at Camp Las Pulgas in California

AFTER WE LEFT THE STATION, Gary poked me on the arm and proclaimed, "This is it Steinbacher, this train is bound for the west coast—our days of wine and roses are about shot, and we'll be Marines when we drop into Pendleton."

The train slowly traversed through the deep valleys of Pennsylvania, arriving at 1700 hours in Buffalo, New York. Upon entering the busy station, we were told there was a six-hour layover until the next train left for Chicago. Gary had a cousin living outside of Buffalo and he quickly called her from the nearest phone booth. As soon as he hung up, Gary showed a wide grin, "We're in luck, Steinbacher, her husband Jack is picking us up in 25 minutes." When we walked into his cousin Mary's kitchen, she had prepared a table full of luscious food, including cold cuts, cheeses, hot macaroni salad, and some chocolate chip cookies for dessert. After filling our stomachs and visiting with our gracious hosts, Gary and I said our goodbyes and Jack drove us twenty miles back to the grey, dreary old train station. I never forgot about those two people who went out of their way to give us a break on the long trip that would carry Gary and I far away from our homes.

By midnight we were on the train, clanking towards Chicago. After sleeping only a few hours, I stepped out of the train and entered the sprawling Chicago station. The large station resembled a military camp, since many Marine, Navy, Army, and Air Force personnel were milling around waiting for the Santa Fe Special that would take us all to California.

After a three-hour layover, I boarded the bright orange Santa Fe Special and sat with Gary on the upper level. I noticed immediately the smooth ride when the train got rolling—a vast improvement compared to the swaying and bumpy trains from Williamsport and Buffalo.

Later that afternoon I met many Marines I knew from boot camp and Camp Lejeune. Like me, many had orders for the 1st Battalion, 26th Marines. Some, however, were Vietnam bound after a short stay at Pendleton.

The next two days passed quickly as I socialized with other Marines at the cafeteria, where we could drink beer. On the last day, the orange diesel pulled the passenger cars through the snow-covered Rocky Mountains and then, like magic, we emerged into lush, semi-tropical Southern California, where palm trees rose from the landscape.

At 1300h, I stood outside the train station near Los Angeles waiting for a bus to take me to Camp Pendleton. An hour later Gary and I rode up the coastal highway north towards our final stop. Camp Pendleton, mainside, was a well-maintained and landscaped base compared to Camp Geiger. After stepping off the bus, we were met by a Sergeant who checked everyone's orders. I soon learned that all men assigned to the 26th Marines would be staying here at mainside overnight and then would take a bus to Camp Las Pulgas the next day.

While walking to the mess hall the next morning, I witnessed a stunning scarlet sunrise coming over the rugged mountains east of Pendleton. An hour later, I looked out the window of a bus, driving through scrubby, hilly country. We descended a hill into a large valley, where I caught a glimpse of my new home, Camp Las Pulgas, nestled on the valley floor. The bus passed many large buildings, grey Quonset huts, and then stopped in front of a lot of concrete buildings with windows.

We dragged our heavy sea bags out on the street between the rows of barracks and waited until a Sergeant came by with a roster containing names. "Private Steinbacher, you're assigned to Alpha

Company, 3rd Platoon," as he pointed, "those barracks to your front." Gary, on the other hand, was assigned to Delta Company.

Camp Las Pulgas, May 1966

As I settled in, I noticed only ten men occupied the barracks. I soon learned that many more men would be gradually arriving to fill the roster of the Battalion. While we waited that first week, I was on work details: raking leaves, digging out dead shrubs, and cleaning the barracks. In general, it was slack duty. During the second week, the barracks filled quickly, and I finally met our platoon commander: First Lieutenant Van Dine—crew cut, lean, about 21 years old, exuding confidence, and ready to lead thirty-nine men in the platoon. He told us we would train to become a BLT, Battalion Landing Team, and our training would be rigorous. Hell, I didn't expect anything less, because the training over the past months had followed the same pattern, pushing men to their limit!

I met some of the non-commissioned officers the next day. Sergeant Collen, a veteran of the Korean War, was Platoon Sergeant. My squad leader was Sergeant Freeman from Tennessee, who had over three years in the Corps. Others included Corporals Falone, Donaldson, Stumpenhaus, and Mendez. While Mendez had already completed one tour in Vietnam, most of the other remaining members had less than six months of service.

Two members of Walter's platoon

As I looked around that day, I realized that a diverse group made up our platoon. One man was from Puerto Rico, another was a Navajo Indian, thirteen were African Americans, and twenty-six were Caucasians. In May 1966 in the Marines, African Americans were called 'Splibs,' and they were fully comfortable with that name. Whites were referred to as 'Chuck Dudes.' I wondered how they arrived at the name. A Splib from Kentucky explained the origin saying, "It came from 'Charles,'—the always present white person who discriminated back home concerning job offers and other benefits whites enjoyed." Regardless, those names worked for us.

On a hot Monday morning, three days later, training commenced for Alpha Company with a six-mile forced march over 'Sheep Shit Mountain' and a few mountains beyond. No surprise, since we needed to be in superb physical shape to stand a chance of surviving the stifling temperatures in Vietnam.

On the next forced march, we met A Company's Executive Officer, First Lieutenant Getlin, twenty-two years old and in excellent shape. We took our first break on the side of a grassy hillside where a western diamondback rattlesnake was rattling not far off. Lieutenant Getlin was addressing the company about training in the coming weeks when he glanced towards the rattling sound, said, "Excuse me a minute," and walked towards the snake in the grass. He picked up the four-foot squirming rattler and proclaimed, "While we're here I will give some tips on these guys, because we'll encounter many of them up close during the next two months." Then he pulled out his sharp Ka-Bar knife, letting the agitated serpent bite the blade while white poison trickled down. Following that demonstration, he backed away, sliced off the snake's head and threw the body into the grass. Oh yes, we got the message—that man was not to be fucked with. He was a leader of men!

The following days, I settled into my training, focused on learning everything I could about combat tactics, fireteam functions, and squad tactics. In fact, I caught a break early in my training days when Sergeant Freeman designated me a point scout. I embraced that role since I wanted to be up front, in control of my own destiny and the destiny of the men following me. Moreover, I sure as hell didn't want some 'big city' kids stumbling us around in the boonies. Yes, they were considerably better street fighters than me, but that's the beauty of the human race: we all bring different skill sets to the table.

May passed like a shooting star flashing through the night sky. The battalion kept extremely busy conditioning our bodies, marching and running over the hills of Pendleton. We also had classes where we learned about the Vietnamese culture and language. Those classes taught us to respect the natives—no abuse permitted. Likewise, we were trained in the humane handling of prisoners of war.

Fittingly, on Memorial Day the battalion was granted our first weekend liberty, off base. Gary and I caught a bus on Saturday for Hollywood. That morning we checked into a clean room, one block south of Sunset Boulevard. We walked around the boulevard that afternoon, checking out the hot cars cruising down the famed street. In fact, I even spotted a few shiny Thunderbirds like mine.

Later that afternoon we both chowed down on tender steak at an up-scale restaurant on the Strip, after which we boarded a bus for Dodger Stadium where Sandy Koufax pitched for the Dodgers. Gary and I were thrilled to watch that famed pitcher throw his sharp curve ball. Yes, we could see that ball break from the upper deck. Following that exciting game, we took a bus back to the Strip.

The Strip was a flurry of activity at night, with bright lights and young men and women buzzing down the street riding in Corvettes, Dodge Mopars, Pontiac GTOs, and other rods. You're damn right, I felt a little jealous. If I were back home I would be racing up and down Third and Fourth Street in Williamsport in my T-bird. But, I felt glad to enjoy time with my old hometown friend.

After strolling around for an hour or so, taking in the action, we retired to our hotel room. The next morning, we enjoyed breakfast in a quaint restaurant—quite the contrast to eating in a noisy mess hall! Gary and I then spent the next four hours exploring the area of Hollywood where movies were produced before boarding a bus at 1300h to head south towards Pendleton. Back at Camp Las Pulgas, we separated and went to our respective Company areas.

Gary Lorson and Walter at Camp Las Pulgas

On Tuesday morning, A Company humped into the mountains for an operation to fight 'aggressor forces' who were lurking in the pine and cactus fields. I was given the opportunity to be a fireteam leader on that operation, charging and screaming orders to other men who were charging and shooting blanks, attempting to take the hill from the aggressors. Hell yes, I acted super aggressively—

I knew that 'pretend' training had no real steel rounds coming towards my body!

I was assigned to a group of Marines that would train the rest of the Battalion in amphibious operations the second week of June. In general, our group demonstrated techniques used when climbing down and up on landing nets thrown over the side of the ship. We also demonstrated boarding and exiting Amtracs (amphibious landing craft). By the end of the week 800 men witnessed our demonstrations. For me, it was a welcomed break from pounding the snake and prickly cactus-laced hills.

The following Monday our company went aboard an old, grey LST, or Landing Ship Tank, to prepare for a Battalion operation making landings from ship to shore. During the first exercise we had to climb down rope nets slung over the side of the ship. What a murderous task, as we had fifty-pound packs and rifles strapped over our backs! As we took steps down, the waves pushed our bodies back up as much as four feet, all while the nets (and we) were slamming off the bouncing ship. Below, the landing boats were also bouncing off the ship. Lose your grip on the ropes and it was a long drop into the boat, or worse yet, you could get pinched between the ship and the landing craft. Thankfully, we all made it into the landing craft without drowning or getting crushed.

We returned to the ship that night and early the next morning we squeezed into Amtracs in the ship's hold. The giant jaws on the front of the LST opened, and one-by-one the 'tracs splashed into the water. I felt scared as I huddled with many other men in total darkness while the operators above, only a few feet above the water, steered the lumbering monster towards shore. A bit later the machine touched the beach sand and the ramp opened. In seconds we hit the water and ran headlong toward the beach objective.

After engaging the aggressors in war games that morning, we once again found ourselves in Amtracs churning towards the waiting LST. When our Amtrac attempted to grind up the ramp into the ship's hold, it slipped off the side of the ramp and we splashed into the water like a lead ball. I slid against the side of the Amtrac in the darkness and it felt like we were going to roll over. In training we were warned that an overturned Amtrac means everyone drowns. What an ironic event that would have been—the newspapers would report: "Twenty Marines perish in an Amtrac while training for Vietnam duty!" Much to our relief, the bobbing 'trac by some miracle leveled out, and I heard the roaring engine and the treads clawing up the steel ramp and into the hold. Twenty Marines would see the next sunrise.

We went ashore the next day and rode buses back to Camp Las Pulgas—our final operation at Pendleton ended. A day later the entire battalion assembled at the drive, in theater, to be briefed by a general. His opening words: "1/26 will see combat in South Vietnam." That didn't surprise us since we had already heard rumors regarding our fate.

That final weekend in June, Gary and I caught a bus to Tijuana, Mexico, where we would have a 'legal' drink before leaving California. In Tijuana we secured a nice room for eleven dollars and then hit the town. The bars we visited were tame compared to the wild stories told by other Marines. For instance, the female dancers were fully covered, and the interiors of the bars were well maintained. Generally, we had a time, drinking and talking. We both knew that communication would be difficult after we boarded our respective ships.

At midnight we bought a bottle and retired to our room where we slammed down a few more drinks and then hit the beds. We had to be back at the base by late afternoon and were a bit concerned about getting backed up at the border. By 0700 hours, we were up and dressed in our summer khaki uniforms. I glanced out the window and down at the street corner where I spotted a man selling tacos. After a quick drink, Gary and I checked out of the hotel and bought four tacos each for breakfast. "Two for a quarter, not bad huh? Steinbacher?"

"What the hell, Gary? This town never sleeps—the 'red light' girls are on the streets already."

We walked around until 0900 hours and quickly found a bus that would take us across the border and back to Pendleton. As expected, the border crossing consumed an hour, but we made the trip to Las Pulgas in time to check in before 1700 hours.

Walter visiting Del Mar Beach, California, July 1966

Marines at Camp Las Pulgas began packing bags and equipment the first week of July in preparation for the movement south to the San Diego Naval Base where three ships awaited us. Simply put, 1/26 was marching off to war!

Walter, ready for deployment, July 1966

After the barracks were cleaned and our sea bags were sent to San Diego, I had slack time during the rest of the week. Two nights Gary and I played basketball against Marines from across the country. The competition was fierce, and I loved competing against the best players. During that final week, we were also granted liberty every night, and I took advantage by exploring Riverside, 12 miles from Las Pulgas, near the ocean. I wasn't old enough to drink in California, and most of us were below the age of twenty-one, so I enjoyed sunset walks out on the long pier overlooking the vast Pacific Ocean. One night I watched a movie, *Night of the Grizzly*, starring Clint Walker, a six-foot-six actor popular at the time. Ultimately, the week passed quickly, and Sunday morning Gary and I went to Mass at the quaint Spanish-style church that rested on a small hill above Las Pulgas. After church we talked a while before going to our company areas to square away our remaining clothes that we'd be carrying on the ships.

As the hot sun came up over the easterly mountains on Monday morning, we leisurely ate our late breakfast at the mess hall before joining our fellow Marines under the canvas roof of a ten-wheel truck. At 0900h, the convoy started moving slowly out of Las Pulgas, with 1,200 men under the canopy covers, truck after truck, traveling the sixty-five miles to San Diego.

By 1300 hours, we reached our destination and jumped out of the trucks at the base near some docks. The dock area buzzed with activity. Giant overhead cranes on rails were loading supplies onto ships. The smell of diesel fuel, spewing from the boats and large lift trucks, filled the air. Sergeant Freeman came by and pointed to the *Vancouver*, our home for the next few months. Twenty minutes later, we walked up the gangway and boarded the ship where we were directed to our sleeping quarters below deck. I grabbed a bottom bunk in a narrow hold, about thirty feet long and eight feet wide.

We were granted leave in San Diego later that afternoon, but we had to be back on the ship by 2300 hours. Our fireteam—McClure, Pierce, Falduti, and I—went to center city San Diego. For excitement we walked around, taking in the bright city lights, the foxy girls walking by, and the busy traffic speeding down the streets. After enjoying coffee and a donut, I stopped at a pay phone to call home one last time.

Fighting back tears I told Mom and Dad that my ship was leaving port at 0900h the next morning. Surrounded by the noise of downtown San Diego, I hung up and dialed Diane's number. I told her I'd send a letter upon reaching Hawaii and said, "Goodbye, Diane." Then I thought, 'She's sixteen, waiting for a next letter from a man headed to war!' After my phone calls, our fireteam took a cab back to the dock, boarding before 2230 hours.

The next morning at 0900h the whistles blew and over the intercom I heard that we were casting off. While the ship began to steam out of the harbor, a small crowd of Marines, including myself, went back to fantail to watch the water churning behind us as the powerful engines powered forward. To the left, the *Iwo Jima*, a converted World War II aircraft carrier, loaded with helicopters, was also on the move. To the right, the *Thomaston* cut through the waves. First Battalion, 26th Marine Landing Team— 1200 young men and equipment—was on the move! We were some of the best trained troops America could put on the field in July 1966. Thankfully, we were joined by likewise, highly skilled Navy men to support us and navigate the ship, since we Marines knew little about operating a 600-foot-long floating city. In the distance, under the bright morning sky, I watched the United States of America disappear from my view. 'I can't turn back now, I am floating to an unknown world and events!'

* * *

The next few days I spent getting acclimated to life aboard my new floating home. First, I quickly discovered the Navy cooks served tasty food. Second, the physical activity was relaxed compared to the rigorous training at Pendleton. Third, after light physical training following breakfast, I had free time to write letters, visit the small PX, and watch a movie on deck at night.

The three ships steamed into Pearl Harbor on July 12th. I was on the flight deck, looking at a half-sunken ship in the harbor, which served as a stark reminder of the surprise attack of December 7th, 1941. Within an hour after anchoring, we were granted liberty to explore Honolulu and Waikiki Beach. Luckily, I met Gary on the dock and we took a bus to town where we spent the day strolling near Waikiki Beach. While near the water we took a few pictures of sites, such as the distant Diamond Head Mountain and the beach. Later we enjoyed some luscious food in town and slammed down a few drinks, since Hawaii had a drinking age of eighteen. Plus, as I recall, all drinks were a dollar regardless if it was beer or a mixed concoction. Gary and I parted around nine that night, and I told him we should try to get together when the ships docked in Subic Bay in the Philippines.

Gary Lorson in Hawaii, July 1966

The next day I went into town with some of the Marines in my squad. We walked around, enjoyed some drinks, and went back on board early that evening.

Before the sun came over the eastern horizon, our three ships were in open water steaming away from Hawaii. I could sense the urgency for the battalion, in that we appeared to have a time limit regarding travel from one destination to another. Only time would tell—I knew a Private First Class like me would be the last to get the word.

The next several days passed quickly for me; each day marked the same routine—breakfast, P.T., free time. The slack duty gave us time to contemplate our mission in Vietnam and events occurring back in the states. In no way were we blind participants headed to Vietnam, and discussions on the deck after dark revealed our thoughts. One night, Corporal Stumpenhaus, who left the University of Missouri to serve, asked, "Are we doing right, intervening in Vietnam?"

One Marine responded: "I don't know either, but this ship is not taking us on some fucking vacation cruise!"

Another Marine with two and a half years' experience noted, "As Marines, it's good to ask questions, but we will be at the tip of the spear when we land—we do not have the luxury of talking from the safety of home, the United States."

After breakfast, a few days later, the company assembled on the flight deck. "Listen up," our captain spoke, "we are approaching Iwo Jima and we will stand at parade rest until we pass that island." He didn't have to instruct us as to what event occurred on that eight-square-mile island in February and March 1945. We knew the 1st Battalion, 26th Marines took many casualties while taking that rock pile from the Japanese Army. The symbolism was obvious: the 1/26 of 1966 had big shoes to fill.

The *Vancouver* entered Subic Bay on the 22nd of July. Other ships from the United States packed the harbor, including a giant aircraft carrier loaded with jets. It was a bustling bay of ships, men, and equipment. More importantly, we all shared the same knowledge—Subic was only a short stopover.

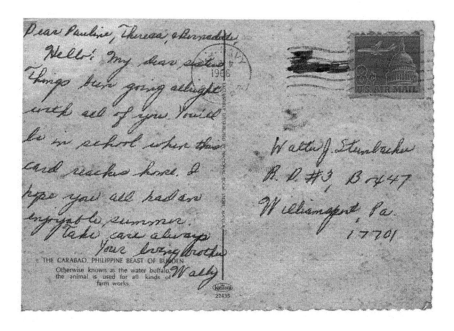

Postcard home from the Philippines, September 1966

Later in the day we went ashore to be fitted with light jungle utilities, along with two pairs of jungle boots, and a green camouflage cover for our helmets. That night we went on liberty to Olongapo, a town just across a narrow, muddy, sewer-polluted river. After crossing the bridge, I jumped into a Jeepster with a group of men from the platoon. The driver took us into the city about one quarter mile. I stepped out of the Jeep and up onto a dirty board sidewalk. Most of the sidewalks were only boards laid down haphazardly; very few were concrete.

As I glanced around the street I saw many neon lights flashing. My God, every doorway appeared to lead to a bar. Soon I sat at a large table inside the first bar I saw, only feet from the Jeepster. Sitting with me were seven or eight Marines from our platoon. Even before our drinks were served, the 'red light' girls came strutting to our table. Hell, one sat down on the Marine across from me and ran her hand down into his pants! What a dubious education I received. Likewise, most of the Marines sitting with me were sharing the same experience for the first time. Yet we all relished the diversion, watching foxy women, listening to American music coming from the band, and enjoying the drinks. In general, I enjoyed the night and took the liberty boat back to the ship before the midnight curfew. The next day the company also had liberty; however, we were forewarned of a one-day training exercise starting the following morning.

Sure enough, Alpha Company went ashore in liberty boats at 0800h. We were combat equipped with rifle, pack, flak jacket, and our flashy new boots. We fell into Company formation and the Captain informed us of a march into the mountain. Olongapo and Clark Air Force Base had a backdrop of tall jungle mountains. Soon we were in a column marching towards those hills. Damn, the booze of the last two nights began pouring out of our bodies like a gushing, leaking pipe. Then, the salty Gunnery Sergeant Runnels, who fought in the steamy jungles of the South Pacific during the Second World War, barked, "How do you men like this 110-degree heat? Vietnam will be same, and worse!"

Behind me, Pierce grumbled, "Southern Georgia was an ice box compared to this sweatbox."

Later that day I ran out of water, and I began tapping bamboo trees to fill my canteens. That water was pure and I didn't need the nasty halogen tablets to kill all the bacteria. That afternoon I learned that we were staying the night in the jungle. No surprise to me, since command constantly prepared us for a harsh, unknown destiny. That night we listened to many spooky, unknown jungle noises. The next morning A Company walked out of the jungle mountain and back to the base. My body felt drained of all moisture from sweating.

Slack duty didn't last long; three days later the *Vancouver* churned out of Subic Bay and headed for Mindoro, another Philippine island, for more jungle training. We were told Mindoro had an aboriginal population living back in the mountains and that an armed rebel group roamed freely in the jungles. As a result, some live ammunition was issued before helicopters lifted us to Mindoro from the ship.

At 1600 hours near a sugar cane field, the squad and I jumped out of the chopper. Once the entire company was on the ground, we moved out past rice paddies, and toward higher ground, into thick jungle cover where we formed a perimeter. That night I shared watch with Pierce, one hour on, one hour off—practicing for conditions in Vietnam. We moved further back in the hills the next day. I saw a few monkeys and some birds. Sweat dripped down into my eyes from the oppressive heat.

In the early morning two days later, in column, the company was on the move, marching to the ocean. Word passed back that the captain refused helicopter extraction for A Company; therefore, we were humping our way to the ocean. Whether the captain actually refused extraction, I never knew, but we were in the jungle and I suspect it would have been too thick and difficult to get choppers down.

As we pushed over another mountain, a light rain started bouncing off my helmet. Around 1400 hours we encountered a fast-moving muddy river and a rope had to be tied off on the other side to enable us to cross. The river crossing proved to be extremely dangerous and slow because the water rose neck deep with a strong current that ripped at our bodies. Crossing over, I slung my rifle over my back so I could keep two hands on the rope. It took a half hour, but A Company made the crossing without losing a man. Over the next hour we walked through farm country, scattered with bamboo and thatch homes near the rice paddies. The natives gave us curious looks as we passed through their land, but some smiled and waved.

As the afternoon waned, I stumbled up onto a narrow road and angry shouts came back the column. "This road will take us to the ocean? Hell, how far away is the Ocean?" We'd been walking for over eight hours and my feet burned as if I walked on hot coals. This did not surprise me, considering my feet were wet all day, and probably the skin began to blister. Bitching from my fellow Marines about sore feet passed up and down the column.

As it started to get dark, Lieutenant Van Dine started singing, "99 bottles of beer on the wall, take one down and pass it around. 98 bottles of beer…" and the chant continued. He attempted to distract us from our pain as we pushed closer to the water. Most likely, his feet were bloody and blistered like mine.

It was dark by the time I hit the sandy beach, and we quickly set up a perimeter and opened cans of C-rats since we had not stopped to eat since noon. Word passed around that we would be picked up by landing boats in the morning. Still, we had to establish a watch system until morning since Filipinos were observed watching us when we arrived on the beach and we had to protect our equipment from theft. The watch was short because we had a tight perimeter. I took the first half hour and then alerted the next Marine. At that point I threw myself down on the wet sand

and didn't remember anything until the sun rose from the east the next morning.

Pierce sat on the sand close by, spooning some meat from a can when he said, "Hey Stein, I heard that brutal hike yesterday covered 20 miles." To me, it felt like forty miles, especially considering how my blistered feet felt.

A bit later we had a beach party in the ocean, soothing our dirty bodies, sore muscles, and more importantly, our blistered feet. The salt water burned our feet, but it would help heal the sores.

By 0900h two landing boats were slowly positioning in the shallow water to take us back to the *Vancouver*. I splashed through three feet of salty water and ran up the ramp, anxious to get back to the safety of the ship. Twenty minutes later we were back in the hold and out of the bouncing crafts. When I got to the bunk I took off the salty, sticky utilities and put on some dry clothes. I applied ointment to my bloody feet and slipped on my cheap shower sandals. Barely five minutes passed when, over the loudspeaker, the ship's captain said, "Be advised, in less than 48 hours 1/26 Landing Team will make a landing in South Vietnam." Damn, that announcement was like dropping a hand grenade down into our hold.

Our platoon erupted with complaints: "What the fuck, these people are crazy!" "Cut us some slack, we just came back from a hell operation on Mindoro!"

Five minutes passed and Lieutenant Van Dine came down in shower sandals to brief the platoon. "We will be riding in landing boats and the initial mission has our battalion supporting an Australian push against the Viet Cong." Our destiny would begin to unfold soon.

* * *

The day after coming aboard from Mindoro Island, we stumbled around the ship in shower sandals, attempting to heal our blistered, bloody feet. Even Captain Velasquez limped around on sandals. In preparation for the landing, I placed extra socks, three C-ration meals, and a plastic poncho in my pack. When I finally threw myself into the bottom bunk at 2130h my body wanted rest, but questions danced in my head as I pulled the sheet to my chin. The first question nagging me centered on my life: was this all there was left of my time—twenty and a half years? The second burning question, how will I perform when all hell breaks loose, and deadly bullets are coming my way? I could not answer either question; likewise, no one else in that small hold could predict their fate.

The next thing I knew, the clock struck 0400 hours and we started going topside to eat the traditional high-protein breakfast of steak and eggs. After chow, I shouldered my backpack and picked up my M-14 and ammo from the armory. Then we began to scramble into a twelve-foot-wide and thirty-foot-long landing boat, after which we watched the large, grey steel ramp at the aft of the ship open, allowing water to flow into the hold. On the walkways, just above us, Navy Coxswain skillfully handled ropes tied to the landing boats. Those ropes prevented the boats from bumping hard into other boats or the bulk-head of the ship. Then, the Navy Coxswain shouted, "We're under way," and we slid into the water, bouncing high with the waves. Within minutes, all the boats were speeding side-by-side towards the shore—Vietnam at last!

Down inside, we hunched down, rifles between our legs pointing towards the bright, hot sky. As I looked around, I saw young men, eyes staring straight at me, faces expressionless; I shared their state of mind. What the hell lurked on that sandy beach and the thick jungle beyond?

I didn't have to wait long. I snapped out of my trance when Sergeant Freeman yelled, "Lock and load." Everyone slammed a 20-round magazine into their M-14. Seconds later, the heavy steel ramps smashed down on the water and I jumped into two feet of water, rifle ready. Like in slow motion, I touched the sand and attempted to run fast as the fifty pounds on my back and the heavy clutch belt bounced and slowed me. Finally, I dropped down after an eighty-yard struggle over the sand. I was five feet from the jungle, but I kept my head against the soft sand. A bit later, Lieutenant Van Dine came down the long line of prostrate Marines, and as I looked up he said, "You can all peek your heads over the top now, there is no one shooting at us."

Further up the beach, however, a few snipers were snapping rounds at one of our sister companies. Ten minutes later we were moving out. The 2nd Platoon had point, and 3rd followed in column. Immediately we splashed into a swamp, water sometimes up to our shoulders. Moreover, the stench and the mud sucking at our feet, combined with the fierce sun burning down on our steel pots, brought out the bitching!

Falduti yelled, "What a fucking slimy hole."

Just ahead, Pierce replied, "Welcome to the Nam, you could have joined the Navy and been back on the dry ship."

Then I piped in, "What the hell's all the strange noises? Hey Pierce, there's a frigging monkey hanging from the tree to our right, chattering at us intruders invading his paradise. Damn, check out the green bamboo viper wrapped around the bamboo tree."

I shuddered as I thought, 'Thirteen months is an eternity. How could one live through that timespan in this spooky land?' Furthermore, we still needed to meet the guys that we're supposed to destroy, the Viet Cong and the North Vietnamese Regulars. A while later, as we sloshed from the watery, slimy swamp onto dry earth, a village appeared out of the trees, just ahead. Then we met our first Vietnamese women, some balancing heavy sacks on their shoulders, followed by barefoot children.

At noon, 3rd Platoon took the point, moving away from the village into the thick jungle. After slowly working our way through a maze of vines, tall trees, and bamboo thickets for another hour, word passed up the column to find a suitable location for a night defensive position for the company. Ten minutes later, our platoon found a semi-open area with some tall trees scattered around. Corporal McClure placed our fireteam fifteen feet apart in order to cover about thirty feet to our front. I was teamed with Pierce and we didn't dig foxholes. A bit later I started my first night watch in Vietnam and discovered some of the eerie night noises in the jungle. Frogs croaked from the ground and trees, and crickets joined the frogs with their constant chirping song. Still other strange sounds I could not identify yet joined the chorus.

After about an hour, staring into the darkness, it appeared that the trees and brush were moving. I twitched my head back and forth to stop that illusion. When I poked Pierce after my three hours of watch, my eyes were bugged out. '390 more nights of this shit?' I despaired. After another three-hour watch, the sun started shining through the misty morning light. I had not slept one wink.

I shouted at Falduti, "Get any sleep, Falduti?"

He retorted, "Fuck no, I think monkeys were throwing objects out of the trees. I was spooked; I thought the Viet Cong were throwing grenades."

Soon after daybreak, we slopped down some cold C-rations and Sergeant Freeman assembled the squad for a briefing. "We're going on a 500-meter patrol, west of our position. Stein, you have the point."

My time had arrived after all the intense training of the past months. Training was one thing, but this was the real thing, with real danger lurking somewhere out in that vast jungle. Minutes later I moved out twenty yards in front of our fireteam. Instantly, my senses of sight, smell, and sound kicked into high gear and functioned at break-neck speed. My eyes were darting side-to-side and straight ahead and up towards overhead trees. I knew Viet Cong sniped from trees.

As I moved ahead, all remained quiet except for the jungle creatures, like the little brown monkeys chattering in the branches, birds swooping among the trees, and a large snake slithering through the tall elephant grass to my right. The sights and sounds were exotic to me. Vietnam's ecosystem had vastly different birds, snakes, animals, trees, and grasses compared to the natural world found back on the mountain in Pennsylvania.

Before twelve o'clock we stopped for a quick C-rat meal. Then Sergeant Freeman gave me a compass bearing for our return to the perimeter. As we were sneaking back, I stopped the patrol once; I had spotted my first punji stakes hidden in the grass. I pointed at the stakes, so Pierce could warn the column. A bit later the patrol reentered our position. Nothing more to do that afternoon but prepare ourselves for another long night gazing into the bleak, dark jungle.

Night two in the jungle, 81-millimeter mortars lit up the sky with flares, creating strange chirps and then shadows, as the flares came to earth on parachutes. Later, on the far side of the company's position, some spooked Marines let loose with bursts from their M-14s, followed by angry shouts, "Stop firing, stop firing!" We were all spooked!

The next two days were uneventful. Late in the afternoon of the fourth day, word came down that choppers were in the air to take us back to the ship. By 1500 hours 3rd Platoon unpacked below deck. Before I had my pack emptied, Lieutenant Van Dine appeared at the door. "Listen up: in less than 36 hours, the battalion is making another landing."

"Jesus Christ, oh, fuck, fuck that, cut us some slack," echoed around the narrow room.

Van Dine smiled, "Are you guys finished? A Company will be a blocking force for the Australians, who are making a big push against a large force of North Vietnamese troops."

Thirty-six hours later, we were assembled on the *Vancouver*'s flight deck. The temperature read 129 degrees. My God, sweat cascaded down into my eyes from my hot head, covered with the steel helmet. A bit later, one CH-34 at a time swooped down on the hot deck and picked up a squad, until the entire Company was plucked off the ship. Then the choppers turned toward Vietnam's coast. Ten minutes later, I jumped down into the five-foot-high elephant grass. Sergeant Freeman quickly organized the squad: "Our platoon objective is that high hill 400-yards to our front."

Our progress was slow in the sharp grass. The sweltering heat had soaked my body, like a rain storm had hit me. Within ten minutes, heat casualties were on the ground. What a fucking blistering day to make a landing! Just above, a chopper circled, ready to land and pick up heat casualties. By the time I reached the hill I had consumed the water in both of my canteens.

We rested at the top and waited for resupply of water from the chopper. After we filled our canteens, the company moved again. We slowly advanced through mixed thick jungle, breaking out into an opening covered with elephant grass. By 1700h, I dug a deep foxhole with Pierce on a small hill. Our front was thick with brush and trees. First, we set out trip flares and strung tin cans sixty feet in front of the hole and we camouflaged the hole with brush and large leaves. We were ready in our comfy hole below ground to take down the expected NVA force, who were reported to be moving in the Company's direction.

That night, Pierce and I slept very little; however, all was quiet, except for the usual jungle creature noises. The next three days, while running short patrols, the Company had zero contact with the NVA. However, the heat continued to drain my body of moisture, like a giant sucking sponge.

Late the fourth day, we broke camp and started the company column towards the ocean. We were to be picked up by large landing craft. As we broke out of the jungle, near the ocean, the Navy landing craft were waiting. The ramps were lowered and weary, hot Marines scrambled on board. As soon as the seamen powered the crafts out into the choppy surf, they started handing out ice cold San Miguel beer. The scene looked like a drinking frenzy, as dehydrated Marines gulped down the cold beers. I took a small swig. Almost instantly, men scrambled for the side of the bouncing landing craft, puking over the side. The gift of cold beer from the Navy men was noble; however, dehydrated bodies could not hold the icy beer after four days of drinking very warm water!

In fact, most of the Marines contracted a bad case of dysentery, and without exception, we all lost ten to thirty pounds due to the body-sapping heat. Despite that, we had something to cheer about: the *Vancouver* steamed south towards Subic Bay for some much needed rest before the next landing operation.

For the next ten days, the men of the landing battalion relaxed, drank, and of course some hooked up with the girls hanging out in Olongapo's bars. The code: live high today, because as we all knew, some bad shit was destined to blast the team on some future landing in Vietnam. Likewise, I knew the fun in Subic would end; however, I needed to see Gary before the next operation. I caught a liberty boat to the *Iwo Jima* to connect with him.

Later that day we went into Olongapo, drank, danced, and talked about old times back on the mountain. At 2230 hours we parted company on the dock where liberty boats picked up Marines and Sailors for trips back to the various ships.

I hollered after Gary, "Keep your head down, jarhead."

He shot back, "You too, Steinbacher."

The next day, the 13th of September, Lieutenant Van Dine briefed the platoon: "We are leaving Subic tomorrow morning, prepare for another landing." No one had any questions; we all knew we were not heading to a Boy Scout camp-out.

* * *

Early the next morning, I stood on deck as large tug boats pushed the *Vancouver* around to point us in the direction out of the bay. We were on our way—three ships, 1,200 Marines, and hundreds of Sailors, steaming towards the South China Sea and Vietnam.

On September 14th, we were all stir crazy—we had an entire day to wonder and think about what the hell kind of event would happen the next day when we went ashore. On the other hand, we did have time to prepare our gear, pack, and C-rations. Rifles and ammo would be doled out in the morning. Also, the chaplains held services and the Protestants had private services. The Catholics had communion, and the chaplain made the sign of the cross, thereby giving us general absolution instead of private confessions. We were ready—we could all go out and die in the jungle tomorrow.

Headin' In to Do Battle With Reds in Viet Nam

Before the battle, armored personnel carriers weave a pattern on the sea as they head for beaches just south of the demilitarized zone in Viet Nam. The operation landed over 1,200 men of the 1st Battalion, 26th Marines, for an assault on Communist positions.

USS *Vancouver* and landing craft from Operation Deckhouse IV

On the 15th, I was out of the narrow bunk and dressed by 0400 hours and went to eat another classic breakfast of steak and eggs, the high-protein combination to prepare us for a hard day's work.

By 0600h, the *Vancouver* took on water as the giant landing ramp sunk below the water line. The other Marines and I loaded ourselves inside an Amtrac, and in seconds the door slammed shut and we dropped into the South China Sea. When all the Amtracs were out of the ship, we slowly plowed towards shore.

Fifteen minutes later, the machine clawed up on the soft sand and down came the ramp as we rushed out onto a vast sand shoreline. The jungle appeared to be a half-mile west. Next, Sergeant Freeman told the squad to kick back and wait for orders to move out.

Much later that morning, salty Gunnery Sergeant Malone came along and shouted to Sergeant Freeman: "Get your squad together, we're going for a ride." Three minutes later I was on top of an Amtrac speeding across the sandy beach towards a distant tree line. When the three Amtracs closed to within 100 yards of the tree line, Gunnery Malone began screaming and pointing. There I spotted a man running near some hooches. The Amtracs stopped, and seconds later 13 men were on the sand cranking hot M-14 rounds at the runner. Damn, I didn't see any rifle in the man's hand; however, at that distance, he could have hidden the weapon. After we stopped shooting, we climbed back on the Amtracs and sped back to our original position. I remember asking myself when I slid down on the sand, 'What the hell was that exercise about?' Sometime in the early afternoon, we received orders to saddle up as choppers were on the way to lift the Company further inland.

Ten minutes later I was in a chopper as it powered up in a cloud of sand, and soon, out the open door I saw the green jungle below. We were moving away from the ocean. A short bit later, the pilot prepared to deposit our human cargo. Within minutes, the entire Company stood on the ground and Sergeant Freeman briefed the squad. "Our platoon will file out after 2nd Platoon." Soon we were moving through flat, brushy country. As we moved further inland the brush mixed with taller trees. I didn't see any villages, Vietnamese, or animals. The area looked downright spooky and was too quiet.

Around 1700 hours Corporal McClure came up and growled, "3rd Platoon is moving past 2nd Platoon, to take the point. Stein, you're up!" Fifteen minutes later, I moved out on 150 percent alert, fifteen yards ahead of Falduti. The stakes were raised for me. Unlike a small squad patrol, I now had 180 lives behind me. Furthermore, the only fact I knew was that we were moving northwest, but where in the hell were the North Vietnamese? About forty-five minutes later I smelled something foreign—smoke? food? My left hand dropped behind my back to signal for Falduti to stop and alert the column.

Next, I slowly stepped forward in the thick, low jungle, searching ahead for the source of the strange smells. Ten steps later, I knew—four feet to my front was a camouflaged foxhole with more holes to the right and left of the first one. Furthermore, I noted that pits were dug for cooking rice. (We saw examples of cooking pits while training.) I silently gasped and thought 'Damn, I am standing on the edge of a large North Vietnamese camp hidden under the thick canopy.'

Although the NVA force was absent, it was likely that a scout or two were left behind, and probably at that moment were watching me. I quickly slipped back to Falduti and told him to signal back the column, to get Sergeant Freeman to come forward. In minutes, Freeman kneeled beside me. "What's up Stein?"

I replied, "Sarge, we're at the edge of an NVA base camp."

Quickly, Freeman instructed me to push forward and establish a temporary perimeter, while the rest of the company moved up. I slipped across the camp about eighty feet, and went down on one knee, while the rest of the platoon set up on either side of me.

Soon 2nd Platoon came up. They would establish a perimeter, exactly where our platoon set in. Our platoon would return to set up where I spotted the camp. When I stood to move back, Denny Eaker, from my hometown, moved into my position. He whispered, "Stein, this area gives me the shivers." Then he patted me on the shoulder, "Take it easy tonight!" Denny was on his second tour in Vietnam and he carried a Bazooka rocket launcher and a 45-caliber pistol.

After getting back to my original location, 3rd Platoon hastily set up across from 2nd Platoon. In fact, the 1st, 2nd, and 3rd Platoon positions formed an oval shape no more than eighty feet wide by 120 feet long. There was high ground to my right. A bit later, total blackness and silence settled in around us—180 men hunkered down.

That night Pierce was my team mate. On my third one-hour watch at about 0100 hours, behind me across the perimeter I heard loud shouts: "Halt, who goes there?" then clanking noses (AK-47 safeties being switched off) and in that same second, blood curdling screams from the NVAs echoed over my head, followed by intense rifle fire from the many AK-47s. In that fucking split second, my life—all our lives—would be forever turned upside down. At the same time, my heart erupted into a pounding machine.

The air space around me lit up with bright streaking green tracers as brush fragments began cascading down on me. Likewise, my ears started ringing from many rounds traveling at 3,000 feet-per-second, passing close and chewing up the red earth around me. Then, from across the camp, I heard excruciating screaming as fleshy bodies began getting hit by hot steel, followed by shrieking calls, "Corpsman, Corpsman up!" We were losing men! Moreover, the rifle fire from our weapons and the NVA was like a crescendo, never letting up. Then the NVA began launching mortars into our perimeter, shaking the ground around us and sending more hot steel zinging through the air, wounding and killing more Marines. Likewise, our mortars went into action, thumping back at the NVA.

After the first shock, I finally got my shaking body under control and shouted at Pierce from a few feet away, "Jim, you still with us?"

"Yeah, Stein," he screamed back, "this is some kind of hell."

I had my bayonet fixed, and my focus switched from flying deadly steel to the real possibility that the NVA could sneak through the thick cover to my front and come lunging out before I could react. Though I wanted to let loose with a full automatic clip towards the green tracers coming from my right, I restrained since I knew Marines were also in that area.

As the shrieks from the wounded, the noise from the heavy rifle fire, mortars, and hand grenades popping continued, I could hear through the noise Captain Velasquez and Gunny Malone shouting encouragement to keep shooting. I wondered how in the fuck any of us were going to survive; the NVA were fully engaged and not running. Then, Corporal McClure shouted out from the next position, "We have Naval gunfire on the way. Bury your heads—they have to call it in close to get the North Vietnamese off our backs." We had a Naval forward observer with us and he had plotted grid coordinates and radioed a ship many miles from our position.

While the intense firefight continued on the ground, above I heard the loud whistles from incoming giant shells. When the first rounds impacted, the violent concussions vibrated along the ground and I felt my body lifting. At the same time zinging steel, the smell of cordite powder, shell after shell continued smashing ever so close, with heavy smoke enveloping the perimeter. My God, when will it stop? Suddenly the barrage ended and the NVA fire slowed to sporadic rounds zipping towards us. The incredibly accurate Naval gunfire did the job on the little bastards! But, the moaning of the many wounded continued.

A bit later, all rifle fire ended, and we settled in, anticipating another attack before dawn. After intense hours of waiting, in the distance I saw the first morning light from the rising tropical sun. Somehow I was still breathing to witness another sunrise.

After I chowed down some hot dogs and beans from a can, I saw Jim Logan, an M-60 machine gunner from 2nd Platoon coming across the camp. He began naming the men who missed the sunrise. "Lieutenant Crawford, Rice, Denny Eaker[†]..."

I exclaimed, "My God, Denny... I talked to him last night. He's from my home town!"

"Yeah," Jim continued, "nine dead, twenty-nine wounded, and some of the wounded are barely hanging on! Sergeant Evans was shot twice through the chest, twice in the legs, and once through the hip. He's a tough man. He was sitting against a tree, smoking a cigarette when I came over."

Then I heard them, Chinooks pounding away, approaching from the east to resupply us with ammunition and food, and take out the wounded and dead. Next Falduti, Pierce, and I were ordered to pick up ammo and C-rations for the platoon. When we made it to the landing zone, there were wounded Marines huddled together waiting for evacuation—bloody battle dressings wrapped around arms, heads, chests, stomachs, and legs. Likewise, some were doped up with morphine to numb the pain, while others still were moaning. The dead were half-assed covered with ponchos, and as the Chinook dropped down, the damned ponchos started blowing off the forever dead young men.

Quickly we off-loaded the supplies, and the first chopper loaded up with fucked-up human cargo. The circling Chinook would take out the rest of the wounded and dead. As soon as the first bird lifted out, we hustled back across the perimeter with C-rats and ammo. Freeman met us, and he announced the day's

---

[†] LCpl Dennis Keith Eaker (died 17 September 1966).

mission. "Third Platoon has the point, we'll be moving within a half-hour. Stein, you're up!" I knew what that meant. I would be out front for the entire company, once again.

At 1130h, I crossed over the blood-soaked ground and made my way into the jungle which was occupied just a few hours ago with the North Vietnamese army. I was alone, fifteen yards ahead of the next man, and I knew that death could descend upon me in one tenth of a second. Regardless, I remained calm, and relished the responsibility; I was the eyes and ears for the company.

As I moved over the first hundred feet, I noticed empty AK-47 brass and blood-soaked marks where the NVA had dragged their dead and wounded earlier that morning littered the ground under my boots. I continued another two hundred feet then put my arm down to warn Pierce to hold up. I slid back to Pierce and asked him to pass the word back to send up Freeman. Five minutes passed and Sarge came up. "Hey Sarge, could I vary the compass bearing one degree to get us away from this trail? It appears we are following the general path where the NVA took out their dead and wounded." In seconds, we both agreed that breaking a new trail would make it more difficult for the NVA to double back and ambush us.

Five minutes later I moved out, rifle in my left hand, machete in my right, hacking the bamboo and brush to make a path for the coming Marines. I marveled at the wild beauty of the jungle as I slowly moved through the tall tropical trees, the twisting vines, colorful birds, monkeys, and snakes.

Around 1600h word passed up to start scouting out a good area to set up a company perimeter for the night. Fifteen minutes later I crossed a small, clear stream and spotted a hill ahead. I hand-warned Pierce to hold up the column, and I cut my way up the hill to survey the area. It appeared to be an ideal area for the company to dig in and defend for a night. I motioned to Pierce, and in minutes the column moved up and Marines began digging foxholes. Our platoon set up to the left and to the right, looking down towards the stream. After Pierce and I dug and camouflaged our hole, we headed down to the stream with Lieutenant Van Dine to rig some booby trap grenades. We placed trip wires across the path and hid the grenades in thick foliage overhead, then tied the wire to the grenade pins. Presto! Trip the wire, yank out the pin and boom—dead or wounded NVAs, and we would be warned of an incoming assault. The Viet Cong and the NVA were masters at setting ugly booby traps; however, we Marines were learning fast.

Perched on high ground, Pierce and I settled into our cozy foxhole by 1930 hours along with the rest of the company—such a vast improvement compared to the low valley the night before. After a long night of staring into the darkness, the hot sun began shooting thin rays through the jungle canopy. While no humans appeared, the jungle creatures made plenty of harmless noise all night.

The new day started with a quick gourmet meal of cold beans and franks, after which Pierce and I went down to the stream and carefully disarmed the booby traps. Once done, we scrambled back and filled the foxhole with red earth. By 0800 hours, Alpha Company slowly moved off the hill as 2nd Platoon had the point and our platoon brought up the rear. I still didn't know where we were headed, only that we were on a northwesterly compass bearing. In oppressive heat, we made our way through a maze of bamboo thicket, tangled vines, and trees. We called it sweat and slim!

The column stopped around 1600 hours as we broke through into a semi-open area. Word was passed back that the company was to set up a defensive perimeter that would become the battalion command center. I started digging and Pierce began stringing cans and rigging trip flares to our front. He also cleared some brush to give us better open fields of fire, since the next two-man position was thirty feet away. Once the sun set, we dropped down into our hole and I took the first watch.

All was quiet until around 1230h when Jim was on watch and I attempted to catch some Zs. I was startled awake by a full burst of rifle fire from Jim's M-14. "What the hell Jim, are we being probed?" A green trip flare was popping to my left front, and shadows from it were dancing about.

Pierce slowly spoke, "Stein, I don't know what's out there, but we have another serious problem; I have a grenade in my hand with a pulled pin, but I still have the spoon held down!" After releasing the spoon on a hand grenade, the holder has about five seconds to get rid of the killer.

"Jim, we have two choices: throw the fucking thing, or find the pin and ring and reinsert it!" Sweat was dripping off my forehead as I groped around the bottom of the pitch-black foxhole. I got lucky, found the pin, and very carefully slid it in the tiny hole that holds the spoon. "Now Jim," I whispered, "roll the son of a bitch away from the hole. We'll dive down, and if it explodes, we'll still be alive." The wire must have been seated properly—it didn't go boom!

Seconds later, Corporal McClure slipped over to our position. "What the fuck is happening with you guys? You have the whole perimeter jittery."

"One of the flares went off and I wasn't taking any chances," muttered Jim.

McClure retorted, "Okay, keep your ears on and your eyes open. Maybe the NVA were probing, maybe not."

On the second day guarding the battalion perimeter, September 19th, as we were chowing down some C-rations, I heard loud, chattering small arms fire about a klick north of our position. "Damn, Jim," I yelled, "that sounds like a nasty firefight."

I left the foxhole to monitor the radio in Falduti's foxhole. He looked up, "Delta Company must have run into a shitload mess of North Vietnamese." He turned up the volume and we listened to the violence erupting from small arms, mortars, and screaming Marines. The Howitzer 105 artillery began pounding the NVA's positions, joined by streaking F-4 Phantom jets, strafing and dropping canisters of napalm. 'My God,' I thought, 'we could end up in that deadly battle!'

My focus diverted a bit later to other events about to unfold when Corporal McClure appeared at the foxhole with news. "Guess what—3rd Squad has an ambush patrol tonight. We move at 2100 hours."

Around 2030h, Freeman briefed the squad: "We will take the narrow road that follows north and west. We'll set in about three hundred yards out, near the road. Stein, you're up." Under a moonless sky, at 2100h, I stepped out on that road, ten yards ahead of our thirteen-man team. The darkness provided an ideal screen for a squad sneaking to an ambush site. I was in no hurry, and I stopped often to listen for foreign sounds. After all, out there somewhere other men were intent on snuffing out my young ass. Thirty minutes later we quietly slipped off the road and crouched down like hungry tigers waiting for the prey to appear—North Vietnamese troopers.

Around 0200 hours a rustling noise off to my right perked my ears. Pierce and I couldn't make out the source of the noise in the pitch blackness. We had to hold our fire until we were sure the noise was human. That strange rustling kept us on edge until

0600h and the glorious appearance of the sun. To my right stood our tormenter, a water buffalo that was munching on golden rice straw. Pierce growled, "We should shoot and eat him for payback for tormenting us most of the night!"

A half hour later we were back at the battalion command perimeter, where we were met by Lieutenant Van Dine. "We need a squad to fly to Dong Ha, and then ride shotgun on tanks that will return to our location. From here, the tankers will push on to assist B, C, and D Companies, who are heavily engaged with hundreds of North Vietnamese, less than a klick from our position." Minutes later, a CH-34 was setting up to drop down to take us air bound. In seconds we were flying toward Dong Ha. Thirteen Marines all sitting against opposite bulkheads, M-14 in our hands and between our legs pointed skyward, faces dead serious. We were now combat veterans, ready for any contingencies thrown at us.

Twenty minutes later, the chopper deposited us on the tarmac at Dong Ha. The airfield was busy with many planes and choppers landing and taking off continuously. Next to the flight line, huge stockpiles of war materials were stacked high. My misconception that this war was small changed immediately—on the contrary, this large base, close to the DMZ, suggested that the United States was here to stay in a big way!

After hustling across the tarmac, we were met by a sergeant who hollered, "Follow me, I'll take you to the mess hall for some chow." Mess halls in Vietnam? None of us had been to an in-country mess hall yet. Our mess area consisted of eating cold food out of a can while sitting on the red earth. Minutes later the sergeant led us into a large, neat hut, complete with long tables down the full length of the building. We grabbed aluminum mess plates, which soon were piled high with eggs and bacon, accompanied by real milk, coffee, and orange juice. Once we devoured the tasty chow, we grabbed our rifles and walked a few hundred feet to the waiting M-48 tanks armed with a 90mm gun and a 50-caliber machine gun.

As I climbed aboard, I sensed a power surge running through my veins. I felt invincible sitting on that heavily armed steel monster. I wondered, 'What mortal human would dare challenge us and this machine?' My idle thinking was halted when we jerked forward toward the thick brush outside Dong Ha. I was on the lead tank with the fireteam, two tank operators, and a man behind the 50-caliber. As we approached a possible ambush site, the machine gunner lit up the brush and trees with many short bursts. Tankers didn't fuck around!

As our tank clanked down a narrow road, around 1500 hours, suddenly there was a violent, loud explosion to the right under my perch, which lifted my body skyward. Flying steel smashed back through the low jungle, and smoke rolled into the air. I quickly checked my ass and legs for blood and found none—the bottom of the tank had absorbed impact of the large booby trap. The tank operators inspected the damage and found a four-foot section of the track had been destroyed. The tank commander told us they carry extra tracks to repair damage, but they wouldn't be able to complete the repair before dark. Thus, we would have to set up a defensive perimeter, and spend the night there. Swiftly, the two tanks behind us came up and started smashing into the low brush to provide us fields of fire if the NVA attempted an assault that night. At the same time, our squad entered the low tree growth and acted as lookouts while the tankers started tearing apart the blown tracks.

As the sun faded to the west, we pulled back in and settled in for a long night behind the three tanks. Twenty-three Marines in a sea packed full of North Vietnamese troops—sure I was scared shitless; however, I knew the twenty-two other men around me shared one common thought—the enemy would not take the tanks until we all lay dead on the jungle floor!

When it turned pitch black, we observed total silence; not a whisper could be heard, but in the distance, we watched flares lighting up the sky over the battlefield where B, C, and D Companies were still engaged with a dug-in enemy. The flares kept me focused on alert, minute-by-minute, until finally there in the east, that beautiful, bright sun peaked over the South China Sea. I had survived one more hairy night in the bush.

For some unknown reason, the NVA did not attack. They sure as hell knew our location after the mine exploded the day before. At first light our squad went into the bush on watch, while the tankers resumed repairing the blown right track. Then, behind me I heard the call, "Mount up, mount up, we're moving." I climbed back on top of the same tank, and within minutes the three-tank convoy was clanking northwest to reach and assist our embattled sister companies.

Around noon the tanks halted near our perimeter. Freeman shouted, "Everyone down, we must hustle back to take up our defensive positions, to protect the battalion head-quarters and the 105 Artillery." As soon as we hit the ground, the brave tankers turned and headed due north, straight to the other side of the jungle where sharp cracks of small arms fire and mortars were exploding.

When I got back to our foxhole, Pierce and I rechecked our trip flares and tin cans to our front before dropping into our home in the dirt to eat some C-rats. As we ate, we listened to the savage battle taking place due north, hearing small arms, mortars, our own 105s firing, and just above an F-4 Phantom screaming in and dropping napalm. That's all we could do—listen and stay alert, since our company was stretched razor thin protecting the battalion command post and the artillery.

As the dark set in, the fight north went silent. Then at about 2300h, Pierce and I witnessed a bizarre scene in the sky. There, a red streak in a crooked arc headed to earth, followed by a weird noise, a roar, like *rrrrrrr.*

Pierce whispered, "What the hell is it?"

I said, "I don't know, Jim, but I think I can hear a low flying plane in between the red bolts streaking toward the earth. Maybe someone will clue us in tomorrow."

The next morning, Lieutenant Van Dine came around checking our positions, and I wasted no time asking him about the strange bright light show in the sky last evening. Van Dine smiled, "That show came from an AC-47 Air Force plane, firing M-60 machine gun rounds at a rate of 6,000 rounds per minute. Somewhat like a modern-day Gatling gun [a precursor to the machine gun.] In fact, word is that beast can hit every square foot of a football field in one minute." Pierce and I didn't say anything; we just shook our heads.

Van Dine also briefed us about the savage fighting between B, C, and D Companies and at least a battalion of entrenched NVA troops in the villages of Gia Binh and An Dinh. He continued, "Some of the bamboo and grass houses are, in fact, reinforced concrete and timber bunkers."

I clearly remember commenting, "No cakewalk for us in this Nam hole, huh, Lieutenant?"

He again smiled, "No!"

Pierce and I watched another air show that night from our good little Air Force buddy. Still our perimeter remained quiet the entire night—no probes by the NVA.

The next hot morning around 1100 hours the magic word came down from Corporal McClure: "We're flying back to the *Vancouver,* after the artillery is lifted out by the Chinooks." In preparation, we covered our foxhole and pulled in all the trip flares, slapped on our red earth-colored packs, and waited for the birds from heaven to take us to a safe place.

At noon, I was snatched skyward into a sturdy CH-34, which headed east towards our water transportation to the *Vancouver*. What a rugged bunch we must have appeared to be to the clean Navy personnel as our chopper deposited us on the deck of the *Vancouver*. Most of us had not shaved in ten days, and our helmets, clothes, and boots were stained by the red earth of Vietnam. Furthermore, if they looked us in the eyes, they would have recognized that we witnessed the horrors of war, up close and personal.

It was soothing to get a few gallons of water on my sleep-deprived body and to get some chow to eat that was warm, as opposed to the cold C-rats. After chow, rumors floated about some slack duty on the Da Nang perimeter that was complete with real tin roofed huts and cots. Who knew? We were told another battalion was taking our place as a landing team, and were headed for Da Nang. Operation Deckhouse IV was over for 1/26, at a cost of thirty-six killed and 167 wounded Marines. More than 250 enemy dead.[†]

[†] Command Chronology [BLT 1/26], 01 September 1966, 1201060196, US Marine Corps History Division Vietnam War Documents Collection, The Vietnam Center and Archive, Texas Tech University
https://www.vietnam.ttu.edu/virtualarchive/items.php?item=1201060196.

Sunday, September 25, 1966
Dear Mom & Dad,

Hello! From your son who just came aboard ship from an eleven-day operation just a few miles south of the 17th parallel. What can I say?? I could write a twenty-page letter on what took place since September 15th, but I don't really feel like talking about this damn war.

I can say it was hot, the nights were long with little sleep, the foxholes were uncomfortable and constant mental strain. You probably know about Denny Eaker from Duboistown by now. All I can say, he was a good Marine and a good American.

War is hell on this earth! A little brighter side of the story. The 1st Bn, 26 Marines smashed the North Vietnamese regulars in the area to a great extent. God knows how Gary made out!! How is he doing?

Oh! Yes! I received some mail from home while in the field. It really upped my morale a lot.

How are things at home lately? I was happy to receive a letter from Theresa and Dad today. We have more mail coming today so I might get more. Thanks for the article on the Irish, Dad. It looks as if they should have a good team again. I am anxious to find out how they made out in the first game. Boy! The world series starts quite soon.

The National League will go right down to the wire again, I guess.

Where am I going now? I will be stationed near Da Nang on a perimeter for 90 days or three months. Then I might go to Okinawa for a while, I am not sure. I'll write the details when I find out the definite word.

Time to go so I'll write soon.

Love always,

Wally

P.S. Thanks for all the letters and prayers.

Cpl. Dennis K. Eaker, 19, City's First War Casualty

Mr. and Mrs. Thomas P. Eaker, Sr., of 832 Arch Street, were informed of the death of their son, Marine Lance Cpl. Dennis K. Eaker, 19, who was killed on Sept. 17, 1966, in action in South Vietnam.

Cpl. Eaker is the first Williamsport casualty in the Vietnam War and the second in Lycoming County. He was with the First Battalion, 26th Regiment, and was in the current Operation Deckhouse in the vicinity of Gio Linch District, Quang Tri Province, when he was killed.

He enlisted when he was 17 and served one of his first two years in Vietnam. After a tour of duty in the states he was again assigned to Vietnam and had been there about four weeks.

Native of City

Born in Williamsport, Cpl. Eaker attended South Williamsport schools and was a member of South Williamsport Methodist Church.

Dennis K. Eaker

Also surviving are six brothers; Thomas, Jr., James, and Charles, all of this city; Robert, of Columbus, Ohio; S/Sgt. William, with the army at Fort Ord, Calif., and Sgt. Donald, with the air force in Turkey; four sisters, Mrs. Margaret Fox, Mrs. Sharon Alexander, Mrs. Mary Hill, and Mrs. Bonnie Baines, all of this city, and his paternal grandmother, Mrs. Effie E. Dunkle, of Ellwood City.

Arrangements are being made for the funeral to be conducted here in the near future.

Williamsport Sun-Gazette, Sept. 19, 1966

Rubbing from the Vietnam Veterans Memorial Wall

Chapter 3:
Third Platoon Up

R&R in Taipei, November 1966

ON SEPTEMBER 26TH the ships docked just after dark in Da Nang's Harbor. I was out on deck with Pierce and Falduti checking out the city lights as Pierce shouted, "Look at the bright lights—Vietnam has real cities." We both thought only rice paddies, swamps, and jungles existed in Vietnam.

The next morning, we went ashore in landing boats and the company waited near some buildings built with plywood, two-by-fours, and covered with shiny tin roofs. They looked like luxury living quarters; could they be our new home?

Around 1000 hours a number of trucks halted near A Company's troops. Minutes later we were riding on one of those trucks, bumping along over rough paved roads leading out of Da Nang and through a nasty-looking outskirt town—Dog Patch Alpha. "What a fucking slum," Falduti screamed over the noise of the trucks. The convoy kept moving out into the countryside, where we shared the dirt roads with Vietnamese locals who were walking and riding bikes. I already knew that the false rumor about some slack duty near Da Nang held zero truth. Where in the hell were we headed this time?

Ten minutes later the answer came when Sergeant Freeman spoke, "We're entering Hill 55; this will be the battalion headquarters." From the back of the truck someone shouted, "Hey Sarge, where are those comfy wooden huts? All I see is thousands of feet of concertina wire, run-down sandbag bunkers and a few canvas tents." Freeman just smiled—evidently, he thought the same.

A bit later we exited the truck onto the main hill complex where we had a quick C-rat meal. Around 1400 hours we were back on the trucks, heading down a steep grade towards a plank deck and a river lined with pontoon boats. A creaky sensation hit my body when the truck crossed over. We could see that the

Seabees were starting to drive large wooden pilings in the river bed, to construct a more permanent bridge.

After crossing the river, the trucks bumped along a rutted road about mile and then stopped. Corporal McClure stood and said, "End of the road for us." When I jumped out of the truck, I was already locked and loaded with my M-14. Back to the war! Soon, the platoon moved out on a muddy Amtrac path, our squad in the rear. I noted a wild, abandoned countryside: no people, dogs, water buffalo, and no hooches.

Fifteen minutes later we entered a perimeter manned by a unit from the 9th Marines—one of the first combat Marine battalions to land in Vietnam in March of 1965. They were rotating back to Okinawa the next day. Damn, they looked crusty and tired, with shoes brown and tattered clothing. More importantly, their faces and eyes revealed that they had seen some bad shit over the past months.

When I looked around the perimeter, I suspected we were occupying a former village. There was a stone well near what appeared to be a shot-up pagoda, and other small elevated dirt spots indicated where hooches rested not long ago.

Before dark, McClure came back from a briefing with the Lieutenant. "Listen up, this position will be our base of operation for at least two weeks. We'll run patrols and ambushes every day. Oh, one other thing—this area is a Free Fire Zone."

Falduti interrupted, "What the fuck is a Free Fire Zone?"

Corporal McClure quickly retorted, "Well, no living creature should be here but us and the Viet Cong. The people—kids, women, and old men were relocated to another area. In other words, if it moves, we can shoot."

I asked, "What if we do see women and kids?"

"Hey Stein, they're not supposed to be here! Fuck it!" Pierce muttered.

After McClure walked away, I said, "What kind of war are we fighting now? Up north it was all North Vietnamese regulars. Now, we have to deal with kids, women and old men? Who the fuck is who?" Regardless, we didn't have much time to hash over the subject, since dark quickly set in and I had the first watch, down in a hole, peering out into 'no man's land.'

The next morning, the platoon from 1/9 walked out of our position and the perimeter now belonged to our platoon. Three ambushes and three patrols later (about a week) 2nd Squad, led by Lieutenant Getlin, A Company's executive officer, ran a supply run returning from Hill 55. As we neared a small bamboo grove, the lead Amtrac stopped suddenly, and Getlin jumped down and ran towards the grove. He quickly drew his 45 pistol and blasted rounds into the thicket. My God, in living color three Vietnamese men ran like spooked deer, rifles in hand, attempting to reach the tall, thick grass twenty yards from the bamboo grove. They didn't know their path to safety led them into full view of another Amtrac loaded with Marines. In a split second I let loose a quick burst on full automatic as Marines behind me stood and fired over my head. Damn, my ears rang!

As we jumped off the 'trac and ran towards them, the Viet Cong were face down, lying in the short grass. One Marine blasted a few more rounds at them to make sure. Beside me, Sergeant Freeman said, "Go ahead Stein, search them." I stared down at a man, hit through the back and sides with numerous rounds. Barefoot, he wore black silk pants, topped with a white silk shirt. I bent down and pulled a wallet out of his pants. The contents were the same that I carried in my wallet—a single photo of a girl standing next to a banana tree; another picture appeared to be his family—mother, father, brothers, and a sister. The wallet also contained a few paper money bills, but no ID cards. As I looked at the bodies one more time, they didn't look all that dangerous now that they were dead. And, they looked older; perhaps they fought the French thirteen years ago? Regardless, I was still alive thanks to bold Lieutenant Getlin. If it weren't for him, they might have picked a few of us off the Amtracs that day, or perhaps some future day.

The next day headquarters up on Hill 55 sent our squad a message with a big pat on the back for a job well done. We were not impressed. Our basic mission required us to kill or capture any VC or North Vietnamese troops that crossed our path.

* * *

Two days later our squad prepared for an early morning patrol east of our base. Lieutenant Van Dine also joined the patrol. At 0900h I started east, with Pierce right behind, followed by our squad. I moved slowly since I was unfamiliar with the patrol area. The terrain was flat, with scattered banana trees and sharp elephant grass that slashed my hands and face.

Ten yards into my patrol, I spotted a blown out concrete building to my left, and guessed I was still in the Free Fire Zone. An hour later I noticed a long tree line to my right about seventy-five yards away. I proceeded slowly, then *zzt, zzt*. Damn, sniper fire from that same tree line—*zzt, zzt* again! I dropped down into the four-foot-high grass and my world reduced to one foot. That is, I should have been blasting away, but I could only see grass. Forty feet behind me, Lieutenant Van Dine yelled, "Stay down, I am calling 105mm artillery on that tree line." I heard him on the radio, "945654, first round Willy Peter [what we called white phosphorous]. I'll adjust from there."

The round whistled as it came down. It was short—thirty feet behind me. White sparks flew like a 4th of July firecracker, spraying out like a fan. Some of the hot Willy Peter hit Sergeant Freeman. Freeman was a hardass; he didn't want a medevac chopper as he wanted to stay with us. Then the Lieutenant, back on the radio, "945654—fire full effect." I buried my head, covered my helmet with my hands, and hoped the 105s would hit seventy-five yards over my head. In seconds, screaming rounds came overhead and impacted the tree line as the ground shook and smoke rose into the air. No more sniping.

When the smoke cleared, our fireteam, McClure, Falduti, Pierce, and I smashed our way through the tall grass to survey the damage and maybe flush out some Viet Cong. I soon discovered inside the tree line there were seven hooches—a small village. Near one hut sat many earthenware crocks filled with rice. But, no people or animals were present—it was too quiet. McClure radioed Van Dine. Soon after, he shouted, "Burn everything."

Quickly we kicked over the crocks filled with the golden rice, then we lit the dry thatch bamboo huts with our Zippo lighters. White smoke puffed straight into the air to be seen for miles. We rejoined the squad, and by 1300h we were back at the patrol base. An hour later, after choking down another C-rat lunch, Lieutenant Van Dine debriefed our squad. He began, "No more burning hooches; battalion saw the smoke from Hill 55." Someone asked whether we were going to be disciplined or court-martialed. "No, no," he added, "I know this is not the Second World War, because that village would have been torched back then, but this war is different."

Sergeant Freeman spoke next and quickly raised hell with me and Pierce. He said, "You guys were up front and should have instantly slammed forty rounds into that tree line." He was right, and I learned. I thought, 'Wait until the next time I get sniper fire—I'll be blasting away!'

Thirty-six hours later, a battalion stationed south of Hill 55 called upon 3rd Platoon to assist in a big push. Our platoon would be on the western flank, while the unit from the south would sweep north. In preparation for the operation, no one had to tell me to carry all the ammo I could, or to pack at least three days of rations.

The next morning with the blazing sun in my eyes I stepped out of 3rd Platoon's position, with Pierce and the rest following. I headed east towards the burned out village, but before reaching it, I changed direction north towards the Song Yen river that flowed east past Hill 55. When I changed direction to the north, around 0930 hours, I heard jets and saw them to my front, strafing the area near the river. Another fast mover came in, dropping Napalm. When the second jet pullet up, rifle fire erupted from the Viet Cong. Hell, they were blasting away at the Phantoms with AK-47s. Can't say those Charlies didn't have balls!

Regardless, we swept in that direction. If the jets didn't kill all of them, they'd be waiting for us when we cross the rice paddy south of the river. Just then, Freeman ordered, "Spread it out, crossing the paddy!" Ten minutes later, I was about eighty yards from the tree line when, *zzz-t, zzz-t.* Damn, I knew it, the jets didn't get all the Cong. Instantly, I went to the ground and tried to pick out signs of our tormenters; I knew they were just inside the trees. Not wasting time, I ripped one clip, aiming low. Pierce, beside me, also blasted away. I rolled left and put another twenty rounds where I spotted puffs of smoke coming from their hiding location.

"Damn," I shouted; fifty feet behind me came the cry, "Corpsmen up, Corpsmen up!"

I had to keep firing, and another clip from my M-14 chewed into the tree line. The sniper fire stopped—maybe Pierce and I found some flesh with our M-14s. As I slammed in another magazine, Lieutenant Van Dine shouted, "Stay in place, I am calling for a fire mission."

About that same time, just east of our position in another paddy, a violent eruption of fire commenced. The Marines sweeping north must have collided with a large Viet Cong band. I could hear their M-60 machine guns pumping away, along with M-14 and M-79 rounds. The Viet Cong were also popping hundreds of rounds back at the Marines. Seconds later, screaming noise erupted as the 105 rounds started chewing up the Viet Cong positions to our front among smoke and flying dirt. "Get some," shouted Falduti, twenty feet behind me.

After a medevac took out a Marine shot in the shoulder, I was on the move again, walking towards the tree line, splintered by our artillery. I didn't advance far—*boom!* Seventy-five feet behind me someone stepped on a fucking booby trap. Hell, I had just come through that area!

Word passed up—Jim Leone, from Louisiana, had been hit badly in his legs and was losing blood fast, so we held up for a medevac chopper. Turns out Jim had missed the operation up north last month and had rejoined the platoon only two weeks ago. Lucky him, if he lived, his tour would be up and he'd be back in the 'World' soon. After the medevac lifted Leone out of the paddy, the Marines to our east must have called for a fire mission, because 105s began whistling overhead and began exploding 300 yards to our east. Following that, a gunship helicopter swooped down and let loose load after load of rockets. I saw their smoke trails before they detonated, hopefully on top of the Viet Cong.

While we watched the air show, we stayed in place in case the Viet Cong broke out of their thick tree line to our east. Unfortunately, no easy targets appeared, and I was back on my feet, slowly working my way towards the trees ahead—my eyes searching for booby traps. A while later, the platoon was busy digging foxholes to prepare for night time defense. Pierce and I dug our hole on the edge of a paddy near the river. About eighty yards ahead to our left was a small village of hooches.

After we ate our evening C-rat meal, I spotted a man strolling towards our foxhole, holding something in his hand. I kept my eyes focused on him as he neared our hole. "My God, Jim, he has a bottle," I exclaimed as he came closer.

Then, he stopped with his hand outstretched and said, "Marine, you drink."

What the hell? Whatever is in that bottle couldn't hurt me as much as the bullets I encountered this past day. I took the cork off and slammed down a long swig. What a smashing sensation—it burned in my mouth and all the way down my throat. Instantly I broke out in a sweat. "Wow, Pierce, this stuff will beat any of that southern brew you drank back home!"

Jim grabbed the bottle and took a good hit. "Damn, Stein, that sake [rice wine] is good shit."

We each took another swig and thanked the old man. He bowed slightly, then walked to the next foxhole.

Twenty minutes later darkness settled in, and true to form, the Viet Cong began sniping just to harass us. The sniping continued until midnight and then I guess they decided to get some sleep.

At 0700h the next morning, Corporal McClure informed the fireteam that the platoon was moving west in an hour, proceeding until we hit the road that would take us back to our perimeter. An hour later we were on the road. Another bull shit operation was over... and I was still breathing!

* * *

Later that day after the operation, Corporal McClure informed the fireteam of a movement, about three quarters of a mile north. He told us, "We will replace another platoon at that patrol base."

Early the next morning we strolled into the new patrol base. Wow, I saw sand-bagged bunkers topped with tin and sand bags to protect us against mortar rounds. Hell, with our luck, we wouldn't be at this location long.

That afternoon, 3rd Squad had a short patrol to the west of the base of operations. We were still in the Free Fire Zone and I spotted an area where hooches once stood. 'What a spooky site,' I thought. 'What the hell happened here before we came?' Screw it. I was determined to stay alive.

Later, coming back, the patrol stopped at a green, lush banana tree that had bunches of green bananas hanging down. Up for anything to provide some joy, we quickly devised a plan to pick the luscious fruits. Pierce and I hoisted up Falduti, and he ripped the beauties free. After returning to our bunker home, we placed them on the hot tin roof to ripen.

The following day, Corporal Falone's squad caught the day patrol. They headed east and at noon encountered a small force of Viet Cong. In the bunker, we listened intently to the brief fire fight. And, the medevac was called to take out another wounded Marine. Damn, it was Doc Jones, shot in the shoulder. Doc was the Corpsman who returned from liberty in California adorned with two bright tattoos, USN on the one forearm and USMC on the other. Doc was well liked and a very skilled Corpsman; we needed him to help save our lives. Our ranks were reduced by one here, one there, wounded or dead—wondering who the hell was next.

The next three days were quiet at the patrol base, then the mission changed again. Sergeant Freeman broke the news, "Tomorrow, be ready to move at 0800 hours. The platoon's new home will be Hill 1, on Hill 55."

Walter outside bunker on Hill 1

After a two-mile hike under the hot, biting sun, we walked onto Hill 1. The hill was a long finger on the eastern part of Hill 55, and the road from Da Nang passed through the center of the position. Ten minutes after arriving, our fireteam was assigned to the bunker on the western end, facing south, across the river. It was a massive piece of land, containing many small villages, rice paddies, and intermingled thick jungles. Similarly, the view north of our position was a mix of the same terrain, features and villages. More importantly, those six square miles were also the home operating base of an unknown number of Viet Cong. I wondered how in the hell thirty-five Marines could patrol, ambush, and cover our own perimeter, along with being prepared to move out for larger operations? It was overwhelming!

A day after arriving at my new home, I caught a break. I was picked, along with three other Marines, for guard duty close to Da Nang. Within an hour, Pierce, Rioux, Falduti, and I were bumping along on a six-by-six truck headed towards Da Nang. Fifteen minutes into the trip we passed through Dog Patch Alpha, a rough shanty town on the outskirts.

We drove through an open gate, 500 feet behind the town onto a larger base. I saw many huts built of plywood, covered with tin roofs, and wire screen covering the first four feet of wall to keep out the helicopter-sized-blood-sucking mosquitos. As we piled out of the truck, a Sergeant Curry met us in front of one of those fancy huts and said, "You'll be staying in this hut and you're required to stand one, two-hour watch each night, at one of those large bunkers you see 200 feet from this hut." He added, "chow down on C-rats for lunch; tonight at five, trucks will take you to a mess hall one mile west."

That night, after devouring a meal of hot beef, mashed potatoes, and canned corn, Pierce, Rioux, Falduti, and I left the mess hall and we spotted a large group of Marines gathered around a makeshift stage. On the stage, I saw a man and a woman dressed in western clothes topped with cowboy hats. Hell, I quickly recognized the couple—Roy Rogers and Dale Evans, the popular singing duo who were television and movie stars. What a bonus to distract us from the war for an evening! We watched the show and then returned to the base.

Later I caught the midnight to 0200h watch in one of those giant bunkers situated on the wire perimeter. I spent the two hours talking to a guy from Tennessee who worked in supply on the base. He told me large amounts of supplies arrived daily to support the war. He complained that more storage sheds were needed to keep the supplies.

I took off my boots when I got back to the hut and laid back on the canvas cot, but I could not sleep. Machine gun and rifle fire broke out down near the bunker that I just left. The Viet Cong must have been probing the wire and got caught. Bright tracers and zinging rounds streaked all over our perimeter. I thought, 'I hope they get the little Charlies before they come running by my hut and try to pitch satchel charges in the front door.'

When the firing ended, I instantly felt uneasy sleeping in those comfy huts. I had been in the mud, jungle, and paddies too long. At least out in the boonies I could have some control over my unknown fate. We had four more days of slack duty on the base before catching a truck back to Hill 1.

* * *

On November 1st, 1966, I was happy to be back with my squad on Hill 1. The easy duty in the rear was only a diversion, because I already formed a bond with the men in the squad and the platoon from the past action we shared.

I learned that our patrol area from Hill 1 included the villages of Bich Bac and Thai Cam (1, 2, and 3) to the northeast. But the patrol also included Xuan Diem (1 and 2) to the northwest, and Duc Ky (1 and 2) and Quang Dong (1 and 2) to the south. That area was a vast piece of land for thirty-five men to cover.

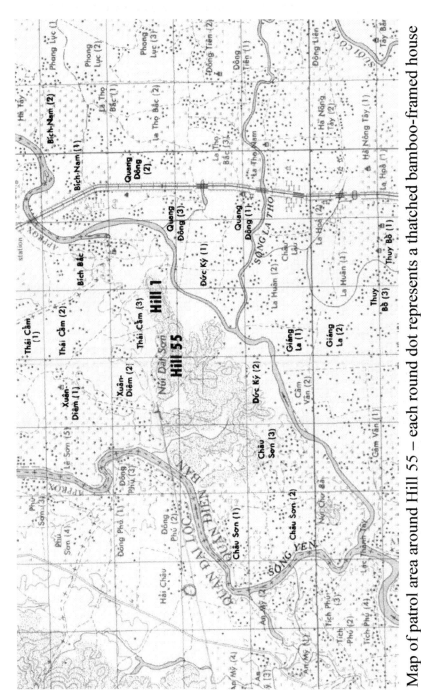

Map of patrol area around Hill 55 – each round dot represents a thatched bamboo-framed house

Source: 6640-4, Chuck Carlock Collection, The Vietnam Center and Sam Johnson Vietnam Archive, Texas Tech University.

Another duty added to our mission involved providing security for the Navy Seabees who were constructing a sturdy cable suspension bridge over the Song Yen river, southeast of Hill 1. Providing security meant placing a fireteam out in the rice paddy while Seabees dangled above the muddy water tying off the cables. In fact, the third day of construction, a Seabee was wounded in the arm while working on the bridge. Our 81-millimeter mortar crew responded by pumping twelve mortar rounds out towards the tree line near Duc Ky (1). The Viet Cong stopped sniping after that barrage.

I had not gotten into a routine the second week, when 3rd Platoon was ordered to make ready for a movement to An Hoa, a base about 12 kilometers southwest of Hill 55. Our mission at An Hoa required our platoon to fill in defensive positions while the 5th Marines were out on a big operation in the mountains.

As I jumped into the bed of a canvas-covered six-by-six truck the next morning, the rain fell in torrents. I knew the route was a sniper's haven, the road was often booby trapped, and at that time the trucks would be slowed by the deep mud. Three miles south of the Hill, heavy sniping hit the convoy. At once, two 50 calibers mounted on two trucks began chewing away at the tree line to our north. We had to stay huddled in the trucks. Five minutes later, the snipers were silenced, and the trucks slowly ground forward on the slimy road.

Fifteen minutes later we came to a river, the Song Thu Bon. The bridge was a shaky, dangerous pontoon, anchored on both sides by wire rope cables. I knew if one of those cables failed, we would probably be swept away and would drown in the deep, muddy river. After a nerve-rattling twenty minutes, the trucks continued spinning towards An Hoa.

When we entered the town of An Hoa, just outside the base I noticed some houses that were constructed of concrete and their electric lights shone through the fog. I had learned earlier that the town had a power plant, cement plant, and a coal mine—a sharp contrast to most Vietnamese villages that were candle lit at night.

The trucks entered An Hoa, a large complex, complete with large sandbagged bunkers, tents, and concertina wire stretched around the perimeter. As 3rd Platoon jumped out of the trucks into the pelting rain, we were taken to two tents furnished with canvas cots sitting on pallets; underneath, the monsoon rains flowed like a small stream. Hell, at least I would be dry at night after completing my watch, in a bunker near the wire.

That night I stood guard in a dry bunker near the concertina wire. When I got to the bunker, my watchmate turned out to be a guy from near Linden, Pennsylvania, a small village across the Susquehanna River from the homestead. We spent three hours talking about home, while artillery blasted away, and flares illuminated the area to the front. I remember thinking about the 5th Marines, somewhere out in this heavy rain, engaging the Viet Cong and North Vietnamese. I knew I had luxury duty compared to them.

The 5th Marines were choppered back to the base three days later, and 3rd Platoon was relieved of guard duty, and I found myself back in a truck, heading once again for that first dangerous bridge crossing. Around noon we crossed safely, and the truck continued north under the smashing rain and fog. It was so dreadful that we didn't even have sniper fire before reaching Hill 55 an hour later.

* * *

Upon arriving at the main Hill 55, the trucks were stopped and 3rd Platoon was placed on standby. 'My God, what a low blow,' I thought. 'The platoon might get at least a half day of peace. No way!' Sparrow Hawk was an operational name given to a full company ready to move in an instant. We knew to pack three days of C-rats, all the clips of ammo we could carry, and two canteens of water. We chain-smoked cigarettes and wrote what could be our last letters home, all the while feeling anxious about what action would be ahead.

Very early the morning of the second day of standby, a Marine poked his head through the tent flap and said he saw bright flashes of light to the northeast. He added, "It appears some base is taking mortar rounds." Then Falduti popped in the tent and said he listened to radio transmissions, and it sounded like Da Nang got slammed from "Rocket Alley." Rocket Alley was an area northeast of Hill 55, where the Viet Cong slipped in at night and mortared any base of their choice. Not three minutes later, Sergeant Freeman shouted, "saddle up, choppers will be on the landing strip at the bottom of the hill in ten minutes. 3rd Platoon is joining two other platoons on a night time sweep along a river northeast of our present location."

In seconds, I quickly stepped towards the bottom of the hill. I could hear the beat of choppers approaching, and soon the first bird sat down, blowing dirt in my face. Minutes later I felt the pilot power me off the ground with the rest of the squad.

Ten minutes later I felt the chopper slowly descending towards the ground, where we jumped into a muddy rice paddy—slime and muck that was Vietnam. God, what a ghostly scene confronted me as I caught my breath. The sky and paddy were lit up like it was daylight. Overhead, a flare-ship airplane circled, dropping bright flares. What the hell? I was already uneasy conducting a sweep under full light. We assembled on line and started moving west towards a village about a hundred yards away. However, we soon decided the muddy paddy sweep was bullshit, and changed tactics. The new tactic was simple: I took the point and the platoon started slowly moving across a paddy dike, towards the village. At the same time, two other platoons were moving northwest, attempting to flush the Viet Cong in our direction.

I kept advancing slowly under the bright lights; I felt like screaming, 'Turn off the lights!' Then, ten feet further, I felt the earth under my left foot was too soft, and I froze. Falduti stood five yards to my rear. "Falduti, I think I am standing on a booby-trap; pass the word back to get everyone face down on the paddy dike!"

After pulling my Ka-Bar from my belt, I shifted my weight to my right foot while still keeping pressure on my left foot. I began probing around my foot for steel or wires; I found none, but I did feel something soft like a mat. The hell with it—I pulled out my pen light and ripped a straw mat from under my left foot. One foot below I saw razor sharp bamboo punji sticks covered with human shit. I was not sure if they had rigged an explosive under that trap. Regardless, I passed the word back to stay down, that I planned to throw a grenade into the pit. Then, I quickly pulled the pin from the grenade, threw it into the death trap, and threw myself down ten feet away—*boom!*—one punji pit that would never kill a Marine! I wiped the sweat from my face and passed the word back, "We're moving out."

The village loomed ahead as I crept closer, while the flare ship still dropped flares. Finally, I entered the village, moving forty yards further, to give the platoon space to set up. Immediately, we began searching hooches, and poking hay. The natives, old men, women, and kids who would have normally been fast asleep, were staring at us. Maybe they knew where the Viet Cong were, maybe not; we left them alone since we already knew the Cong had melted into the fabric of their country by now. We left the village and called for choppers. At least our leaders knew, there was nothing more to accomplish staying until full daylight. Thus, ten minutes later I was in a CH-34, flying back to my lovely home on Hill 55. I always gathered my thoughts on flights after an operation. My thoughts that time were about how combat was one giant *could have*.

I *could have* run multiple poison bamboo spikes through my foot and leg or experienced an exploding device under the spikes; yet, I was still breathing and walking! Likewise, for the three platoons out in all that nighttime insanity—not one Marine killed or wounded.

* * *

The day before Thanksgiving, I was in the bunker cleaning my rifle when Sergeant Freeman ducked in from the pelting rain. "You're going to Taipei, R&R, the day after Thanksgiving."

"Hell Sarge, I never thought that day would come; I put in for Bangkok, but Taipei sounds like heaven compared to this cold rain, and the murky rice paddies."

The day after Thanksgiving, Jim Logan, Jack Rice, and I caught a truck to Da Nang. At Da Nang, we checked in to be processed for R&R, and then we were assigned to a clean, dry hut to spend the night.

After securing my khaki uniform from my stored sea bag in a large building reserved for the battalion, I took a cool shower. Damn, the water ran red as it splashed off my body. I didn't get completely clean, but it was better than a helmet-liner shower! Next, I found a mess hall where my buddies and I chowed down on beef stroganoff. After filling our stomachs, we stepped out in the rain in search for a slop chute to drink some beer. We didn't walk far before we spotted a neat sign that spelled NCO Club. Minutes later, we sat drinking and catching up on news from Marines from other units. Current music played in the background, making me feel like I was already on R&R.

Around 2300 hours we went back to our hut. As I laid down on the dry cot, hearing the hard rain pounding the tin roof, I thought the war had disappeared that night.

The next morning, we ate a hot breakfast—real eggs, bacon, pancakes, coffee, and fruit juice—then we hustled back to our hut to dress in our neat khaki uniforms; no stinky jungle utilities today as I headed to a fantasy world without a rifle in my hand.

At noon I was on my way, sitting in a four-engine Pan American commercial air liner, complete with sexy American flight attendants. Later, they served us food and drinks. I was getting primed to have a great time.

When I stepped off the plane, the weather was chilly, but soon I was in a U.S. government bus that took me to a processing center. At the check-in station we were told where the best hotels were located, and other locations to explore while in Taipei. Following our briefing, we walked down the busy street, bright with neon lights and Chinese letters, flashing everywhere.

Our first mission began at a clothing store where I spent $50 on some quality clothes and a pair of shoes. Minutes later we were quite the trio, strutting down the street in clean civilian clothes, barely thirty-six hours removed from mud, jungle, and vicious firefights.

Next, we checked into a modern nine-story hotel, paying with vouchers given to us at the check-in station. A bit later, we were back on the street searching for a bar to get some food and drinks.

We entered the first restaurant/bar on that busy street. Hell, the menu was printed in Chinese, but the gracious waitress translated it to English. I ordered a fried rice, eggs, and mixed vegetables dish. The food was top shelf compared to C-rats! After the food, we headed to the bar next door where modern tunes were vibrating. Before we could enter the bar, three movie-star-looking girls came up to us. One eying me had shoulder-length dark shiny hair, a sweet face, and wore a mini skirt. She was a real heart stopper! I quickly told her we were going into the bar to have some drinks and maybe dance.

Minutes later we were enjoying a cold beer and listening to great American tunes, played by a live band in the corner. I danced with the same sweet girl, but I discretely told her I was going to get a good night's rest, and that I'd be around the next night. We downed a few more drinks and went back to the hotel where we had separate rooms on the same floor. My room was small, but clean, and had a small bathroom with a tub. Before bed I filled the tub and slipped into the hot water with a sweet-smelling bar of soap in my hand. Within seconds, the bathwater turned reddish brown, the color of Vietnam's earth. It was no surprise to me since my last good bath occurred in California in early July!

I slept well that night on that soft, clean mattress. It was quiet, and I felt safe. At 0800 hours, Jim knocked on the door and asked me if I wanted to attend a mass at a church a few blocks away. I thought that going to a real church, without rifles, in a safe city sounded like a novel idea. To our surprise, American families and U.S. troops filled the church, most of them on R&R. The large contingent of Americans proved that Vietnam's support personnel were widespread in South East Asia.

After church, Jim and I met a young man who cleaned the rooms. He wanted to learn how to speak some English, and we seized the opportunity to make a trade. He taught us some Chinese—in exchange, we taught him some English. After he finished cleaning our rooms, we three shared a lesson, which benefitted me in the coming week, communicating with the locals.

Jack Rice, Walter, and Jim Logan outside restaurant

Sunday afternoon that same young man offered to take me, Jim, and Jack to some tourist attractions around Taipei. The first featured a man pushing a cart mounted on rails. When Jim and I were being pushed up a hill, we offered to get out, but the man pushing insisted he would do it without our help! He was one tough hombre, all 120 pounds. Later that afternoon, I saw how the Chinese constructed beautiful terraced rice paddies on the steep slopes overlooking Taipei. They were true man-made works of art!

Walter and Jim Logan riding rail cart outside Taipei

The young man took us to an upscale restaurant to cap off the day—what a treat spread before us—various vegetables, fish, and meats, and we could relax on real chairs at a table, unlike sitting on mud-soaked pants munching out of a can.

That evening, Jim and I checked out another bar close to the hotel, where we had a few drinks and danced with a few foxy girls. Then we retired to the lobby of the hotel, where syndicated TV shows of *Gunsmoke*, starring James Arness, and *Have Gun Will Travel*, starring Richard Boone, played every night at 2300 hours.

While watching, we drank beer and pretended we were back in our home living rooms thousands of miles away!

The next two days passed too quickly for me as we duplicated the same routine. We explored the town during the day, went to the bar and danced, and ended the day in the hotel lobby, drinking and watching those classic TV shows.

Wednesday morning, I woke to loud popping-cracking sounds, like rifle fire. I jumped out of the bed and looked out the window at the sidewalk below. Hell, firecrackers were exploding on the street and sidewalk. To me, it appeared that the dressed-up people were celebrating a happy occasion, but what? Later, the young man who cleaned my room explained that firecrackers are set off on wedding days.

That evening, Jim, Jack, and I decided to explore another area of Taipei. Later, while walking near a busy intersection, a man started pestering us concerning some beautiful girls he had for us. I politely told him, "Not tonight." He continued to harass us loudly, and that drew a mob of young men who began to surround us. Odds appeared to be 20-to-3, and they looked damn menacing. In unison, we stepped out in the street to flag down a moving cab, and the driver slammed on his brakes whereupon we scrambled into the cab. I screamed at the cabby to get the hell moving. I recall asking Jack, "What's up with those people? We come here to spend our money, but they wanted to do us in? We could have taken plenty of them down, but there were too many to make a clean sweep!" At that moment, I was disgusted with South East Asia and wanted to go home.

Thursday, our friend the cleaning guy told Jim and I about a section of Taipei that had stores like those found back in the states. He was right—the stores were decorated for Christmas, complete with bright lights and green vines stretched around poles. I felt like I was transported back home at Christmastime. I stayed quite a while in the last store I visited, just to extend the illusion that I was home, shopping in Williamsport.

We caught a cab around 2100 hours back to the hotel. Once in the lobby, I stared at the telephone hanging from the wall and thought about calling Diane and my family. I sat on the bench by the phone and attempted to make a decision, since I knew it would cost about $85 for three minutes—three-quarters of a month's salary. But I also knew that the next time they saw me, I might be in a wooden box, silent, eyes closed forever. My emotions finally sealed the decision, knowing I couldn't bear to hear their voices and then have to say goodbye again. I would remain strong and await my unknown fate in Vietnam!

I wanted to stay close to the hotel on Friday, since early Saturday morning I would be on board a flight back to Da Nang. That evening I enjoyed a few drinks and some dancing with a cute girl at a bar a block away from the hotel. Afterward, I told her I was going back to the war the next day and retired to my room. I already felt anxious to end this fantasy week and get back with those Marines living in the mud and murky water of Vietnam.

Saturday morning, Jim, Jack, and I were in a cab headed to the airport to catch the 1000h flight back to Da Nang. Soon I was in the air, heading back to my real home—the bush and those incredible men with whom I would be forever bonded.

Chapter 4:
Back to My Groove

Walter's fireteam bunker, November 1966

THE TWO-HOUR FLIGHT on Pan American Airlines went smoothly, and when the plane hit the runway, I looked out the window to thick fog. Ten minutes later, I walked down the portable steps into the driving rain. 'I am back,' I thought. 'Where else but Vietnam does it rain that hard?' By the time I reached the R&R check-in hut 100 feet away, I was soaking wet. Despite that, I received good news when the Marine in charge told me I would have to wait until later the next day for a ride to Hill 55!

After getting a change of dry utilities at the bunk hut, Jim, Jack, and I went to the mess hall. After eating, we went to the NCO club for some drinks and music, where I enjoyed every minute, drinking and talking with Marines from other areas of Vietnam. Their views appeared to match my thoughts concerning the war—it became larger each day!

That night I had a good night's sleep on the cot in a dry hut. The next morning, I enjoyed crisp bacon, eggs, and toast before heading to the armory to get my trusted friend, my M-14. I would need it back on Hill 55 and in the country bordering it.

At 1400 hours, our transportation back to the war pulled up close to the R&R hut, and in seconds I was in the back of the canvas-covered six-by-six, sitting on the attached wooden bench, M-14 in my hand, pointing towards the canvas. In no time, the trucks were outside of Da Nang, splashing and spinning along the mucky road leading eight miles south to Hill 55.

When I dropped down from the truck near my bunker, I learned that 3rd Platoon was set in on the eastern end of Bich Bac; I sure as hell wouldn't attempt to walk out in that open country alone, so I asked the driver to drop me three-quarters of a mile east. We turned around and I jumped out on the road. I found the platoon dug in around the eastern end of Bich Bac. The rest of A Company had surrounded the remaining part of the ville.

When I rejoined the squad, men hurled the usual questions of someone returning from R&R: "Hey Stein, how were the girls and the booze in Taipei? I thought you got lost in Taipei and decided to stay." I remembered, and simply smiled. I was happy to be back with those men!

A bit later, I opened a can of C-rats for the first time in nine days. After eating, I smoked a cigarette as I sat on the ground beside the foxhole talking to Rioux when *zit-zit-zit*. Damn, ears ringing again—the Viet Cong were sniping from across the river to my south. A split second later, I slid down into the foxhole; Rioux looked over smiling, "R&R is over, Stein, welcome back to the fucking Bush!" *Zit-zit-zit*. Then the M-60 machine-gunner moved closer to the river and popped a few hundred rounds back. The Viet Cong went silent, for now. Hell yes, I was back in the groove; I needed those sniper rounds to reset my focus on survival!

During the night the Viet Cong snapped a few more hot rounds at us from across the river, just enough to keep everyone alert. At first light, the County Fair began for Bich Bac, even though the village was surrounded. A County Fair was a Marine Corps invention designed to establish good will with the people who lived in the villages where Marines operated. No one was allowed in or out of the village. A team of Marines entered with an interpreter and two Corpsmen. ID cards were issued to adults and the Corpsmen checked the general health of the villagers. During this operation, ARVNs were assisting by pushing through the village from west to east, driving any Viet Cong into our laps. What a cluster—all I heard for fifteen minutes was M-16 gunfire with no return fire from Viet Cong. "What the hell are they blasting at?"

Rioux replied, "They're crazy and undisciplined. I am staying deep in our hole."

When they finally emerged from the trees to my front, I discovered they were sniping at small birds in the trees. I felt relieved to get out of that village with those crazy ARVNs on the loose! When I got back on Hill 1 before dark, I heard that the people had celebrated Mass in the little French church. Maybe we did spread some good will that day.

* * *

A week after the County Fair, 3rd Platoon was placed on Sparrow Hawk for the Battalion. We were moved to tents on the main Hill 55 complex and we waited for the next crisis that demanded shock troops (rapid reaction). We didn't wait long. At 1300 hours the first day, Lieutenant Van Dine opened the tent flap and ordered, "Saddle up, the platoon will be boarding trucks in fifteen minutes."

When I stepped outside the tent, the rain felt like a small waterfall hitting my helmet. Someone behind me said, "We're going out in this flood? We'll need boats in the paddies today." Within 5 minutes, the convoy sped down the hill and crossed the massive wooden timber bridge the Seabees completed three weeks prior. It replaced the shaky, Civil War-style pontoon bridge over the deep swirling river. In fact, the Seabees did a brilliant job driving large wooden poles deep into the river bed, and fitting the wooden bracing between the poles, and laying 12x12x14 timber flooring—all while taking sniper fire from distant Viet Cong.

The road south from the hill was muddy with deep ruts. Consequently, the trucks labored to keep from getting stuck. After twenty-five minutes, plowing through that gauntlet of deep mud, the trucks stopped. We jumped out into slime almost up to our knees. The rain relentlessly pelted our bodies. "Listen up," the Lieutenant spoke, "the platoon will be security for some Amtracs stuck deep in the paddies, about 500 feet south of this road."

In seconds, we started moving, spread out through fog and muck towards the disabled 'tracs. It was like the earth wanted to suck me in for invading its privacy. Soon we found four Amtracs with their crews, close to an abandoned village—we were in the Free Fire Zone. Pierce and I started digging in the mud in front of a destroyed concrete structure. We finished the foxhole quickly, but not before water filled the bottom. 'Who gives a fuck,' I thought. 'We were already wet and miserable.' I gathered some banana tree leaves to camouflage our hole, and together we rigged two ponchos overhead and climbed into our sweet little home in the mud.

That night I slept only a few winks. The human body does not rest well when soaking wet and shivering. Besides, the noise from falling water kept me awake.

At first light, first squad prepared for a daytime patrol. That patrol meant our squad would have the night ambush. Marines did not sit idle; they're out and about seeking Charlie and possible action. During the day, Pierce and I passed the time smoking a few cigarettes, eating two C-rat meals, and talking about the Civil War. I was entertained by Jim's hate for General Sherman's infamous destructive march through Georgia in the late summer and fall of 1864! We also talked about our homes and families—light subjects compared to the strife surrounding our present situation.

As expected, third squad had a 'fun time' ambush planned for 2100h. The ambush site was a tree line about 250 yards south. No compass needed to reach that tree line, since from my foxhole I had observed that location during the daylight.

At 2100 hours, with rain falling and fog enveloping the land, I started slowly towards the ambush location. The earth sucked at my feet and it took twenty-five minutes to get to the site. The rest of the squad then moved in and sat down in the mud to watch a path running parallel with the trees. Hopefully we could intercept the Viet Cong attempting to blow up the disabled Amtracs. No such luck.

Four hours later, Falduti slapped my arm, "We're moving," which meant I would be on the rear, heading back to our patrol base. I alertly brought up the rear, knowing that in the thick fog, a Viet Cong could sneak up and grab my ass before I had time to recoil. Twenty-five minutes later, I heard a voice from my front shout, "Who goes there?" Damn, did the patrol point forget the password? (That night it was Williams-Ted, the famous hitter who played for the Boston Red Sox). Then, *zing,* an M-14 round screamed close past our heads and my ears rang!

From the front, Sergeant Freeman shouted, "3rd Squad coming in."

We started to move again, and there he was: PFC Justis, a bright-eyed Splib, nineteen years old from Cleveland, Ohio. "What the hell Stein," he growled at me. When I walked past him, he continued, "I came close to opening up with the M-60!" Justis was a machine gunner, and a damn good one, too. That gun had a firing rate of about 550 rounds a minute. If he had opened up on us, there would have been many dead Marines laying in the mud. Instead, he exercised restraint on a patrol that screwed up on a simple password, and he only fired a warning shot. My tears fell on the paper as I wrote this paragraph; without a doubt, thirteen men in our squad, myself included, would forever owe our lives to PFC Justis!

Our stay at the position extended into the fifth day and we were without food. Helicopters could not fly because of the thick fog; likewise, trucks could not reach us for resupply since the road flooded. As a result, Lieutenant Van Dine, Freeman, and two other

Marines decided a meat hunt was in order. He figured there had to be a few pigs left over from when Vietnamese farmers occupied the area.

After the meat hunter detail went out at 1300 hours we began a search to find a few cigarettes. Falduti finally came forward with two smokes he found in his pack. Soon, about ten men were huddled under a dry corner of the concrete structure where part of the roof had collapsed. Overhead, we had some hats and clothes draped over the rafters to dry. What a sight we were, passing around those two wet cigarettes, enjoying a simple pleasure. Then, *zt-zt-zt-zt*—sniper fire. Damn, a utility hat came tumbling down and when I picked it up, a neat little hole punched through the fabric—a round from Charlie the sniper. In the distance, out near the road, in all that fog and rain, a sniper or two watched for a target.

We quickly organized a small group to patrol and sneak out towards the road to find any signs of human movement. We kicked around for half an hour and then went back to the perimeter. The Viet Cong melted into the landscape to wait another day for a Marine target.

Around 1500 hours, the meat detail returned, appearing out of the fog dragging a freshly gutted pig. 'We're going to chow-down tonight!' I thought. The pig was quickly rigged on a crude bamboo spit and a blazing fire was started by igniting dry bamboo with C-4. An hour and a half later, I chewed on a charred chunk of pork. Who cared that it was well-done? It killed any possible worms or strange disease carried by the pig. Likewise, standing around with me in the rain, young men with wet dirty hands and bodies were enjoying the moment, ripping at the cooked meat—food, what a small and simple necessity. I loved them, because I knew I would never die alone.

A few days later, the relentless, heavy rain let up and a heavy tracked tank machine with a large cable winch arrived from Da Nang. Soon, that beast yanked the Amtracs from the slimy field to our front. Then, later that afternoon, we shock troops boarded trucks and left that perimeter and headed back to the hill.

* * *

In the days following the operation south of Hill 55, the onslaught of heavy rain continued. Despite that, we continued to run patrols and ambushes. We walked through two feet of water in the paddies, as the muck under the water pulled at our legs like a giant suction cup attempting to swallow us whole. In that same water, leeches waited to ambush us—to bore into our lower legs, arms, crotches, and even our faces, if we happened to fall into the water.

Another menace was jungle rot, or ring worm, that looked like a two-inch round red sore which appeared on lower legs and faces. Scratch the sores and blood flowed. Treatment was foot powder that dried the rot until our lower legs became soaked again, and again, and again—virtually every day!

The third day back our squad prepared for a daytime patrol that took us to Xuan Diem (2), a village northwest of Hill 1. At 1300 hours Pierce, on point, left Hill 1 and we proceeded north towards Thai Cam (2) village. Twenty minutes later we turned west, sloshing in a knee-deep paddy. As I spied the village of Xuan Diem (2) in the distance, I heard rifle fire break out on the other side of the ville. Hell, there must be another Marine unit in that ville while we are advancing from the east. The rifle fire shut down, and we pushed forward in that direction until the squad entered the center of the long group of hooches.

We were not alone. There was another Marine unit in the village, down on the ground and spread out. I recognized

Lieutenant Dennis, Gary's platoon commander in Delta Company. My God, there beside Dennis was Gary, kneeling with a radio on the ground beside him. I quickly walked over. Gary looked up, "How the hell are you Steinbacher?"

I retorted, "Good, how about you? Where was the Cong fire coming from?"

He noted, "Oh, across the river, it wasn't much."

What an incredible moment—two life-long buddies, meeting on the killing fields of a war zone. Gone forever were those easy, care-free days back near the mountain in Pennsylvania. Likewise, gone were those boys of summer and autumn competing in baseball, football, and basketball.

Gary had that 'don't give a damn attitude': the stiff upper lip, the eyes, the soiled skin, clothes, and boots—a carbon copy of myself. I cherished the few minutes we had, but we both had to depart. We had jobs to do. His platoon needed to get back to the western end of Hill 55. Our squad had to move south to Hill 1 and wait for the next mission. An hour later, 3rd Squad was back in our perimeter after a no contact patrol, but who cared?

Christmas approached in that war-torn, rice-rich farmland. On December 22nd, two village elders from Bich Bac came to the barbed wire on the road outside of the 3rd Platoon, A Company's position. An older man with a long white goatee blurted a request to talk to our chaplain, Father John. Later, Father rode up in a Jeep, dressed in jungle shirt, pants, and jungle boots, appearing to look like any other Marine, rather than clergy.

Speaking in broken English, the old man asked Father, "Could you celebrate a Mass in our church on Christmas Day?" Father John quickly agreed and the two men's faces lit up like a new morning sun. They thanked Father and hurried back to Bich Bac to announce the good news to the villagers. Promptly, Lieutenant

Van Dine assured Father John that 3rd Platoon would provide security in Bich Bac. It was a friendly village and our patrols in and around the village had never tripped any booby traps.

Lieutenant Van Dine informed the platoon that the people of Bich Bac had come to the wire to ask the battalion chaplain to say mass on Christmas Day. Starting the next day, our platoon would rotate a squad to guard the church. The mission served as a nice diversion from the daily grind of patrols, nightly ambushes, snipers, and booby traps. We thought, by comparison, this would be easy duty. A squad promptly set up a perimeter the next morning around the church to stop the Viet Cong from disrupting the Christmas service.

For us, back on Hill 1 on December 23rd, it was business as usual—outpost duty for Rioux and me. Our mission was to watch the suspension bridge and ambush any Viet Cong attempting to cross the river towards our hill. Around 2000 hours, Rioux and I slipped through the sharp concertina wire and slid down the hill towards the thick brush where we could observe the bridge. The rain pelted down on our helmets and made sounds like hail bouncing off a steel roof. We were wet and cold. Vietnam's temperature during the monsoon was often chilly, especially when you were soaked to the bone.

In minutes we hunkered down in the brush with a poncho pulled over our heads. After about two hours of peeking around the poncho to view the bridge, I got highly pissed off at the insanity of our mission. Hell, it was near impossible to see the bridge through the fog and darkness; likewise, the Cong would have to literally trip over us before we saw them. "Rioux, I need a cigarette." I slid out a plastic bag tucked in my soaked jungle utility pocket, and somehow lit a cigarette under the poncho—who cared if Charlie threw a grenade under the poncho and put me out of misery! We cupped our hands around the cigarette and shared it until it died from wetness.

Somehow I endured the intolerable weather conditions that night, and as dawn broke I saw the river had overflowed its bank. As a result, the deep, rushing water blocked the bridge on both sides. A bit later I called radio watch on the hill and informed them, "Op 1 was coming in." Rioux and I clawed our way up the slippery slope to our bunker. Inside the bunker, water was pouring down from a large leak. We fixed the tarp, packed more sandbags on top, and stopped the leak, whereupon we ducked back into the rugged hut.

Mission accomplished for Rioux and me. Now we could attempt to get some rest, since we were excused from other duty the rest of the day.

* * *

Ten miles south of Da Nang, a small, sturdy cement church rose up above the lush banana and bamboo trees in Bich Bac. Pockmarks from bullets were visible on the wall from prior firefights. To the south flowed a lazy, muddy river, the Song Bau Xau. To the north a mucky road curved towards Hill 55, the combat base of the 1st Battalion, 26th Marines.

On December 24th, in preparation for the Christmas Mass, the Vietnamese women, men, and small children carefully swept the wooden floors, dusted the pews, and knocked down the cobwebs in the church. It was as if they found a lost treasure, to attend Mass once more in the old French church.

Christmas morning dawned a grey, rainy day—common weather, especially since the monsoon season had been in full fury the past two months. All was serene that morning in Bich Bac; the Viet Cong didn't even throw one sniper round at the church.

Maybe they, too, sensed that the day was holy and decided to take the day off.

We saw Vietnamese appearing out of the fog from all directions, walking briskly towards the church. Word had obviously spread to other villages prior to Christmas. The women and young girls were dressed in white silk tops and black pajama pants and the men and boys wore black silk tops with white pajamas. Some were bare-footed, as was common, while others wore shoes fashioned from a piece of old tire with a strap between the toes. In fact, their simple attire reflected the practical life-style of the Vietnamese farmers in that fertile farm valley.

Just before 1000 hours, Father John arrived in a mud-caked Jeep escorted by two Marines who would later serve as altar boys. The Vietnamese waited patiently until Father entered the church, and then quietly seated themselves in the front pews. Although twenty-five Marines strongly desired to be in the church, some had to remain outside as a security force. Graciously, just before Mass, several Protestant men volunteered to remain outside in the downpour to man the foxholes. The rest of us entered, leaving our weapons in the back of the church. A rare occasion for all—the rifle would be out of arms reach.

In preparation for Mass, the two Marine alter boys placed fresh linen on the altar and lit two candles brought by Father John. There was no electricity in that little church, but the windows provided some welcome light inside.

The Mass began around 1000 hours and some of the Vietnamese prayed out of missals that they must have cherished and kept safe for many years. The setting in the church was one of simplicity and warmth, even though the sun was absent, and the rain pinged on the tin roof. There were no lavish decorations such as poinsettias, red ribbons, pine boughs, or bright lights. On the contrary, two small vases of colorful garden flowers adorned the altar. The chaplain wore his green jungle pants under his robe, with his mud-caked boots below. The humble Vietnamese sat in the front pews, and were joined by foreigners—eighteen- to twenty-one-year-old Americans from thousands of miles away. Together, in a chance meeting, they celebrated Christmas Mass.

After the Mass ended, Father John turned to the Vietnamese and replied: "Are there any Christmas hymns you desire to sing?" They gazed at him, murmuring among themselves, acting confused over the inquiry. Then, in Vietnamese, they started to sing, probably an old familiar piece. The Church's walls suddenly were filled with the most beautiful lyrics echoing from their sweet voices. In fact, it sounded as if a legion of angels descended into the church, singing on high! The sheer beauty of the song sent chills pulsating down my back.

When the song ended, the Vietnamese slowly filed towards the rear of the church, their faces filled with smiles of joy. Although those smiles probably masked some sad thoughts concerning their prospects for the future, they celebrated the fact that after many long years they were once again able to have Mass in their church.

The Marines walked towards the back, heads held high while tears streamed down their faces, parting the red earth stains, creating tiny furrows down their cheeks. They reflected joy and memories of past Christmases shared with loved ones in South Philadelphia; Stone Mountain, Georgia; Buffalo, New York; Slick, Oklahoma; South Chicago; Bald Eagle Mountain, Pennsylvania; Trenton, New Jersey; Louisville, Kentucky; Jackson, Mississippi, and other corners of the United States.

The Vietnamese and Marines knew in their hearts and minds, as we left the safety and warmth of the church and stepped into the driving rain that we would be stepping back into the uncertainties of the ongoing war. The Vietnamese had to return to their homes and continue farming surrounded by constant strife. Likewise, the 3rd Platoon could not march down the murky road and go back to 'the World'—a mystical land and time that once existed in our lives—the United States of America. December 26th would dawn, and with it more patrols, ambushes, booby-traps, and operations.

Nevertheless, for one hour in time, on Christmas Day in 1966, in the charming French Catholic Church in Bich Bac, South Vietnam, a group of tenacious Vietnamese, Father John, twenty-five American Marines, and two Navy Corpsmen shared together peace on earth and good will to all men.

Walter with Corporal McClure (Oklahoma), Lance Corporal Pierce (Georgia), and Lance Corporal Falduti (New Jersey)

Chapter 5:
Radio Man, Up

View of river and countryside from Walter's fireteam bunker

TWO DAYS after Christmas, Alpha Company was on the move again—our mission: to conduct a County Fair in Thai Cam (2) village, one and a half kilometers north of Hill 1. When our platoon left the hill around 0500h, the rain gushed out of the sky, instantly soaking us to the bone. Even so, the movement went quite smoothly, and the company had the village surrounded within the hour without anyone tripping a booby trap, as so often happened in the dark. Third Platoon moved into position on the eastern end of the village without incident. Sergeant Freeman set our squad up in two dry hooches. What a break! We could skip digging foxholes in the mucky rice paddy just fifteen feet away.

Vietnamese homes were cozy, with hard dry dirt floors and wide overhanging thatch roofs that kept out the driving rain. Each hooch also had a cooking area separate from the sleeping quarters. The cooking stove was a simple hardened clay device, about three feet high with a ten-inch hole cut in the middle to hold the fuel. A steel grate held a large pot on top—a very efficient system.

That afternoon we decided to have chicken for supper, for two reasons. First, a few birds were flying and squawking overhead. Second, eating chicken instead of C-rations appealed to our taste buds. Catching the wild chickens proved to be quite a project, but we finally cornered two fat hens and sliced off their heads with our trusty Ka-Bars. We skinned the birds and dumped them into a pot of boiling water. An hour later we sat around chewing on tough chicken, but who cared—we enjoyed the moment. Another simple pleasure distracted us from the constant insanity always enveloping our lives.

Despite the fact that the Viet Cong sniped on and off most of the night, we enjoyed the dryness provided by the cozy Vietnamese hooch that evening. Tracers whizzed overhead while we simply stayed low and waited for dawn to break.

When first light appeared, a Vietnamese woman came to the hooch. She immediately started screaming at us. Likely she was upset because we slept in her house the evening before, or possibly she missed her chickens—hell, I didn't know. On the other hand, we suspected she could also be a Viet Cong nurse, since we found a large cache of medical supplies in a small side room. The cache included large battle dressings, healing ointments, and other items that could be used to treat wounded men; however, we couldn't prove they were hers.

Freeman advised us to get ready to move out. The County Fair had ended, and we headed to the road as long as the Viet Cong stayed clear. The Charlies must have slept in, because we hit the muddy road leading back to Hill 1 without a shot being fired. Twenty minutes later, I was back in my sandbagged home on Hill 1, shaking foot powder on my wet feet. Mission accomplished— no medevacs needed!

The day before the New Year, some new 'boots' that landed in the country two weeks prior relieved 3rd Platoon on Hill 1. Our next mission was two days of slack duty on Hill 55 inside a dry tent, complete with a dry cot and nothing more to do than write letters to everyone back home as we listened to the water falling in sheets on the canvas overhead.

That afternoon I sat my helmet liner outside to fill up with water for a shave and some slight bathing. By the time darkness set in, I was half-assed clean and decked out in dry socks and jungle utilities, a rare luxury! In fact, another luxury waited for me 150 feet further up the hill—a bar hall, or rather a rugged tent with tables made of scrap wood and some wooden benches to sit on, where I would drink a beer or two on New Year's Eve.

I draped my poncho over my shoulders so I could stay dry, even if only for a few hours. When I opened the tent flap and stepped out into the darkness, I stumbled and fell into an old foxhole filled with three feet of water. "What the hell," I shouted at Rioux, "I forgot about that hole, now I'm soaking muddy wet! Frig it, Rioux, lets go down those beers, I am not changing!"

Later at the rugged beer joint, I enjoyed the moment, drinking, talking, rifle back in the tent. Some other poor bastard Marine was out near the wire in a leaky bunker, peering into the fog and darkness waiting for Charlies to trip the warning flares rigged nearby.

On New Year's Day 1967, in the dark tent, I wrote a letter to Mom and one to Diane by candlelight. Later, I joined other platoon members for steaks in the makeshift mess hall, just 300 feet north, on Hill 55. Before dark, we saddled up, rifles in hand and spread out in a column. We walked down the slippery road towards our defensive position on Hill 1. Happy New Year 1967!

* * *

The day after New Year's, I attended Sunday Mass in the church tent on Hill 55. After Mass, Father John asked those in attendance if anyone was interested in riding shotgun for him the next few Sundays. We looked at each other in surprise, but no one raised a hand. 'Why not,' a thought flashed through my brain. It can't be any worse than a daytime patrol on Sunday. I raised my hand and committed a mortal sin—I just violated a golden rule in the military: never volunteer for anything! Regardless, I was committed, and Father briefed me about my duties riding shotgun. He told me I would be in the back seat of a Jeep watching the surrounding countryside while the driver buzzed down the road.

That next week I survived two patrols, an ambush, and night perimeter watch every night. On Sunday morning I waited outside my bunker to be picked up by the Jeep driver and Father John. At

0930h I jumped into the back of the Jeep loaded with my arsenal of weapons. I packed my M-14, complete with 200 rounds, an M-79 with 10 rounds, and a shoulder fired anti-tank weapon—an M-72 LAW rocket launcher. I was well-prepared to meet any violence the Viet Cong might throw at our one Jeep convoy. Surprisingly, we encountered zero Viet Cong snipers during the five-mile trip to and from Charlie's Ridge.

A week later, when Father John's driver stopped at my bunker, a light rain fell, and fog rolled over the hill. Per usual, I was loaded with an assortment of weapons.

A bit later in our trip, when we turned left at the intersection of the Da Nang road, I heard a loud explosion to our west in the same direction we were traveling. Two miles later we spotted the explosion site. On its side in the rice paddy was a large bus that had a deep gash on its side and a hole in the underbelly. In the slimy paddy next to the bus, lay the dead alongside numerous squirming men, women, and children—some badly wounded. What a fucking bloody mess of humanity!

On the other side of an eight-foot wide hole in the road, a Marine colonel just arrived with other Marines. He immediately called for a medevac chopper to take out the wounded. It would require a Chinook to take that many wounded and dead.

I quickly jumped out of the Jeep and walked around the giant hole and asked the colonel if I could be of assistance. He told me thanks, but he and his team would handle the evacuation. Soon we heard the Chinook overhead and it was on the ground in no time to take out all those unlucky souls.

Our Jeep driver slowly went around the giant hole and we continued towards our destination. I looked back one last time and thought about the outcome if it had been our Jeep that tripped that giant booby trap set under the road drainage pipe. The probable outcome would have been a gruesome site for the Colonel and his team; they would have had to pick up parts from three unknown Marines who had been buzzing down that road fifteen minutes earlier.

A half hour later, Father John delivered Mass at a makeshift church tent on Charlie Ridge. The driver and I hit the road around 1300 hours. Father John was going to be flown by chopper back to Hill 55 a while later. As we traveled back, I was on high alert since I knew the Viet Cong were aware that our Jeep had to come back along that same route, and they might have a cute ambush waiting for two lone Marines. However, we made it safely back to Hill 55. Maybe the fog and rain screened our five-mile trip.

The next Sunday, after cleaning up with another helmet-liner shower, I asked Falduti to take some pictures with my Instamatic camera that I had just bought from Falone. We walked across the perimeter to the command bunker that faced the river and Duc Ky (1) Village to the south. As I positioned myself against the sandbagged bunker for the first picture, a loud clap smacked my ear drums. I had a split-second before becoming a target for the sniper somewhere south across the river, 700 to 800 yards away.

I screamed at Falduti to take the frigging picture as I bent down to pretend to tie my shoe string. In fact, bending down a little, instead of jumping behind the bunker was an act of defiance. I dared Charlie to take another shot, but none came; however, I knew I had violated another cardinal rule: never diddy-bop around the skyline in full view of the valley below and Duc Ky (1) beyond the river.

Ten minutes later, I rode high on the back of the Jeep, shot-gun man for the Chaplin and his driver. Five miles of dangerous road and possibly my next meeting with the waiting Grim Reaper were ahead of me. "It doesn't mean nothin'," I murmured to myself.

Walter pretending to tie his shoe while taking sniper fire

* * *

Late that same Sunday, after running the gig as shotgun for the Chaplin, Sergeant Freeman met me at the Jeep. He told me to come to the command bunker as soon as I got my weapons secured. A bit later, while walking across the perimeter with the M-14 slung over my shoulder, I wondered what surprise awaited me in the command bunker.

Upon entering, Lieutenant Van Dine announced the surprise, and didn't stutter. "Stein, the platoon needs a radio operator, and you're it!"

Hell, I felt like I just got run down by an angry water buffalo. "Lieutenant, I am a point; I don't know anything about operating that bulky radio."

He quickly countered, "I will not put a radio on a FNG, because I don't think a newbie could handle the pressure like a combat veteran."

I knew it was useless to protest further; therefore, I told Lieutenant Van Dine, "I'll give it my best shot."

I immediately went to find Fred Stevens, the best radio man in the platoon to secure some on-the-job quick training. The radio was about 12 inches by 12 inches square, four inches thick, and heavy—about thirty pounds. Furthermore, there were many dials, and each had a different function—helicopters, artillery, jet fighters. I was intimidated, but I started writing numbers down that corresponded with all the important frequencies.

After working with Fred about an hour, I went back to my bunker and thought: 'This is great. Now I am a big fat bullseye for the Viet Cong.' Radio men were favorite targets for the VC—knock out the radio and communications were crippled.

I didn't have to wait long for my baptism as a radio man. Corporal Menendez stopped by the bunker the next morning and informed me that I was going out with his squad. The mission: a County Fair at Xuan Diem village. Second Platoon requested a squad from our platoon to reinforce their operation. When I left the Hill at 1000 hours, the monsoon pelted my body much like a machine gun belched bullets. When I stepped into the paddy east of Hill 1, I sank in over my knees, and I felt the bulky radio pressing down on my shoulders. I hated the job already. I should have been up on point.

While sloshing along the edge of a paddy, 400 yards later, I heard the loud shrieking sound of 105 rounds overhead. Then I saw the rounds impact, thirty yards to my right. Quickly, I jumped off the paddy for cover; however, it was the wrong move. Deep water swallowed me and my head went underwater by the heavy weight on my back. Somehow, I twisted my body around and pushed my head above water while I clawed my way out of that water hole.

As I spit slimy water out of my mouth, I grabbed the receiver on the radio and screamed, "Alpha 6, Alpha 6—Alpha 2, we have

105s falling on our heads. Get them the hell off our backs before the whole column is butchered!"

"Alpha 2, calm down, get me some map coordinates for your location."

Quickly, Corporal Menendez and I plotted our position on the map. I pressed the receiver, "Alpha 6—Alpha 2, our position reads 954328."

Alpha 6 replied, "I'll get them off your back!" Three minutes later, Alpha 6, back on the net: "Alpha 2, artillery secured. They were firing plotting rounds for future missions, and they didn't know your unit was in that area."

"Roger, Alpha 6, thanks!"

That was my baptism operating the radio. I had calmed down when I called in our location. No matter how much I longed to be back on point, I knew that I could handle this.

The column then was on the move, slowly splashing west of the sea of water. At noon, the reinforced platoon set in around Xuan Diem (2). Jimmy Price and I started digging our five- by two- by three-foot-deep foxhole on the southeastern corner of the Village. After completing our dirt home, we propped two poncho halves over it, then camouflaged the ponchos with banana leaves. We were ready to defend our dangerous position on the corner until the next day.

While we watched out over the rice paddy, the rain continued its assault and the fog rolled in, and the business of the County Fair started in the village. ID cards were checked and villagers with health problems were examined and propaganda pamphlets were distributed—winning hearts and minds. On the other hand, reality for Jimmy and me meant a long, wet, dark night staring out into the thick fog, waiting for the boogeyman to come.

I remember later that night telling Jimmy, "The Viet Cong could crawl in here and hand us a hand grenade before we see them."

"You're right Stein." Jimmy was a man of few words; nevertheless, it was comforting to know I would not die alone that miserable night, if fate might have it.

Around 2300h, explosions thirty feet west interrupted the rhythm of the driving rain on our foxhole cover. Hell, the explosions sounded very close to the next foxhole to our west. Then, I listened on the radio—"Alpha 6, Alpha 6—Alpha 2 [2nd Platoon commander] we are taking mortar rounds!"

I said, "What the hell is happening? Those loud pops sounded like hand grenades to me." Furthermore, if they were mortars, more would be falling on us. After about fifteen minutes of quiet, I heard on the radio that an underground tunnel had been found and a Marine had dropped down into the hole to search for Charlie.

Ten minutes later Corporal Menendez came to our foxhole and ordered, "Stein, we need you and the radio on the north side of the village. A Marine who was poking around down in the tunnel has a bad leg wound that is bleeding profusely, and we must get a chopper to take him out."

Seconds later, I slammed the heavy radio on my back, and stumbled through the fog and rain to a rice paddy just outside the village. Next, I slipped off the radio and pulled out my penlight. I needed to change frequencies to match the chopper's radio. Finally, I reached the chopper and Corporal Menendez plotted our six numbered coordinate. The pilot rogered me, "We'll get your man out."

My God, how in hell would he locate us under the thick fog cover? In a flash, we started gathering the little brown boxes that previously held our C-rations. Then, I heard the *woop-woop* of the

CH-34. They were close, and I pressed the receiver, "You're close, we'll give you some light."

Seconds later, we lit those small brown boxes, and the pilot was back on the net, "I see the fire, I am dropping in." Coming down, he switched on his lights and disregarded his own safety, making him a good target if the Viet Cong saw the chopper. In seconds, in a whirl wind of water spraying over our faces, he landed. We loaded the badly wounded Marine onto the chopper and the pilot quickly powered-up and out of the paddy, bound for Da Nang. Now, I could go back to my hole and wait for daylight.

The night passed quietly; perhaps the Viet Cong ran short of hand grenades. Finally, day broke, but no cheery sun appeared, only fog and monsoon rain. Jimmy and I gobbled down a can of C-rats and stayed in the foxhole waiting for word to move out. Around noon, Corporal Menendez came by to brief us. "Our squad will bring up the rear when we leave the village, in about 15 minutes."

'That's just great,' I thought. 'Our squad got screwed.' The rear of our slow-moving column would be an ideal target for the Viet Cong before we reached the road.

A half hour later, I was on the move right ahead of Corporal Menendez, since radio operators had to be close to the unit leaders. About a klick south east of Xuan Diem (2), around 1300 hours as we approached Thai Cam (2) village, my ears popped like a lightning bolt had just passed by. It was not a lightning bolt, but steel rounds searching for my flesh. 'Damn, they spotted the radio, I am a dead man!' I thought. I instantly struggled through the muck towards a bank to my left that might give me cover.

Stone Mountain, the Marine ahead of me jumped down over the same bank, only to find deep dangerous water. I saw his head sink under the water. In a flash, I hurled myself down into the water, found his neck, and managed to get his head above water. I screamed, "Grab my rifle, I'll pull you out!" Somehow, I yanked him out of the water and up to the paddy dike. He coughed slimy water out of his mouth, still in a daze. In those seconds, I noted heavy fire coming from the village tree line, fifty yards away. 'Screw the radio that's pressing me into the muck and water, I am a rifleman now.' I fired twenty rounds of full automatic into the tree line where I saw rifle flashes and movement, then three more clips on semi-automatic. The geysers of water that splashed skyward around me as the Viet Cong tried to send me to hell, suddenly stopped.

Further east at the other end of the village, I could hear snipers, still harassing the lead elements of the column. In return, I could hear the M-60 and other M-14s plastering the village with hundreds of rounds. Following that heavy fire, the Marines ahead of me arose out of the thick fog and shouted, "Pass it back, move up, move up, we have a walking wounded man, but the M-60 will cover us."

As I passed the machine gunner blaring away at the tree line, I saw the heavy rain pelting down on the hot barrel, sending puffs of steam skyward. "Keep blasting away, guys," I screamed. Our machine gunners always amazed me. The M-60 was a heavy, twenty-three-pound beast to carry. Furthermore, those daring men were constantly covering our asses, most times exposing themselves to enemy fire.

The column was back on the road ten minutes later, but the trucks were not there to take us to Hill 1. No one even bitched— we were happy to continue the three-quarters of a mile to the Hill. Any small hardship did not compare to the last twenty-four hours of boogeyman time.

Back on Hill 1 thirty minutes later, the squad had our usual debriefing following a mission. As I suspected, Corporal Menendez gave me hell for breaking contact with him when Charlie opened fire on our rear element. He said, "I could have called artillery on the VC if I had a radio."

I countered, "You may be right, but on the other hand, our platoon had a County Fair recently in that village; would Battalion have given us freedom to call artillery inside that village?"

He didn't answer. Regardless, even though we disagreed, I liked Corporal Menendez. He was on his second tour in Vietnam and a solid leader. When I walked back to my bunker in the rain, I was happy to still be walking.

* * *

Three days after the County Fair the platoon said good-bye to our platoon commander, Lieutenant Van Dine. He was transferred to a new assignment and would be missed, especially by us veterans from the training days in California and the landings made the previous summer. We were informed the new commander would be Staff Sergeant MacGregor, who was in the Reserves for fifteen years and volunteered for active duty in Vietnam.

Two days after Staff Sergeant MacGregor took command, our platoon was assigned a mission one-and-a-half miles east of Hill 1. The mission placed us inside the 11th artillery battalion perimeter. The position had bulldozed sand banks, ten feet high, that surrounded the interior; a secure base, where snipers were put out of business, because they couldn't see anyone inside moving around.

Encampment inside 11th Marine artillery perimeter

The platoon spent one glorious slack day in that base, and we even played tackle football in the soft sand, all of us reliving memories of smashmouth games back in our home towns. However, our fun and games were brief, because the next day our squad moved to guard an abandoned railroad bridge, one-half mile west. Guarding the bridge prevented easy access for Viet Cong units crossing and harassing us from the south. In addition, our platoon would run patrols and set ambushes west and south of the river, an area unfamiliar to us.

I didn't have to wait long for my first adventure into that strange area; Corporal McClure gathered 2nd Squad together at 0900h the next morning. Our mission was to patrol west along the abandoned railway bed. Fifteen minutes later, Pierce, on point, started slowly west, towards a village, Bich Nam. Three hundred yards out, he gave us a hand down, and passed the word back for McClure to come up. I went with Corporal McClure, radio on my back. Jim kneeled down and pointed with his rifle at a tunnel hole hidden under elephant grass. We all knew what could be waiting in that tunnel—booby traps, VC—in general, nothing healthy for the trooper who entered alone.

Walter posing on the disused railway bridge east of Hill 55

"Screw this," McClure shouted. "Let's search around for more holes, I don't want any of my men to be killed or maimed down in those rat holes." A few minutes later Pierce discovered another hole about seventy-five feet away from the first one. McClure made a quick decision, "We'll blow the holes shut. Get to it, Stein; rig some C-4." I usually carried C-4 and detonating wire in addition to the radio, pack, rifle, ammo and water. I went to work, inserting one end of the wire into a two-by-eight-inch piece of C-4, poked my head and shoulders down into the tunnel, and dug a hole in the stinking earth where I packed in the C-4. Then, the two Marines holding my legs pulled me out. The same was done with the other hole.

A bit later, I pulled the detonation wires out seventy-five feet, touched the wires with the detonator, and boom! A red and white plume shot in the sky, probably visible for some distance. Then, we watched the area closely for escaping Charlies coming from a tunnel we may have missed. None came, but while we watched, the radio buzzed, "Alpha 3-2, Alpha-6 [A Company commander on Hill 55]. What the hell is happening out there?"

I quickly answered, "Alpha 6, we just blew up a tunnel complex."

Alpha 6: "Were the tunnels searched before blowing them shut?"

"Negative, 6," I transmitted.

He did not question me further. "Roger, Alpha 3-2," and I 'Rogered' him back.

Corporal McClure heard the transmission on the radio and replied, "We don't have any dead Viet Cong to drag out of the holes, but neither do I have any dead or wounded Marines to throw on a chopper!"

I thought about Captain Velasquez's reaction to our actions. He *had* to ask me about a search of the complex, but I had known the man since he took command the prior April. He was one hell of a leader, never asking more of the men he commanded than what he asked of himself to endure.

A half-hour later the patrol was back at the bridge. That afternoon I spent some time talking to Staff Sergeant MacGregor, and discovered he knew some people from my hometown. I also learned that he had a cabin, twenty-five miles south of my homestead. Instantly, I felt at ease working with him, and we began to plan hunting together at his cabin after the war.

As darkness set in, Corporal Falone's squad crossed over the bridge and headed west to set up a night ambush. Falone was a two-and-a-half-year Marine veteran and an outstanding squad leader. He was also an original member of my platoon when we formed in California.

I switched on the radio as soon as the patrol went out because I had to monitor transmissions from the patrol. Around 2130 hours, Alpha 3-3 called in their first check point. All was quiet. But then, a half hour later, I heard a fierce volume of rifle fire erupt about a half-mile west. Alpha 3-3 broke on the radio: "I think our point bumped into a Viet Cong patrol, we're taking heavy fire."

I saw bright tracers cross the skyline. Some came in my direction. Sarge MacGregor sat in with me and listened to that firefight. We growled, "What the hell did 3-3 smash into out there?"

Then, the next minute, the rifle fire ended. On the radio I heard, "Alpha 3, Alpha 3-3. I am coming in."

"Roger, 3-3."

Falone's patrol crossed over the bridge thirty minutes later, and he stopped at my position. With his unique New Jersey accent, he said, "Stein, we were damn lucky out on that paddy dike! My point and the Viet Cong point exchanged gunfire. My point took a round to the chest, but it didn't penetrate his flak jacket, but it stung him and knocked him down. Then, all hell broke loose and we exchanged hundreds of rounds, before Charlie grabbed his hat and fled west." He continued, "I think we dinged a few Charlies, but I thought better against feeling around in the dark looking for dead or dangerous wounded men."

I replied, "Good call, Falone. I am happy you brought all your men out of that boogeyman land." Then 3-3 made their way to the artillery perimeter and to safety.

Corporal Robert "Keith" Stumpenhaus inside the
11th Marines artillery perimeter

Two days later while eating my noon C-rations at the bridge, I met Lieutenant Kilhenny. Fresh from Officers' Training School, he would be our new platoon commander after some on-the-job training. He stood at 5'10" and 150 pounds, with eyes filled with fire to command a platoon in combat. However, Vietnam was not standard school combat, and he would have to learn the hard way, just like all of us veterans. But also, I had serious concerns because I would be his radio man. That required me to follow him around on operations and patrols. 'Somehow,' I thought, 'I'll have to give the man a chance to lead, if he doesn't get dinged first.'

Third Platoon's mission at the bridge and the artillery compound ended the next morning and we humped back to Hill 1. My vacation was over, because when morning broke the next day, Lieutenant Kilhenny requested that he join Corporal McClure's patrol in Duc Ky (1), west of our position. Damn, it had to happen sometime—my first patrol following the 'boot' Lieutenant. Furthermore, I hated tagging after anyone. On the contrary, I loved being the front man. I was apprehensive when I descended Hill 1 that morning, as the patrol slowly moved west along the river.

When we entered the village at 0930h, Corporal McClure held up the patrol and told everyone to get down and to keep their eyes open. Then, the Lieutenant whipped out a map, stepped out of the tree line onto a paddy dike, and looked back at me. I yelled, "That map tells Charlie the sniper that you're an officer, and officers are prime targets in this war." I waited for a loud pop coming from some hidden Charlie. Thankfully, none came, but the Lieutenant got the hell off the paddy dike in a hurry.

The squad screwed around in that unfriendly village until mid-morning, then Corporal McClure ordered a movement back to Hill 1. When I walked back to my bunker around 1100 hours, I breathed a sigh of relief. We had all lived through that first patrol with the 'boot' Lieutenant.

Two days later, Corporal Falone's squad left Hill 1 just after noon for a patrol south across the river towards Quang Dong (1) village. Sergeant MacGregor, not one to hide back on the hill, was on that patrol. An hour later, sharp rifle fire broke the silence somewhere beyond Duc Ky (1). I was on radio watch in a bunker facing the river and paddies beyond, Falduti with me in the same bunker. Then a squad taking fire from Charlie opened up with a barrage of M-14, M-79s, and M-60 machine-gun rounds. A bit later, the Viet Cong rifles went silent. Alpha 3-3 called in stating the squad was headed back to the hill.

I knew the Cong were safely firing from south of another river, the Song La Tho; therefore, 3-3's patrol could not pursue the Charlies. A bit later, I heard an explosion out near where the patrol was located. Then, on the radio: "Alpha 3, Alpha 3-3. We have one WIA, Sierra Mike," in code.

"Damn, Falduti," I screamed, "that's Sarge MacGregor." Back on the radio, I replied, "Alpha 3, we're calling in a medevac chopper."

"Roger 3-3."

"Need any more assistance, call."

Ten minutes later, a chopper dropped into a distant paddy that I could not see through the binoculars. When the pilot powered up from behind a tree line, the Viet Cong opened up. I could make out green tracers in the sky near the chopper. At the same time, 3-3's men sent everything they had in the direction of the Cong. 'Chew them up buddies,' I thought, watching from a distance. Sure as hell, that steady burst of fire by those young men gave the chopper pilot time to escape and take Sarge to Da Nang and life-saving treatment.

Around 1600h, I made out the point of the patrol nearing the bridge at the bottom of the hill. After the patrol moved inside the perimeter I went to talk to Falone. He told me: "Sarge stepped on a rigged hand grenade trap. His one leg was a mass of blood and flesh, but he was calling cadence for us when we carried him to the chopper. He'll never return to the platoon, but I think he'll live to go back to the World!"

"Falone, he was one tough son of a bitch, and an incredible leader, the platoon will miss him."

Two days later, another adventure was ordered for 2nd Squad. The area for the patrol was none other than the hated village complex, Duc Ky (1). Furthermore, Lieutenant Kilhenny would be with the patrol and I as his radio man. Around 0900h, the point crossed the bridge and headed south over acres of rice paddies. In the distance a tree line hid the village, and the Song La Tho river. I was in super alert mode, because contact with Charlie was frequent in and around that area. An hour later, when the point neared the river, sharp rifle fire vibrated my ears and rounds skipped through the brush around me and the patrol. I went to the ground beside the Lieutenant and emptied a magazine of rounds across the river. Then I heard Joe Rivers blaring away with the M-60 as the Viet Cong were still slinging steel, but not as heavy.

Lieutenant Kilhenny pulled out his map and suggested we call in some eighty-one millimeter mortars. He quickly plotted the Viet Cong's position, and I pressed the receiver. "Whiskey Alpha, Alpha 3-2, request fire mission at 945645."

"Roger 3-2, one Willy Peter in the air." The white phosphorous came screaming down.

"Good location, Whiskey Alpha," I transmitted. "Fire for effect!" I screamed over the loud rifle fire. Then, I called to my men, "81s coming in, heads down!" I heard the mortars leaving the tubes, sounding like dull thumps. Seconds later, the air was filled with whistling rounds overhead, before impacting in the maze of trees and brush across the river. Smoke, dirt, green tree debris, and hot steel fragments zipped through the air. When the barrage ended, the firing from Charlie had stopped. But who in hell knew if those 81s chewed up any human flesh, since we couldn't swim across the muddy water to peek? The next time we strolled near the river, the same Viet Cong, or their replacements, would be lurking on the other side.

Regardless, the patrol proved worthwhile for me because Lieutenant Kilhenny performed with a calm professionalism when he called in the mortars, right when and where we needed them. His performance proved he would be a competent leader to guide the platoon through more bitter firefights.

* * *

The dates for TET vary from year-to-year. That year the holiday period started the first day of February, and both sides were expected to honor an 'unsigned truce' for a week.

The morning of the first day, I slopped across the perimeter to visit Rioux in the sniper bunker. I told Rioux I was bored with sitting around in bunker, and I wanted to scope out the far paddies for him. After about twenty minutes of glassing an area 1000 feet south, I picked up four men in column moving east. They had bundles in their arms, but I couldn't identify the objects they appeared to be hiding. I quickly handed Rioux the glasses. He, too, saw them and commented, "Fuck this shit Stein, we can't shoot, but we'll probably pay later with whatever they're hiding."

Day two of the truce began with rain pinging on the canvas covering over my bunker—the same rain that was falling for the last eighty days. Nevertheless, at 0900 hours I learned I wouldn't have to listen to that pinging rain on the roof, because I was called outside by Lieutenant Kilhenny. "Stein, 3rd Platoon has an unexpected mission. Our company commander wants our platoon to get to Hill 55, ASAP. I was informed that two Viet Cong are marching around a flag stuck in the rice paddies, taunting Marines on the hill."

Minutes later, we had about twenty pissed-off Marines gathered around the Lieutenant, and the bitching began: "Fuck this bullshit. Is 3rd Platoon the only one left in the battalion?" and "Cut us some slack!" Hell, we knew we would be expected to snatch that flag from those two tormentors without killing them.

Ten minutes later, when we moved into position on Hill 55, the Charlies had vanished into the fog, leaving the flag stuck in the mucky paddy. The Lieutenant briefed us: "We're sending out a fireteam and the rest of the two squads will provide cover. Stein, your team is the lucky one!" (That day someone else was humping the radio). Quickly, I had the Marine that carried the M-79 pop about six rounds around the flag to set off any possible booby traps. Then the M-79 rounds sent muck and water rotating into the air around the flag, but there were no secondary explosions.

Immediately, four wet, miserable Marines stepped through the wire out into the boot-sucking mud to fetch a Viet Cong flag. When we reached the flag, three of us dropped to one knee and Falduti pulled the flag and we started back to the wire. One-by-one, each man sloshed back while the others watched the distant tree line of the village, Xuan Diem (2). Five minutes later, I stepped through the wire—not a shot came from the Viet Cong. Who knew why? It was just another morning in the bush.

> *Saturday, February 11*
> *Dear Mom, Dad & Family,*
>
> *It's early Saturday morning and time for a few words home. I might as well tell you all I am getting letter weary. I wish I could throw this pen and paper away and come home. I am a dreamer!*
>
> *Not much new here except that stupid 'truce' is still going on. And, as always the Cong are moving tons of war*

supplies getting ready for us American troops when it's over. In a sniper bunker on Hill 1, we've been observing them moving with rifles about 1500 meters off. What can we do but let them go, knowing they'll be the ones hitting us at a later date. We had to go out and rip a Communist flag down and a sign they put up saying "Welcome Americans to the cease fire for the National Liberation Front for South Vietnam." The stupid fools don't phase us any, we would love to get our hands on all of them (Cong). I am glad this will be the last phony cease-fire in my time over here anyway.

We aren't doing much, but I can imagine what that slimy rat, the Cong is up to. I can't wait to get out in the field again!! Before I get carried away—how are things at home of late? I'll bet you just love that spastic winter, huh? It's getting hot here.

Well, I'll end this letter now so take care everyone.

Your loving son & brother,

Wally

P.S. Be expecting a roll of colored film in an envelope; I am sending it soon!

When our two squads made it back on top of Hill 55, a Marine with a camera wanted us to assemble for a picture, holding the National Liberation Front Flag. We grumbled and snorted because glory was never on our minds; nevertheless, we lined up and told him to get his picture. Wonders of wonders, three weeks later the photo turned up in the base newspaper. Regardless, we were not impressed.

Newspaper clipping, February 1967 – Marine on left holding flag is Walter

Source: Photo by LCpl. J. L. McClory / Courtesy of the Department of Defense.

Chapter 6:
Jackson Brown

Walter with his fireteam members − Corporal McClure,
Lance Corporal James Pierce, and Lance Corporal Falduti

February 12

Dear Mom, Dad & Family,

Here it is early Sunday morning and I am on radio watch. A radio is playing songs on Armed Forces Radio bringing back many memories. At 7:00 a.m., the truce comes to an end.

Not much new around here except the same old day to day activities. Tomorrow our platoon moves to Hill 55 from Hill 1. Boy! We never stay any place very long. We even set up a shower tank while we stayed here and now it's moving time. This is being a 'grunt' for you! Somehow it will all pass, and I'll be able to come home to my loved ones. Truly, it will be the greatest day of my life.

So Bobby Steinbacher is coming over, huh? I was hoping this mess could be ended before my friends and cousins have to come, but it's not the kind of war to end fast.

Things going okay at home? I guess this is the day you go to the hospital Mom. I received the last sports book. Thanks! Yesterday I sent home a roll of film in a little package. The pictures were taken at the artillery battery, and the bridge we were guarding. They are of my friends who came over with me and myself.

You asked me for the addresses of the two guys I went on R&R with. I can get the guy's address from near Phil. (the Irish guy), I am not sure about the other guy. He was wounded in the leg and went Stateside before Christmas.

Take care and I'll write soon,

Love, Wally

THE MONSOON RAINS subsided the second week of February, and we started seeing the sun glowing through the clouds. With calmer weather came increased Viet Cong activity. I could hear firefights within a few miles of Hill 1, which meant B, C, and D Companies were clashing with Charlies.

That same week, Alpha Company served as a blocking force east of Bich Bac. A battalion stationed near An Hoa made a big push north and we were to dig in north of the river and prevent any Charlies from escaping across the river. Sounded like an easy operation for Alpha, huh? On the contrary, forget the word 'easy' for grunts in Vietnam, because when the three platoons moved out in pre-dawn hours, I heard two loud explosions about one hundred feet to my rear. I heard on the radio: "Two men badly wounded by a booby trap." The company was to hold in place until a chopper could take them out. A bit later, after the medevac, we were on the move, and as the sun appeared from the east, Pierce and I started digging a foxhole. We camouflaged our position well and slid into our hole for the day to await fleeing Charlies coming from a tree line seventy-five yards south of us.

Five-hundred yards to the south, a sharp roar of rifle fire broke out around 0900h. The Marines sweeping north had run into a large force of Viet Cong. On the radio I heard a constant roar from M-14s, M-60s, and M-79s blaring away. The heavy fire continued, and I heard 105s whistling over our heads on their way to scratch some Viet Cong. After the artillery erupted, the heavy firing ended, but we didn't spot any easy targets running for the river. For the remainder of the day, I sat under that blazing sun in the hole until finally the radio crackled, "Get ready to move in ten minutes."

By 1800 hours, Pierce and I had the foxhole covered and the platoon moved towards the road north that connected Hill 1, three-quarters of a mile southwest. An hour later, the platoon returned to Hill 1, just in time for our evening C-rat meal before dark set in. After chowing down and having a smoke, it was time for night watch, with plenty of time to think about the next operation and location.

The following afternoon word came down to prepare for an operation somewhere northeast of Thai Cam (2). I was familiar with that piece of real estate, because it was near the location where I almost dropped into the punji pit, on that crazy night push.

Early the next morning, the company moved northeast on the Da Nang Road and we jumped out about two klicks from Hill 1. Two platoons moved northwest, and our platoon cut across a paddy in a northerly direction. Where our other platoons had crossed to my left, explosions rocked the morning serenity. On the radio, Captain Velasquez called: "Alpha 3, can you call a Medivac? We have two WIAs."

"Roger, 6," I transmitted.

I dropped the heavy beast to the earth and started to turn dials in an attempt to come up on the choppers' frequencies. Finally, I heard the chopper pilot. However, 6 came back on the net and called in the coordinates, "956456." Damn, I moved too slowly; he beat me to the contact with the bird. Regardless, in five minutes the two booby-trapped Marines were headed to Da Nang's medical facility.

As soon as the chopper left, our platoon swept northwest to meet up with Alpha's other platoons. Another Marine force swept along the river to our north, and an hour later that unit and ours merged with A Company's 1st and 2nd Platoons. We made no contact with any Charlies, which was unusual—but who cared? That meant we could redirect back to the road south and be trucked back to Hill 55. Two hours later, around 1700h, I was back at my home, the rundown bunker on Hill 1.

Later that week, A Company's commander, Captain Velasquez, left the Company for a new assignment. 'What the hell,' I thought, 'we lost a solid leader who cared for his men's welfare during the past nine months.' Regardless, we were conditioned long ago for losing good men! Lieutenant Bedford, 1st Platoon Commander, replaced him. I remembered him from training back at Pendleton as a hard ass, disliked by some of his men. However, I stood ready to give the man a chance, because the brutal, sometimes bloody day-to-day strife we faced demanded a hard ass to lead us.

Two days later I had radio watch in the command bunker—my first opportunity to talk to our new commander. I concluded after chatting with him that he would be a good fit for our Company.

After talking, he settled in for the night on a cot in the corner of the bunker. While he slept, I monitored the radio. I considered radio watch slack duty, but that radio served as a vital life line for the Company. Sometimes coordinates for Medivacs and artillery were relayed from my location. Also, I recorded checkpoints called in from night patrols about ambushes and warned the perimeter when they came in. All the preceding was very important, but the best luxury of radio watch was writing letters by candlelight and listening to music on the little transistor radio, transmitted from Japan by an angel, Chris Noel. The tunes '500 Miles,' sung by Peter, Paul, and Mary, and 'Winchester Cathedral,' by the New Vaudeville Band, still ring through my spirit. They connected me to that 'lost World' that did not exist for me.

Again, the next night, I had radio watch in the same bunker, hunkered down in my corner writing letters and listening to modern tunes on the radio. All was quiet—I had taken three check points from first squad that patrolled south of the Hill. The quiet ended around 0200 hours when an explosion vibrated the bunker. Outpost One broke on the radio, "Alpha 6, they just blew the fuck out of the crane."

I transmitted, "Keep alert OP One; the Seabees will check it out in the morning."

By that time, Lieutenant Bedford sat up on his cot, wide awake. "Stein, what the hell happened out there?"

"Lieutenant, the Charlies snuck in and set off a large explosive device on the Seabee's crane. There were no shots fired; they must have grabbed their hats and run off."

"Yeah, not much we can do until daylight. I'll try to catch some more Zs before day break." The night passed without any more drama, and the Seabees found the large bucket excavator damaged, but repairable.

Another surprise event for me occurred that morning. I was informed the radio gig for me had ended, and I would be reassigned to my old squad as a fireteam leader. 'What a joy,' I thought. 'I'd be on point again, back where I belong.' Nevertheless, I did pick up much valuable knowledge operating the radio, and that knowledge could help me survive in the future.

* * *

A few days after I put down the radio, Alpha Company was ordered to standby on Sparrow Hawk, meaning the entire Company must be ready to fly out in choppers on a moment's notice. For us, it also required that we move to the main Hill 55, near the chopper landing zone. Hell, I was an old pro; I had been on standby many times before. I knew the drill. A time of high anxiety, smoking one cigarette after another, writing my 'last' letter home, and checking my life line—my M-14.

On that standby I only had to wait eighteen hours. Sergeant Freeman burst through the tent flap at 2200h and shouted, "Saddle up, we need to be at the LZ, ASAP. The Chinooks are air bound from Da Nang." We all were bitching, scrambling, slamming on our packs, bumping into one another. Nonetheless, in less than ten minutes, our Company was waiting in the darkness on the landing zone.

When I heard the *whoop-whoop* of the approaching choppers, I knew this was no drill. In minutes I'd be airborne, flying into some distant black hole. Minutes later, the first Chinook swirled dust on the ground. Hold onto your helmet time! As soon as the first bird lifted and circled above in formation, heavy sniper fire erupted from the south of Hill 55. No secret to me, it came from Duc Ky (1) village. What a spectacle, with green tracers streaking up at the chopper. The second air bound bird also took sniper fire.

I ran up the lowered ramp of the next vibrating Chinook, and sat on my full pack against the bulkhead. Maybe that pack will prevent a round from penetrating the thin skin of the bird, and up through my flesh. As we powered up, I heard the barking of M-60 rounds from our gunners on Hill 55, attempting to silence the snipers. 'Get some, boys—or I could become a crispy critter buried in a heap of smashed aluminum in the next minute.'

Like wonders from heaven, I finally felt the chopper level out. The skilled crew had flown out of that hell trap and thirty Marines in the dark were flying towards our unknown fate.

The CH-46 was a fast, smooth flying machine, and soon the bird descended to drop us in the blackness. Before landing, Sergeant Freeman shouted above the chopper's noise, "Stay close when we pile out; we have to link up with the rest of A Company before we move out." After we hit the ground, the Lieutenant quietly informed us that a battalion of North Vietnamese troops were close by. Good thing they were not sitting in that LZ minutes ago, because A Company would have been in a world of shit. Soon the 3rd Platoon made contact with 1st and 2nd Platoons and we formed into a defensive perimeter to remain on complete watch until first light.

When morning broke, I stared at a prominent land feature to the north—a high, steep jungle mountain. A bit later, the platoon moved seventy-five yards and set up a perimeter near a small stream. I choked down a can of cold C-rats since I wasn't sure what would occur next. I got a hint of our next move when at 1100 hours, from the blue shining sky, a F-4 Phantom veered down towards the thick mountain top at more than 1,100 miles an hour and dropped a load of bombs. On its tail, another F-4 screeched down that let loose another load of destruction. That spectacle continued for two more drops.

My God, intelligence must have reported North Vietnamese parked on top of that monster mountain. I knew we would be ordered to take that hill from the North Vietnamese! And, though no snipers opened on the jets, that fact did not indicate there were none present. It only indicated they were practicing fire discipline, to make us *think* they were not dug in on that mountain.

Then, the dreaded word came down around 1230h. Sergeant Freeman briefed our squad, "The company is climbing that hill to the north," his hand pointing. "3rd Platoon moves first. Stein, you're up!" Quickly, I sized up the monster mountain—I didn't need a compass, because I already saw where the jets had dropped the bombs. I would attempt to sneak in from the east side of the drops, maybe flank the North Vietnamese. I had no illusions about surprising them. If they were perched on that slope, the mountain soil would be splattered with American and Vietnamese blood.

As I began to ascend, I breathed in the hot moist tropical air. I heard the birds overhead singing happy songs, a snake slithering away, and a monkey swinging from branch to branch, screeching loud warnings of our approaching invasion. Vietnam's lush jungles and exotic animals were a natural wonder, but it meant nothing to me that afternoon, because there were 130 Marines behind me stretched out over 150 yards. My job was serious business, sneaking twenty-five yards in front, cutting a path with my razor-sharp machete, traversing back and forth since the slope was too steep to climb straight up. Every step was important and my eyes darted everywhere, with my nose at full alert to pick up any cigarette smoke, camp fires, or human shit.

Walter with Lance Corporal James Pierce

After two and a half hours of hacking, sweating, and slipping, the ridge top loomed near. My hand went down to signal Pierce to hold up. I wanted to scout ahead for NVA activity. Forty yards further, I picked up some camp fire smell; however, no sign of bunkers or fighting holes. Where in the hell was Charlie?

I slid back to Pierce and told him to move up. Soon, I arrived in the blasted area, where massive holes were drilled in the earth among shattered trees, and there, in the fresh earth, 'tire tracks.' (Many North Vietnamese wore sandals made from discarded tires.) And there were fresh graves. They had been here. But, for reasons unknown to me, the North Vietnamese left after that bombing destruction from the F-4s. I didn't care why. I managed to still breathe that stifling hot, tropical air.

Soon, we dug holes to make ready for night time defense, in case the Charlies came back. Another long, spooky night dug in on the same ground that the NVA occupied the night before. Again, we were on full alert, which meant the Company had no sleep for two days. Pierce and I kept poking each other during the moonless night to keep ourselves awake.

When the sun rose over the eastern horizon, I felt like cheering, because I didn't have to fight off charging Vietnamese troops during the night. They failed to show up.

The Company marked the remaining hours of the morning, and at 1300h, I heard the familiar *whoop, whoop* of Chinooks nearing our position. The jets had cleared a secure LZ with yesterday's exploding bombs. Ten minutes later, the mechanical angels from the sky had A Company snatched off that mountain. What a thrilling feeling, lifting off in a chopper after an operation. I was safe again, until the next mission.

* * *

Twenty minutes after leaving that mountain, I scrambled out of the Chinook on Hill 55 in a cloud of dust. Freeman ordered the squad to get some chow before we headed back to Hill 1. Minutes later, just before entering the rugged chow hall, I heard a fierce firefight in the distant southwest. Then I saw a gunship popping rocket and machine gun fire towards the ground. 'The hell with it,' I had better grab some food while I can. While sitting, eating some beef and real potatoes, Falduti drug a radio up to the plywood table. "Stein, a unit from Delta Company jumped into some bad shit about a klick west of Hill 55." A few minutes later, Sergeant Freeman came to our table and growled, "Guess what, bad boys? Third has been called out again. We will be boarding Amtracs in five minutes, so get your shit together. There's more men; Delta has some KIAs and WIAs laying out there. We will attempt to pin the Viet Cong against the river."

Sounded like a tall order, because we were all without sleep for seventy-two hours. On the other hand, the platoon had been running on fumes for a long time and no one bitched. We had Marines out in those killing fields that needed us, ASAP. When we got underway, I saw a chopper swinging down northwest, and they were taking fire from Charlie. The bird attempted to land and to take out the KIAs and WIAs. It appeared that our platoon on the Amtracs were in a good position to sweep up the Viet Cong and end their boldness.

However, as our lead 'trac sped towards the Cong in a nearby tree line, a blocking force suddenly appeared—a swarm of men, women, and young children ran from a village to my left and surrounded our lead 'trac. They began screaming and pointing fingers at us. Then I heard a yell from behind me, "Waste the dinks!" My God, we all had twitchy trigger fingers. Twelve bone-tired, sweaty Marines held hostage by a mob of screaming people. Then the machine gunner on the 'trac let loose with a barrage of steel over their heads—and still they didn't budge.

Beside me, Corporal McClure yelled, "Let's move them!" Down into the paddy, we jumped and very gently, we started pushing back the people, like a sheep dog does, controlling unruly sheep. Our 'trac started moving away from the people and we quickly ran hard and leaped back on the moving 'trac. Full speed, the three Amtracs raced to smash the Cong into the river. Before we could reach the tree line, the Cong had broken contact and were on the run towards the river. We had missed our opportunity because of the human blockade back in the paddy.

In minutes, the platoon was on the ground and spread out. We began following the river northwest to link up with Delta Company's men. Ten minutes later rifle fire broke out in front of me, then a grenade exploded. I dropped to one knee as the column halted. When the column resumed moving again, I soon saw the reason for the automatic rifle fire and grenade. There, in the bamboo thicket, lay a dead Vietnamese man with a cigarette still stuck in his mouth. I remember turning to Falduti, "Hey what's up with the cigarette?"

"Don't know, but the dude didn't even get a shot off before our point surprised him."

I thought, 'Maybe a little payback—that dude for at least one dead Marine and four WIAs earlier in the afternoon. In fact, better him than me!'

Soon we came upon Delta's unit, and they began to file down off a small hill and in column towards Hill 55, one klick east. A short bit later, the column halted. 'What the hell is the holdup,' we thought. We sure as hell didn't want to be out there overnight— this area was Viet Cong boogeyman country. Corporal McClure went forward to find the cause for the delay. He came back and said, "Stein, the point fireteam is fucked up concerning the location of Hill 55; get the hell up there and get this column moving. It's almost dark."

Instantly, I started moving along the column, with Falduti behind me, lugging the radio. I would need him to call the radio watch on 55 to warn them before bringing the column of men in. By then darkness had set in, but I was able to use a star as a guide to Hill 55. Likewise, I knew the river that flowed past the hill was about seventy-five yards south of our column. Therefore, I would attempt to break out near the bridge that led to the Hill. I moved fast along a dry rice paddy and twenty minutes later I saw the outline of Hill 55. Falduti got on the net, warning the outer bunkers on 55 that we were coming in. Entering 55 in pitch blackness was a deadly undertaking, because many of the Marines on watch were jittery FNGs with itchy trigger fingers.

When I got within 100 feet of the wire, I whistled and called out, "Alpha and Delta column coming in, get your fingers off the triggers." They answered, and two Marines opened the wire gate over the road below Hill 55. Within ten minutes, the rear man was inside the wire.

The tally for the past eighty hours without sleep: sixteen miles walked, an unknown number of dead and wounded North Vietnamese and Viet Cong, and one dead and four wounded Marines. Our reward—maybe sleep in the moldy platoon tent on 55.

Saturday March 18
Dear Mom, Dad and Family,
Here I am again after a hectic week of work. This morning I received letters from Mom, Pauline, Theresa, Aunt Eleanor, Ron, an Easter card from Uncle Bob and Aunt Hatti and Stan. Made me feel great but I felt like

crying at the same time. I am so close, yet so far from seeing all of you wonderful people! Again! What can I say?!

I could write ten sheets on what happened since Wed. the 15th until last night at 10 p.m. They woke us up at 2 a.m. the 15th and said we're going out by choppers. Where? I didn't know. Our platoon landed in the dark in the mountains north of Da Nang. We joined a platoon from H Co. 2/4 and the next day moved through the thick valleys towards a mountain where a battalion of Cong was located. Jets hit the mountain for about three hours, hours before that. We got up the jungle mountain to find a large and neat Cong hideout, but the Charlies got out before we arrived. Thank God! We dug up many graves of Cong. The Phantom Jets did get some of them. It's unreal to see what a 750-1000 lb. bomb does to a mountain side.

We were up there that night without a reinforced Marine Co. Flew out in choppers only to find we had to go on a sweep as soon as we got off the helicopters on Hill 55. They had some gooks trapped near a river and needed another platoon. We got them, and my fireteam had to lead two platoons back to the Hill in darkness. I guess the other unit wasn't too familiar with the area.

That's all I have for now, thanks for your letters and prayers.

Your loving son and brother,
Wally

* * *

I did get to sleep in the moldy tent that night for eight straight hours until 0700 hours. However, an hour later, the most extreme nightmare occurred when I was fully awake. Lieutenant Kilhenny called the platoon together and announced, "Today, we will trade in our M-14s for the M-16 rifle."

Instantly, like a red-hot branding iron touching flesh, my blood began to boil. 'This can't be happening—in the middle of a fucking war, some unknown power is ripping my lifeline out of my hand, for a plastic piece of shit with a cute little handle in the middle, that looks like a kid's Mattel toy!' I thought back on the mountain valleys at home, where people hunted groundhogs with 223s. Here we were hunting big game, and they could shoot back!

An hour later I gave up my beloved M-14 and we all marched down the road towards Hill 1 to try out our new plastic toys. After blasting away with two clips, I walked back to the road feeling hopeless and apprehensive about the piece I lugged. Will it work when Charlie starts shooting with dependable AK-47s and SKS rifles?

The platoon stayed on Hill 55 for the purpose of running patrols and ambushes in other nearby locations south and west. At the same time, I got a new assignment. I would be a fireteam leader and an assistant squad leader. Jimmy Viello outranked me as squad leader in name only, because he had only three months in country. We had to work together on patrols and were a perfect team as he always discussed decisions concerning the welfare of the squad.

Later in the week, the squad was picked for a bastard ambush that took us across the river and then southeast 1000 meters near the ville Giang La (1). I told Jimmy I was out near that area the prior October, and it was a friggin' Viet Cong shit hole. Also, the squad had just added three FNGs, who had not yet been on a patrol or ambush. Nevertheless, I started preparing with Jimmy.

First, we plotted coordinates along the patrol route that we'd use if we needed artillery and mortars. Second, we checked every man's ammunition clips—I was overly cautious because I didn't trust that new weapon, the M-16. When I felt satisfied, all details covered, I wrote a letter home before dark set in. Writing home before a dangerous mission had become a habit, because there was no guarantee that I would witness the sunrise the next morning.

At 2030 hours, thirty minutes before our ambush departure, the three FNGs burst into the tent. They had been up the hill in the bar tent, and I could see by the candlelight that they had more than the two daily beers allotment. Immediately I knew that I had missed one important detail: keep everyone in the tent that evening. I stared at three impaired men. Slobbering, Jack Yoder spoke, "Stein, we've never been on a patrol... what's going to happen south of Hill 55 tonight?"

I retorted, "God damn it men, our job tonight requires us to sneak out 1000 meters and ambush some Viet Cong and kill them!" Their twisted faces revealed their fear, but I understood their fear stemmed from a human factor. They were asking themselves the essential question: 'How will I react when the shooting erupts?'

I quickly told them to get their gear together and be ready to move out in twenty minutes. Then I went outside to confer with Viello. Jimmy looked up from his perch on a sandbagged chair. "Hey Stein, what's up?"

"Jimmy, I think we'll go to plan B tonight—the newbies have had too much booze and that leaves us with only seven effective bodies. But also, I don't think tonight is the ideal time for them to tangle with Charlie. They'll get plenty of chances later. More importantly, our job is to bring everyone, including us, back alive."

At 2100 hours, before moving out, I assembled the squad outside the tent. I only told them that we had to alter our ambush plan. Then, on point, I led them down the hill where two Marines opened the wire gate. I headed to the bridge over the river. Two tank crews and other supporting Marines guarded the bridge on the south entrance, about thirteen in total. Those tank crews held the key to my plan B. I planned on talking to the senior NCO about setting the squad behind the tanks until 0300 hours.

When we reached the tank perimeter, Viello and I talked to the Sergeant in charge. He understood my problem and instructed me to set the men in down an embankment behind the tanks. Five minutes later, I had the squad set in place and I told them to stay alert and no bull shitting. Then Jimmy and I sat down behind the tank. We were secure—if Charlie struck tonight the tanks would do our light work with the monster 90-millimeter canon, 50 caliber, and the blazing flame thrower. The night passed quickly for Jimmy and me because we were checking on the squad every half hour, but that probably wasn't needed because veterans Rioux and Falduti kept everyone alert.

Around 0330 hours, I called the 3rd Platoon radio man and told him to warn the outer bunker near the road that a patrol was coming in. Ten minutes later I thanked the tankers, and in the blackness, I started towards the bridge with nine men close behind. As I spotted the outer bunker close to the road, I went to one knee, as did the squad behind. I whistled to the men in the bunker and heard, "League!"

I came back, "American, Alpha 3-2 coming in." We entered the perimeter and I told everyone to catch some Zs, and that we'd debrief later in the morning. I thought, 'An aborted ambush for sure, but also, the Lieutenant won't have to write the required condolence letters to the parents, informing them their sons were dead!'

When the hot sun peeked its head above the horizon the next morning, we held a squad meeting. I directed my words at the new guys, "First, I understand your fear of the unknown dangers surrounding you—I was a new guy last summer. However, sooner or later you will be shot at, and like magic, you'll be a veteran of war, like it or not. Second, we will not have booze before the next mission, because we all need to be fully alert to keep each other alive in this shit hole of a place."

When the debriefing ended, I pulled Jimmy aside and explained the aborted ambush the night before was my first incomplete mission since coming ashore the prior summer. I also told him I was superstitious, and that I liked to be at the intended location of a mission. On the other hand, our choice of locations the night before worked out for everyone. It gave us valuable time to train the new guys.

* * *

The platoon stayed on the main part of Hill 55 for a few more days, then we were reassigned to a finger on the western fringe of the hill, to fill in for Delta Company. Delta Company was out on an operation attached to some other battalion. In fact, I observed, by then all the companies of 1/26 were constantly on operations, patrols, and changing positions. We were all running on fumes.

Less than twenty-four hours after moving, McClure, recently promoted to sergeant, received an order to run an ambush west near the ville Chau Son (1). He hand-picked a ten-man team and asked me to lead the point fireteam. Sarge informed me a new 'boot' sergeant wanted to tag along. I immediately protested. "We don't need any FNGs out in that spooky area where Delta lost those men two weeks ago." Sarge reassured me he would place him behind me and out of my hair. Just more bullshit I had little control over—too many of our original leaders were ending their enlistments and leaving to go back to the 'World.'

Regardless, at 2200 hours I went down the hill outside the wire and headed for a paddy dike that ran west towards Chau Son (1) and the river. Through binoculars, I observed from my bunker that the farmers used that dike to get to their fields and back to their village, meaning it probably wasn't booby trapped. I moved at medium speed, making sure not to lose contact with the team. A bit later, near 2350 hours, I held up the patrol because I saw the tree line to my front, and beyond that the river flowing southwest. Then Sergeant McClure and I set everyone behind a paddy wall that paralleled a path coming from the river. We were alert like a cat, crouching and waiting for its prey to run. Hell, Sarge and I had stopped counting months ago, the number of night ambushes we'd set since last August.

Everything was quiet on that moonless early morning until 0200h when I heard some racket down near the river. Beside me, Johnny Adams started to twitch. Instantly I grabbed his shoulder and whispered, "Hold your fire, it is a 'mortal sin' to trip an ambush until seeing live bodies sneaking by. Furthermore, if we start throwing steel at the bushes, our position would be compromised, and any Charlies in the area could make us the ambushed!" A bit later, the noise down by the river ended—monkey, water buffalo, Viet Cong, who in the hell knew?

Two more tense hours silently passed watching the path in front, but no unlucky Viet Cong appeared. By 0400h, it was the time set to start for the hill and be back inside the wire before first light. We didn't want to be in that open paddy at sunrise.

When the patrol entered the wire an hour later, the sky just began to brighten from the east. We had met our deadline—the Charlies were denied early morning targets.

I went to the fireteam bunker, threw off my boots, and plopped down on the scratchy cot to grab some rest before the 1000 hours briefing. The squad gathered outside my bunker to hash over the ambush. The Lieutenant joined us, and the first thing he heard came from the newbie sergeant, who questioned my strategy of taking the patrol across the middle of open paddies, instead of sneaking along the river to the south, which offered cover. I shot back, "Go ahead, Sarge, take a patrol along the river. You'll have Marines fucked up after they've tripped booby traps. Furthermore, you may get your head sniped at from Charlies across the narrow river!" He didn't reply.

For me, it was more of the same bullshit. Our continuity as a platoon was constantly disrupted by the influx of new replacements, and the veterans still with the platoon—me, Falone, McClure, and others—grew restless. We longed for someone to come along with some master plan and say: "Here's what we're going to do to end this friggin' war!" Of course, *we* didn't get paid to create 'master plans.' We were paid to execute the tight ropes, running constant patrols into all the dangerous villages surrounding Hill 55.

* * *

Thirty-six hours later, we moved back to Hill 1. Corporal Falone's squad caught the next mission—a patrol across the suspension bridge and south into Duc Ky (1). The patrol left the hill at noon, walking through fog with rain falling on them. As soon as they crossed the bridge, Falduti and I began radio watch in a bunker facing south. A half hour later I lost sight of their movement in the fog. Within fifteen minutes, small arms fire broke out about a klick south. It sounded like Falone's men stepped into some bad shit. I heard sharp cracks from the Viet Cong's SKS and 30-caliber carbines—American weapons captured by the Chinese Army during the Korean War and obtained by the Vietnamese.

'Damn,' I thought, 'the Viet Cong are standing and fighting.'

Then, on the radio, "Alpha 3, Alpha 3-2. We have one Kilo India Alpha and three Whiskey India Alphas. Request a medevac!"

Falduti transmitted, "I'll call for a chopper, Alpha 3-2." My God, Falone had one dead and three wounded men.

Our 81-millimeter mortars went into action, blasting any Cong that were now retreating towards the river. Minutes later a CH-34 swooped in from the northeast, and instantly the Cong ripped off bursts of fire at the bird dropping into the paddy. When the medevac rose up and powered towards our hill, the sniping continued; however, that helicopter crew flew out of danger, towards Da Nang. Five minutes later, 3-2 transmitted, "Alpha 3, Alpha 3-2. I am bringing the patrol in." I spotted the point as he appeared out of the fog, 200 yards from the suspension bridge. Soon, the patrol, minus four men, scaled the hill and trudged back into the perimeter.

I slipped my rifle over my shoulder and walked across to Falone's bunker, where I found wet, muddy, and visibly outraged men. One trooper shouted, "We should go back to Duc Ky (1) and get some payback!" In fact, he voiced an urge that raced through all our minds.

Then Corporal Falone quietly added, "Somehow during the fire fight, we lost Brown's M-16. Don't be surprised if we're ordered to slosh back out to find it."

Damn, the words barely escaped from his mouth when Company Commander Johnson came rushing from the command bunker and exclaimed, "We need a patrol to retrieve that weapon."

Silence overcame fifteen sullen Marines. Corporal Falone then replied simply, "We'll get it done sir."

After Lieutenant Johnson departed, murmurs of dissent bellowed from our group. One guy shouted, "Screw him!" Another Marine followed, "He should be shot."

Falone quickly cut in: "Sure, he's a hard ass, but we need veteran leaders now, rather than a new commander fresh from the states."

We scraped together enough men to run the Duc Ky (1) gauntlet to find that rifle. Falone's men would stay back. Five minutes later, I stepped through the wire, and nine Marines followed over the bridge southwest along the river.

The fog still rolled across the paddy as I moved towards the southern edge of Duc Ky (1), where we would concentrate our search. When I reached the southern edge of the ville, six men spread out behind a dike, while Rioux, Falduti, Pierce, and I started kicking the haystacks, roofs of hooches, and behind fences. But we didn't uncover the missing M-16. What the hell? It had been three hours since the firefight; the Charlies could have found it, or maybe some kid had a souvenir, who knew? Screw this. Now, all we could do was get back to Hill 1 without losing any more men.

I signaled the men in the paddy to take the same route back to the hill, and I would bring up the rear. We moved fast, sloshing through the knee-deep paddy along the tree line. While we moved my head was like an owl's head looking for his next meal, twitching 360 degrees, watching for movement to our south, east, or west. Twenty minutes later, ten wet, dirty Marines were safely back on Hill 1. Amazingly, we patrolled out and back without contact with the Viet Cong. Nothing could be predicted on patrols, but when it happened, it was short, violent, and deadly!

When I set my rifle against my bunker a few moments later, I contemplated two realizations. First, Jackson Brown was one of those rare people we all hope to encounter during our journey through life. His infectious smile and pleasant personality always made people feel welcome. None of us wanted harm to come his way. However, none of us were immune to death in the bush—men died and were ripped apart every day. Brown was now on his final trip home to a heart-smashed family. For us, we would never see his smile again, but tomorrow we would go back to work hunting Charlie.

My second thought: 'Damn, I was proud to be surrounded by all those platoon members that shattering day.' On that second patrol out to Duc Ky (1), everyone felt a powerful urge to destroy twenty-five hooches and every living being in that ville. Nevertheless, the patrol held their cool, like professional soldiers. No one could ask more of America's sons, none over the age of twenty-one.

Members of Walter's squad – O'Brien, Rioux, and Ramirez

Chapter 7:
Who Left the Boogeyman Loose for 96 Hours?

Walter, exhausted and thin, 1967

THE NEXT MORNING when the sun rose, Sergeant McClure left the perimeter with ten men for a patrol north, one-half kilometer to Thai Cam (3). It was most likely his last patrol. He had only three days left and a wake-up, then back to the 'World' with a discharge after four years in the Corps. While his patrol was out, Falduti and I were tuned in on the radio, checking the patrol's progress. Then at noon, McClure came on the net, "Alpha 3, Alpha 3-2. I am bringing the patrol in." Five minutes later I spotted his point man working his way across the wide paddy that separated the ville from our wire.

I watched them approaching the wire from my bunker. Then, heavy rifle fire erupted from Thai Cam (3). Damn, the Viet Cong decided to get some target practice in before the patrol entered the perimeter. Seconds later, as the men were scrambling for cover, I heard a loud explosion, and saw a plume of smoke near the wire. Then, Sergeant McClure was on the net, "Alpha 3, we have a man down." Jim Trice, a Corpsman, stood by my bunker, grabbed his medical bag, and ran towards the wire. Rifle in my hand, I rushed after him. By the time we twisted through the sharp concertina wire, James Dugan was 'shaking and baking' with his M-60 machine gun, sending hundreds of hot rounds at the snipers near Thai Cam (3).

Minutes later the Viet Cong weapons went silent. Promptly, Trice and I found the downed man, laying in a pool of blood. My God, the kid from Oklahoma! As Corpsman Trice quickly bent down to check vital signs, I glanced down and said, "Fuck, he's gone; it doesn't mean nothin'!"

Then, Sergeant McClure pushed through the bush and shouted, "I think his grenades detonated while he was running for cover. Maybe a round from the Viet Cong hit the grenades." Who knew? The kid was nearly cut in half. The Sarge kept ranting, "Screw this shit, I lost a man from my home state on my last patrol," as his face grimaced in frustration and anger.

I heard a CH-34 approaching from the east and five minutes later, under the swirling blades of the chopper, we carefully loaded the destroyed body of the eighteen-year-old kid into the chopper. Back to the 'World' in a bag to another devastated family.

Several minutes later, I leaned my Mattel toy against the rat- and mouse-infested bunker and bent to sit down and have a smoke. But, I never lit that butt, because Falduti rushed over and shouted, "The Lieutenant requests a patrol to Duc Ky (2). He said some Vietnamese came to the wire complaining about mortar rounds hitting near their hooches last night."

I snapped, "Hell yes, the Cong were sniping at Hill 55 last night from Duc Ky (2); if we can't shoot back, our men should pack up and go home!"

I gathered the squad and briefed them about the patrol to Duc Ky (2), but before departing, I stopped at Lieutenant Kilhenny's bunker. I understood he wanted to go out with us, which was fine with me, because it meant he wanted to lead from the front, not watch from the safety of his bunker.

Duc Ky (2) village was southwest, about one and a half klicks on the northern side of the river. When we were about one klick into the patrol I saw a procession of women approaching from the southwest. We held up and everyone went to one knee on full alert. A few minutes later, the lead barefooted woman, dressed in black silk pajamas and bright white skirt, held out her arms. She held something in a straw woven mat. She stopped, screaming in front of me and opened the bundle. Inside, a dead baby was wrapped carefully in a silk cloth, ready for burial. I gasped. Damn, what could I possibly say to ease her pain? I was supposed to be a Marine warrior.

Nonetheless, in my best Vietnamese, I quickly told her we didn't intend to harm her baby, but rather to silence the snipers. What the hell else could I do or say? After that brief exchange, she turned, still sobbing, and led her group of women towards their village. I turned around and instructed the squad to start moving towards our position on Hill 1. Falduti and I brought up the rear.

After returning to our bunker in early evening, I cut open a can of beans and franks for my evening meal. I barely finished the last morsels when Corporal Falone came by and announced, "Hey, Stein, more bullshit tomorrow. I am assembling a reinforced group of fifteen men for a patrol to Xuan Diem (2) tomorrow. Do you want to tag along?"

"Hell yes, Falone, I can't live forever; furthermore, maybe we'll get some payback out in Xuan Diem."

The patrol set out at 0900 hours towards Xuan Diem, one and a half klicks northwest of our perimeter. The sun was on full blast on our helmets and the rice paddies were drying, because the monsoons had ended. Consequently, we could move fast across the treacherous open paddies leading to our target ville. An hour and a half later, my fireteam entered the ville; all was quiet, but I did see some Vietnamese tending to their gardens near their hooches.

Corporal Falone quickly took a team of seven men up a path to check ID cards and search several hooches. The rest of us spread out to watch for movement of people from all directions. A bit later, Falone's men approached from the west. Then, a single shot rang out, but none followed. The next second I heard that hated call, "Corpsman, Corpsman up."

My God, thirty feet from me the new kid, Jake, wasn't moving, while Jim Trice, our Corpsman, leaned over him. I shouted at Jim, and he shouted back. "Forget it, Stein, he's gone—shot through the heart!"

Damn, that sniper had to have been hundreds of yards away, somewhere north of our position. As soon as Corporal Falone brought up his team, he ordered everyone to stay down, because that Charlie was a professional sniper armed with a powerful scope. At that moment, that dead Marine just happened to be the best target for the sniper to make a kill shot. Who knew? Tomorrow any one of us could become that kill shot.

Regardless, we had a dead kid to take back, and Corporal Falone and I decided that nothing short of a B-52 strike would kill the sniper. Furthermore, we both knew no one would give us a B-52 strike to destroy the vast country to the north, simply for one sniper. Therefore, the patrol was put in fast motion towards Hill 55, less than a klick away. We quickly slid Jake's lifeless body on a folded poncho and four Marines, one on each corner, started across that open paddy. I was one of those four, complete with a firm upper lip and a burning rage racing through my body about the kid I carried. He was barely out of high school, in country only two weeks, and should have had possibly sixty more years to enjoy a rich, full life.

The day's sweat and aggravation count: one dead Marine, one professional sniper on the loose, no dead Viet Cong. After pushing across the open rice paddy for nearly fifteen minutes, we made it to Hill 55. My arms were numb from carrying the makeshift stretcher, but it was the least I could do for another beloved fallen warrior. As soon as we climbed the hill, we found the tent where a Marine would put a tag on his foot. The body would be sent to Da Nang, bagged, and would join other bags for the jet trip back to the 'World.'

The next day dawned hot, dusty, and dry. We didn't have time to rest from the mission the day before, because a new order came down from Battalion to conduct a Country Fair two klicks west, in the village of Xuan Diem (1). Around 1000 hours, the platoon scraped together twenty-five men, and we were quickly on the move on a path the Vietnamese used daily. An hour later the platoon had the village surrounded and sealed off against anyone breaking out. Ten Marines went in and searched for Viet Cong, checking ID cards, while two Corpsmen checked people for any health issues. While that occurred, our squad stayed in place on the eastern edge of the village and started digging foxholes for the long day ahead.

About noon, some sharp sniper fire zipped in on the western edge of the ville. Our M-60 gunner quickly sent the Charlie tormentors down their cozy spider holes... dead or alive?

Two hours later, Pierce and I were down in our five-by-three foxhole, when a shot rang out from the next foxhole, forty feet away. "Corpsman, Corpsman up!" I saw Ed Johnson moving; however, Jim Conner was sprawled back, and our Corpsman Trice frantically attempted to stop the bleeding from an ugly head wound. Trice screamed, "We need a medevac now!" Ten minutes later, a CH-34 landed on the ground and four of us loaded another dying man on the bird. Damn, he looked bad—hardly breathing, with blood oozing through thick layers of battle dressings.

As soon as the chopper was air bound I hurried back to my hole and jumped in to join Pierce. Sweating, I blurted out, "What in hell happened in that foxhole?"

"I think Ed Johnson was 'grab-assing' with Jim, and somehow his rifle went off point blank into Jim's head."

I proceeded to tell Pierce about Johnson telling me how to get out of this combat zone. "He told me he could smash my ankle with the butt of his rifle, thereby causing an injury that would make me limp. I told him, '*Who in hell would be your squad leader if I abandoned you and the other men?*' Furthermore, I threatened to put him on point the next patrol for talking such shit. Jim, he shut up in a hurry. But I wouldn't put him on point; he'd fuck something up and get someone else mangled!"

Late that afternoon, Pierce and I were picked to take outpost duty for the night. That duty required two men to set in, fifty yards or more outside any perimeter for the purpose of detecting early probes by Charlie. Moreover, that duty was extremely hairy since it placed us forward, unsupported by the main perimeter. Despite that, Pierce and I casually ate our C-ration grub and prepared for the long night. After eating, we sat in the hole and smoked our last cigarettes. Then we worked our way east and dug another hole near a path where the Viet Cong might sneak through if they probed the eastern perimeter.

Nightfall set in with no moon, meaning Charlie had ideal conditions to prowl around in the dark. It also meant we had to be on high alert. For that reason, we decided to take thirty-minute watches that night. I remember before taking the first watch. Jim said, "Damn straight, no alarm clocks out here; our need to survive keeps us awake in the bush!"

Later, around 0030, I called to the platoon, "All clear with OP1."

The next thing I remembered, Falduti shook both me and Jim and whispered, "What the fuck happened to you guys? You haven't called in since 0030—it's 0300 hours."

"Damn," I said without talking loud, "we checked out for two and a half hours." I told Falduti to crawl back to his position, and Jim and I would watch together until morning.

The remainder of the night passed with Jim and I wide awake, poking one another constantly, until the sky turned crimson and the sun peeked from the east. I felt damned embarrassed that two veterans had fallen asleep on watch and compromised our lives and those of the platoon. On the other hand, it was evident that the last twelve months of constant training, combat, and lack of sleep finally caught up to Jim and me. We talked about our screw-up while chowing down. "For one thing," I told Jim, "we could have gotten our throats slit and then Charlie could have crept up on the platoon. We were lucky again, huh? Eight months of luck with so many around us getting blooded and greased."

At noon, we covered our foxholes, buried our C-rat cans, and the platoon tramped towards Hill 1, leaving behind the people of Xuan Diem (1). An hour later I was back at our fireteam bunker sitting with Pierce, Falduti, and Rioux. We were jovial, eating and celebrating the end of another short operation. That joy shattered five minutes later when Lieutenant Kilhenny stopped at our bunker and announced, "First, Sergeant McClure, Sergeant Freeman, and Sergeant Collen depart for the 'World' tomorrow. Second, Jim, you will be transferred to the 1st Battalion, 9th Marines."

Jim, in shock, looked at me. "That's right," I said, "you heard it right—the walking dead!" The 1st Battalion, 9th Marines were given that dubious title because they were always stepping into some bad shit. However, the truth in Vietnam held that most Marine and Army grunt battalions would sooner or later hit some bad combat, resulting in many casualties on both sides.

After the Lieutenant walked back to his bunker, Jim shook his head and said, "Stein, it's a bad omen; 1/9 is the last outfit I would have picked for my last two months in the zone."

"Maybe not, Jim. You already know Hill 55 is an extremely hot combat zone. Hell, you'll make it back to the World." He nodded and went into the bunker to get his equipment ready for tomorrow's departure.

Early morning the next day, I bid farewell to the sergeants and Jim. Then, like a flash, they hopped up on a truck and sped away in a cloud of dust towards Da Nang. I sat down on a sandbag out of the sun's hot rays, thinking about the leaders who just departed from my life. Any one of them would have given their life for me. Furthermore, I would never see them again, much like all the other dead, wounded, and transferred men before them. On the other hand, I was hardened to that loss, because I was still alive and had to remain strong and focused for the men in the squad that were entrusted to me.

> *Tuesday, April 11*
> *Dear Mom, Dad & Family,*
>
> *I received at least three letters from home the past few days, but I haven't been able to answer them or anyone else's letters.*
>
> *Things around here have been going hard & crazy. The Cong are popping up all over and they're staying and fighting. Every day observers are spotting movement and our platoon goes out on tanks after them. Sometimes I think the only way we'll win the military war is to move the people out (which has been done in areas around here) and tear everything up. I don't even want to tell you what war is like. And believe me, this is as furious as any, as far as I am concerned. I might as well forget about getting out of a line company and a combat zone. Maybe they'll cut me some slack the last month over here. I don't know if I'll get R&R again either. All these new guys have to go once before I can go the 2nd time. Oh well.*

Yes! I received both packages. Boy! I didn't know Gram was 75 years old. I did get the fudge from Aunt Mary. You said Diane has been coming to the house a lot lately! Maybe it's because I don't write her much anymore. Girls are the least of my problems, all I want to do is keep my head 'wired together' and try my best to get out of here soon. War makes a guy 'hard,' I think. By the way, I had a mustache, but I had to shave it. Bn. orders for all of us. All us 'old' guys wore them.

I don't have much more to say so I'll end. Thanks for all the letters and prayers, I need them both.

Your loving son & brother,
Wally

* * *

Jimmy Viello left the platoon; I didn't know he departed until I heard that he had been caught stealing morphine from a Corpsman's bag. Maybe he was disciplined for drug use, or discharged from the Marine Corps. I never did learn what happened to him. As a result, his departure meant I was the permanent squad leader. In fact, it was no surprise to me since I had performed squad leader level work for the past six weeks. I knew that responsibility would come, because the platoon lost many NCOs over the past three weeks. My low rank, E-3 Lance Corporal, meant nothing in Vietnam—time in country counted more, and I already felt I had been there forever.

I didn't have to wait long for the next operation. Lieutenant Kilhenny came up to me when I was cleaning my 'Mattel toy' and told me to prepare the squad for a two-force operation the next morning near the villages Thai Cam (2) and (3). Also, he warned me, "The intelligence people reported heavy Viet Cong activity in that area."

I commented, "I guess that heavy presence is constant, no matter where we patrol since the monsoon rain ended, huh, Lieutenant?"

He nodded and said, "The Amtracs will pick your squad up at 0900h. Tom Jackson will take his squad out towards Thai Cam (2) at the same time. Be careful Stein!"

Later, as I stood watch at the bunker peering north towards Thai Cam (3), I double checked myself concerning the next day's patrol. Had I forgotten any details? Before dark, I assembled the men and told them to carry 200 rounds, one C-rat, 2 canteens of water, and no hand grenades—I didn't have to remind them about the kid from Oklahoma. After reviewing the details in my head, I was satisfied that we were ready for tomorrow's operation—the only question remaining was whether we would bump into Charlie.

The next morning at 0900h, my squad of ten men were around me as I gave them the last frag order. "Tom Jackson's patrol is leaving the perimeter, and as soon as the 'tracs arrive, we will proceed east and be on standby as a reactionary force near Bich Bac." Two Amtracs stopped five minutes later in front of my waiting, anxious men. Quickly, we boarded the green monsters and sped away from Hill 1, leaving behind a cloud of dust. Amtrac crews had two operators and one man perched on top behind a dependable M-30 machine gun. Our two crews were salty veterans from last summer's landings. I knew I could depend on them to inflict deadly firepower against any Viet Cong force.

Two hours later, Tom Jackson reported that all was quiet at his first checkpoint. When that checkpoint was transmitted, we were parked under some banana trees, just north of the dusty road that led to Da Nang. Although we were shaded, salty sweat dripped down our faces. Regardless, the men on the 'tracs were fully focused on the mission, and no one bitched about the harsh weather conditions.

Around 1130 hours, Tom called in his next checkpoint. Barely ten minutes later, automatic weapons spitting out hot steel punctured the hot tropical air—AK-47s and SKSs. Next, I heard Dave Johnson's heavy M-60, firing from M-16s, and pops from the M-79s. Then, more bursts from the Viet Cong. My God, they were standing tough and not running. Seconds later, Tom Jackson shouted on the radio, "Alpha 6, Alpha 6 [our Company Commander back on Hill 1], we have a man down and the fire from Charlie is too heavy to get to him. We're pulling back to a tree line." Alpha 6 calmly relayed back to him to provide map coordinates for 105 artillery support. But Tom did not answer.

Quickly I glanced at the Amtrac operator, he looked back at me—we knew what must happen next. Seconds later the two steel machines were churning across the paddy, loaded with my squad clinging to the straps. I grabbed the radio receiver and squeezed, "Alpha 6, 3-1 needs our firepower; we're on the move!"

Six replied, "Roger."

I squeezed again, "3-1, we are about 200 meters out and closing. We will pass you and will drive the Viet Cong from their position."

Ten seconds later we approached a small bamboo thicket and there, under the shade of the trees, a squad of South Vietnamese troops were wasting away time. I screamed, "Don't blast them, they're friendly!" On the other hand, they were zero help to our squad that was pinned down nearby. Screw it, we must get to our downed Marine.

I kept my eyes peeled at a tree line seventy-five yards north, then I saw flashes and puffs of smoke; they had turned their fire towards us. Then the *zip, zip* of steel broke the air all around our heads. The two machine gunners also saw the puffs and opened with hundreds of rounds, chewing up the bold Charlies hiding in the brush. The whizzing rounds no longer were coming at us. As we closed to within forty yards of the Cong, I saw our man lying face down, straight ahead. As the lead 'trac neared the downed Marine, the operator jerked the machine to the left and stopped, giving us cover to retrieve our man.

I jumped off the 'trac, followed by Spencer, Walker, and another Marine. We grabbed the Marine and pulled his bullet-ridden body into the opened Amtrac door. Blood splattered on my hands as I ran around the Amtrac and let loose, full automatic, towards the tree line. Likewise, the squad followed my lead and we all dropped to the ground as we continued chewing up the thick brush where Charlie had fled seconds before.

Then I heard screams from five men, "Our rifles are jammed."

"Stay down, the Amtrak's machine guns will cover us!" I shouted back. "Frigging pieces of shit," I yelled to Jimmy Spencer, ten feet to my left. Sweat poured down his face—no rounds were coming from his 'Mattel toy' either! I ripped another clip where the Viet Cong last fired, but there was no return fire. Only then was I confident the Charlies had disengaged, and I ordered a cease fire.

A calm silence overcame the battle field; whereas, seconds before, hundreds of hot rounds were searching for human flesh. Like shutting off a water spigot, the chaos of combat ended. Nevertheless, we still had more work—to search for dead and wounded Cong. Four of us kicked around the brush, but we didn't find any bodies, only plenty of blood smeared on the ground and bushes. Clearly Charlie took some hits but managed to drag off their comrades. A few minutes later I ordered the squad, one at a time, to cross over the paddy to the south and hook up with Tom's men in the tree line. A further search for Charlie back in that thick bamboo would have been stupid. Hell, most of our worthless rifles wouldn't shoot. Minutes later I was the last man to cross the paddy and the Amtracs pulled back to join us. Once there, I suggested we rest, eat some C-rats, and take time to clean our worthless rifles.

Around 1230h, both squads mounted the two Amtracs and prepared to advance south towards Thai Cam (3). Then Alpha 6 broke on the radio. I grabbed the handset from Falduti, "Six, we're on the move, approaching Cam-3."

Six, "Roger."

The machines ground across the open dry paddy, closing on the ville. As soon as we saw the village sign we stopped. I was no stranger to the village entrance. The sign in bright colors read, "Thai Cam 3," and the ville appeared like most others in the area—peaceful and serene. Neat little gardens featuring peppers, melons, tomatoes, beans, and various root crops were surrounded by neat bamboo fences. Likewise, the straw-and-bamboo-framed hooches were humble, but dry and sturdy. On the other hand, I knew the Viet Cong lived and operated in all the 'peaceful' villages we searched. The plan that afternoon was to search and attempt to catch some Cong that might be hanging around.

Immediately after stopping, I jumped off the 'trac, followed by my squad. The other Amtrac moved about seventy-five yards west to cover the northern edge of the ville. Our 'trac crew stood by to cover us while I moved on the path towards the sign. Twenty feet from the ville's edge, I passed the word back, "Punji poles on both sides, watch your step." Then, as I passed under the arch—*snap, snap, zit, zit*—hot rounds zipped past my head, and branches and splinters of bamboo bounced off my steel pot. "Damn," I screamed as I dropped to one knee, "where in the hell did that shit come from?" I focused on the tree line on the ville's south side, and I noticed a hooch thirty yards up the path, but did not see any signs of life. On the other hand, nine men were flat on the path, waiting for a command from me. I had split seconds to decide; thus, I calmly ordered the squad to get back on the Amtrac. I would cover them from here.

Five minutes later, our 'trac caught up with the other squad, and together the machines with human cargo on top sped along the northwest edge of the ville. After racing 200 feet, we ground to a halt as a group of Vietnamese suddenly appeared from the ville's edge, screaming and pointing at us. Immediately, I heard shouts from the men to "waste the dinks!" I didn't know why they were agitated. Maybe the invasion of the monster machines sitting in their rice paddy? Or, did they simply want us to go home? Who knew? What I did know was that we had twenty-five sweaty, hot, pissed off Marines sitting on two 'tracs. Furthermore, one dead Marine was inside, and we wanted revenge. "Frig this," I snapped as I grabbed the handset from Falduti. "Alpha 6, Alpha 3-2."

"Alpha 6."

"Six, we're one klick south, we're coming in!"

"Roger 3-2."

Seconds later the operators had the Amtracs at full throttle, with smoke flying out the exhausts, pushing towards Hill 55, leaving the angry mob behind, still shaking their fists at us. Our Amtracs entered the wire fifteen minutes later and clawed to the top of Hill 55 and we stopped at the tent where dead troopers were tagged, sent to Da Nang, and shipped back to the 'World.'

After Spence, Falduti, and I carried Scotty's body into the tent, I threw the tent flap up and stepped back outside. Near the tent I spotted a pile of bloody jungle utilities and boots scattered on the red earth. Instantly, I shouted at the Marine in the tent, "Why doesn't someone burn that stinking, bloody mess outside the door?" Then I caught myself peeking back in the tent flap. "It's okay, Marine, it's not your fault. I am angry and frustrated." Then I told the two squads that we had to hump the one-third mile back to Hill 1. "Stay on the left side of the road down off the skyline where Charlie, the sniper, can't see us."

Fifteen minutes later, nineteen tired, sweaty, and dirty men sat on the hot earth behind Lieutenant Kilhenny's bunker for a debriefing. First, we all agreed that Tom's squad could not have anticipated the Viet Cong were concealed in that tree line. We discussed the hazards crossing open rice paddies. Finally, I informed the Lieutenant about the five 'Mattel toys' that failed to fire while we were still engaged with Charlie. I added, "We were lucky today, because the Amtrac gunners covered our asses; tomorrow, if that junk rifle fails, we could have dead and wounded men lying out in the paddies."

He agreed, and told us he felt powerless, because we all lost the better weapon—the M-14. That ended the debriefing, and I told the squad I would meet them at my bunker after talking to the Lieutenant. We went inside his sandbagged bunker out of the hot sun. He quickly said it was suggested to him that 3rd Platoon run a night time patrol back to Thai Cam 2 in an attempt to capture some VC in their sleep. I didn't question where that order came from, but I quickly asked if my squad was the chosen one. "Yes, Stein, you've been to that village many times before I joined the platoon."

I hesitated a second and replied, "Yes sir, we will go if two circumstances are met: one, we wait until the waning moon a few days away, and two, we leave our noisy flak jackets and helmets here because I want the men to be light with zero noise." I strongly preferred night missions and I had full confidence in my squad's ability to sneak into that ville. The Lieutenant agreed. "Good, we'll wait until the waning moon, and I'll start working on a patrol plan." Then I stepped out into the stifling heat, and with the plastic rifle slung over my shoulder I started towards my bunker.

While walking I began to reflect about my present state of existence. I had no illusions about going home alive or in one piece, and if I did survive Vietnam, how would I ever fit into life back in the 'World'? I had already beaten all odds the past eight months, but as every day passed, I could feel the level of combat increase in our sector. News from all areas in Vietnam was likewise grim. America was losing her sons at a rate of one hundred dead and six hundred wounded each week, and those rates were spiraling upward with each passing week. At the same time, I was no longer the nineteen-year-old kid who went south to boot camp in 1965. On the contrary, I was a 'reincarnated' human life. I was now living a second life, but still in the same body. The unnatural human brutality that war demands had seared my being forever, much like a red hot branding iron burns the rump of a young bawling calf. I reflected a moment on the Viet Cong. God damn! They were a tenacious adversary; their courage showed, hanging fast in the trench-line, facing two charging Amtracs and twelve angry marines, looking for payback. In fact, we marines had utmost respect for 'Sir Charles,' because we had more in common with him than with the people who sent us here to hunt down Charlie. Nevertheless, we'd bump into one another again and the result would be violent; each side would bleed and gut the other out.

When I reached the bunker, Spencer's fireteam and the rest of the squad were busy cleaning their rifles. Spence looked up. "Hey Stein, what's up?"

"Guess what, Spence? Our squad is running a night recon back to Thai Cam 2."

Spence shouted, "What the fuck for?"

"It has been suggested we can nail some VC in their sleep and take them alive."

Falduti, the old salt left in the squad, laughed and then retorted, "Stein, they don't sleep at night. They're out fucking with us."

I barked back, "Hell, it will be a cake; no flak jackets or helmets will be worn, and our faces will be charcoaled. The squad will be silent, like a ghost in the night, and who knows? We could win the war that night with the last reconnaissance patrol in Vietnam. The headline will read: Alpha 3-2 of A Company 1/26 bags five VC in their sleep and turns the tide of the war!"

Steve Wilson shouted, "You're a crazy son of a bitch, Stein."

"I know," I replied. "And the squad is stuck with me."

I moved away from the men and the bunker looking across the rice paddy towards Thai Cam 2, two klicks north, lost in my thoughts, quietly formulating a possible route and a plan for after we reached the village. After a few minutes, I turned, gazing at nine men sitting on the hot ground. They were crusty, sweaty, and didn't even have a hot shower to sooth their bodies and wash the red grime away. All they had was a little water from a jerry can dumped in helmets and then splashed on their faces to wash off the filth. In fact, the last shower that splashed on their bodies was five weeks ago when the monsoon season ended, shutting off the giant nozzle from the sky. Above all, even though their lives were void of any worldly luxuries and surrounded by constant insanity, the marines on the ground were joking and grab-assing like they hadn't a care in the world.

Then, my gaze turned to self-reflection. God damn, how I cared for those young marines on the ground. They looked to me for leadership, but at the same time, I needed them, too. Then a realization hit me like a hammer and calmness overcame my spirit. I no longer had any doubts concerning my present state of existence. This was now my home, and I belonged here with these men. No matter what it would take, I must get them through this life-sucking human meat grinder.

* * *

Two days later, around 1900 hours, we assembled at my bunker before departing: ten men with charcoal painted faces and utility covers on our heads. With no flak jackets to weigh us down and ammo clips tied down tight, we looked light and fast, the same as our counterparts—the Viet Cong. Fifteen minutes later, we left Hill 1 on the road towards Bich Bac, less than a klick northwest. A bit later the squad slid down over the road berm, just 100 yards west of Bich Bac, and hunkered down until dark. My plan was simple—I wanted all Vietnamese in the area to see us go out in daylight and set in near Bich Bac. However, after dark, I planned to vacate the road berm and set out for Thai Cam (3). The squad knew every move that was planned for that night.

Right before dark, our Corpsman questioned me. "Stein, it's suicide to tramp out a kilometer and sneak in that ville. We can stay here, can't we?"

Quickly, I countered, "John, we're committed because the Vietnamese know our location and the Marines on Hill 1 expect us to be due north. What the hell happens if a Cong patrol gets between us and the perimeter and probes the Hill? Then, we could possibly get cut down by our own men blasting in our direction." Finally, I told John, "We're going to Thai Cam (3); you can stay here by your lonesome if you choose."

John remained silent. I knew he thought I was crazy—and he was somewhat correct. Nevertheless, my job that night demanded our squad complete the mission without losing any lives.

At 2100 hours, after our eyes adjusted to the dark, Rioux climbed up on the road and we started north across a dry paddy. Our spacing between men was a few yards because I didn't want anyone to get separated in the blackness. A bit later, we stopped when we reached a paddy dike that ran east and west. That path led to Thai Cam (3), one-third klick west. Twenty minutes later I made out the tree line of the ville and we halted and went down on one knee—no whispering, nothing. Every man knew the next move: watch and listen for any human activity from the ville. The countryside farmers in our operating area were without electricity; therefore, soon after dark the villagers extinguished their cooking fires and candles and retired to bed. Thus, the only humans roaming around were the Viet Cong and the Marines.

After watching and listening for twenty minutes, we slowly crept toward the ville until we reached the arch entrance sign—the same spot where snipers opened fire on us a week ago. Then I took six Marines down the path towards the first hooch. Four men stayed in place to cover us from possible movement from the east. Seconds later I touched Spence on the arm as a signal for him to surround the first hooch. Then Rioux and I slithered inside and flashed our pen lights on three kids and a woman, all sleeping on straw and bamboo beds. Damn, they didn't even wake. We backed out, and the team of six moved fifteen yards to the next hooch. When Rioux and I entered the next home, we found a startled man and a silent, shaking woman with two kids. They sat up from their hard bamboo beds, terror written on their faces as they encountered us. I quickly pointed my rifle at the man and asked for his ID card. I was close enough to see his heart pounding under his white silk shirt.

He handed me his ID card as Rioux checked the woman's card. Although they had cards, sometimes those IDs were obtained from the Viet Cong, not the Marines. Recalling that, my mind worked at warp speed—I could slice their throats with my Ka-Bar or tie them up and take them back to the Hill. On the other hand, what would I do with the shivering kids? I grabbed Rioux's arm and told him to get the squad moving east, fast, while I kept my rifle trained on the man and woman. I told him, "When you get moving, knock on the bamboo pole outside and I will catch up." Shortly thereafter, I heard a soft knock on the bamboo. Then, keeping my gun pointed at the Vietnamese couple, I snapped off the light, slipped outside, and caught up to Rioux. As I walked east under the arch, I planned to bring up the rear and watch for movement behind us, knowing that if that man and woman were Viet Cong, they would quickly organize more Cong and then follow us to ambush us from the rear.

As it turned out, twenty minutes later we crossed the paddy leading to the road near Bich Bac without any contact with Charlie. I called the radio watch on the hill, "Alpha 3-2 patrol coming in from the east."

"Roger 3-2, I'll alert the perimeter." By 0100h our patrol was behind the wire. I breathed a sigh of relief—ten men out, ten men back safely!

The squad joined Lieutenant Kilhenny at 0900h for our debriefing. I spoke first: "Sir, the squad performed flawlessly last night. At the first hooch we searched, the woman and children never knew we peeked in. In fact, the only words spoken were whispers from me giving orders. The next home we entered, we encountered two adults and two children. Although both had ID cards, I remained suspicious. My choices were to either tie them up and bring them to the Hill, slice their throats, or leave them be. Sir, I quickly chose to get the hell out of there because our position was compromised. If we chose to continue searching west, we might have been ambushed and cut off from the four Marines guarding the eastern end of the ville." Lieutenant Kilhenny agreed with my decision to leave the remaining people of the ville to sleep that night.

After the debriefing, we all went to our bunkers. I sat down on my sand-bag chair and smoked a cigarette. I was damn proud of the squad's smooth performance, especially considering that none of them were even old enough to legally drink alcoholic beverages.

* * *

Two days after the night recon into Thai Cam (3), we enjoyed some slack time since another squad was out on the day patrol. Although we had the day off, the war never did. I joined Rioux in the sniper bunker on the southern perimeter. Rioux was a trained sniper. He had left the platoon in January to train with the elite sniper team on Hill 55. Five weeks later he came back to the platoon where he served my squad as a fireteam leader. He didn't talk about his days of training, or his sniping while part of the sniper team. Likewise, I didn't ask.

As soon as we settled into the bunker, a heavy volume of rifle fire broke the peaceful silence of that morning. The fire fight was located near Thuy Bo village, about three and a half miles south. "God damn, Rioux," I shouted, "some Marine unit just stepped on a large hornet's nest!" In fact, I recognized the sound of the weapons used by both sides. Viet Cong were blazing away with

AK-47s and SKS rifles, and the Marines were answering with M-60 machine guns, M-16s, and M-79 grenade launchers. Then I heard F-4 Phantom jets approaching. The first jet screamed down, dropping many tumbling barrels of Napalm, followed by bright flashes of hot flames and sparks showering out. The next jet sprayed the same area with 20-millimeter rounds. I wondered how any living organism could live under that shower of destruction. After the jets screamed away, I heard a CH-34 helicopter, which came from the east and descended into the trees, attempting to land. Was it to medevac some wounded or dead Marines? Hell, I didn't know. I just observed the spectacle from a few miles away.

I knew our platoon could be sent out into that bad-ass village if those Marines didn't get the VC off their backs. Snapping out of my trance, I got back to scanning the area south of the river beyond Duc Ky (1). After scanning with binoculars for nearly ten minutes, I spotted two Vietnamese men sneaking along near the old railway grade, about 1200 yards south of our position. I handed the binoculars to Rioux and he scanned the men. "They appear to be Charlies," he shouted, "and they are hiding something on their left side, away from us." Then, he was behind the 50-caliber. The beast started belching rounds towards the juicy targets. Tracers and hot rounds from the heavy 50-caliber screamed across the 1200 yards in split seconds. I had my hands over my ears to muffle the loud noise. Then Rioux let off the trigger and I resumed scanning the area. The two men I had spotted minutes earlier were no longer visible. "Hell, Rioux, I can't see them now, after your last shots." Rioux looked up and said, "You and I sure as hell aren't going to go out in that swamp, searching for bodies." A bit later after scanning, but hearing no more from that sharp fire fight near Thuy Bo, Rioux and I went back to our bunkers across the perimeter.

Back in the bunker, eating our C-rat lunch of boned chicken fresh out of the can, typical conversation ensued about Marines in the battalion that were zapped recently in combat. Falduti spoke first: "A Marine from Delta Company got sniped off Hill 55 yesterday. He was fucking around, walking on the south facing slope, and a Viet Cong sniper dinged him."

Second up, Jim Spencer, added, "Charlie Company had a man, Albert Johnson, step on a large mine out in Chau Son (3), and I guess what they found of him fit in a shoe box!"

"My God," I replied, "he was in my platoon at boot camp. He was a fun guy to be around, always laughing and joking." I continued, "I heard our former executive officer, Captain Getlin,[†] was killed at Camp Carroll and they found ten North Vietnamese around him when his unit was overrun. He was one hell of a leader! Remember, back in October the day we bagged those three VCs when he jumped off the lead Amtrac and started blasting at them, before they could run in front of our Amtrac?"

Those conversations we had might sound morbid to people back in 'the World;' however, that was our reality—death was possible every second. Even while we talked, a mortar round could drop in and snuff us out. But, one constant I observed from talking to all troops—tankers, pilots, artillery, grunts—no one bragged and gloated about the deaths and butchering we inflicted upon the Viet Cong and North Vietnamese. We simply and silently carried out our gruesome business.

While eating my C-ration breakfast the next morning of ham and lima beans, Lieutenant Kilhenny came to my bunker and exclaimed, "Stein, some members of the platoon will be transferred to 3rd Battalion 26th Marines, you and Rioux

---

[†] Capt Michael Peter Getlin (died 30 March 1967).

included." I would have been less shocked if he had handed me a live grenade!

"My God Lieutenant, what about the squad? I had high expectations of leading them until I was dinged or went back to the 'World'!"

"I hate losing you 'old' veterans, but the transfers came from a higher power. Be ready to move tomorrow at 0900 hours." After the Lieutenant went back to his bunker, I sat down behind the bunker, thinking of the squad, and what would happen to the ten men left behind.

After a restless night with no sleep, I made my way around the perimeter, saying my good-byes to men that would have given their lives for me. Nevertheless, I was powerless, and in one half hour I would be on a truck headed for Da Nang. Someone else would be patrolling the same square miles I had walked the past seven months!

Chapter 8:
Something Big is Stirring in the Scuttlebutt Pot

Khe Sanh squad, 1967 – Rioux, Walter, and Ramirez

AT 0900H the next morning, I sat under the hot morning sun at the Da Nang Airport waiting for instructions to board a waiting C-123, a double turbo propeller Air Force plane. It was a workhorse, hauling men and supplies. Moreover, the plane could land and take off from the perilously short runways often found in Vietnam.

> *Saturday, April 15, 1967*
> *Dear Mom & Dad,*
>
> *I am in the air terminal at Da Nang waiting for transportation North to Phu Bai. I wrote a letter while on Hill 55, but I forgot to mail it. I hope someone picks it up and mails it. You'll probably get this letter 1st. Anyways, I've been transferred to 3/26 and I don't know much about them. What can I say after being with 1/26 for a year. 1/26 will always be my outfit in heart. I've been through so much with them since last April. Here it is a year after I left home. Really something, huh?? Just 3 ½ months and it's so close yet so far away. I'll probably land back in the grunts at 3/26.*
>
> *I don't know what my address will be, but I'll send it as soon as I get to Phu Bai. Phu Bai is about 40 miles south of the DMZ.*
>
> *I hope life is ok at home! Spring must be starting to show up by this time.*
>
> *I'll go now so I'll write soon.*
> > *Your loving son,*
> > > *Wally*

At 0930h, about sixty Marines clambered aboard, wrapped makeshift seatbelts around their waists, and seconds later the fat-bellied beast was airborne, heading north. The flight took about an hour and as I felt the plane dropping in elevation, I knew my next adventure was about to unfold.

After bumping to a stop, I walked down the ramp. I was loaded with my pack, web belt, canteens, and rifle. I dragged a rubber waterproof bag filled with letters from the 'World,' and a few extra sets of clothes. In minutes I stood inside a giant base. "My God, Rioux," I barked, "how big is this place? I can't even see the outer perimeter, bunkers or wire."

As we left the air field, we were given directions to 3/26 Battalion headquarters. The headquarters building was built like a ranch house, about 24x30 feet. Inside, in one corner, were communication radios, neatly set. In another corner a Marine sat behind a typewriter. I thought I had been transferred back to 'the World.' Then, a sergeant appeared from a separate room. He checked a list of names on a tablet. After Rioux and I gave him our names, he said, "Yes, you and Rioux are assigned to India Company. That row of buildings fifty feet from the door is 3/26's area."

Rioux and I slowly started walking down that row of buildings. Each 30x40 foot building had a tin roof and partially open walls with screening running full length to keep out the biting mosquitos. Clean clothed Marines passed us and gave us quick glances, as if to say, "Where in hell did those scruffy creatures come from?" Though I knew why they were staring at us, I suddenly felt horribly out of place. My boots were dirty brown with gaping holes, my helmet was battered, and my jungle utilities were ripped. I can recall saying to Rioux, "Where in hell is the war!?" Rioux said nothing; I knew he, too, was extremely uneasy.

Then we saw a sign for India Company. We checked into the building with the sign and a Sergeant gazed over a sheet and said,

"You and Rioux will be in 1st Platoon, and your quarters will be the next building down."

After finding an empty cot and throwing my crusty water-proof bag on the floor, Sergeant Klindenst greeted me. We shook hands and he said, "You'll be my first fireteam leader and Rioux will also be a fireteam leader in my squad." He welcomed me as his right-hand man because most of his squad had little time in country. I immediately felt at ease with him. Later, I learned that he lived near Hanover, Pennsylvania, about 125 miles south of Bald Eagle Mountain.

I wasted no time asking Sergeant Klindenst about India Company's operational status. He noted, "We're staying in Phu Bai at this time; however, you know how quickly things change in the Nam!" He added, "We have many new boots, since we came over and also some previously wounded people are coming back to the company." I then questioned him concerning night time duty on the perimeter. He smiled, "Some other troopers have duty at night guarding the outer edge. Most of them are *boots* in the Nam."

I replied in disbelief, "You're shitting me, all I have to do is tuck myself in and snooze the night away?"

He said, "You have it!"

The next morning after my first full night's sleep in months, I rolled off the cot and Rioux and I headed for the chow hall, dressed in our dirty, ripped utilities. Plenty of eyeballs were flashing at us. Nevertheless, we entered the hall, grabbed an aluminum mess plate, and moved down the line. When I reached the end of the line, my mess plate was piled high with eggs, bacon, pancakes, and potatoes. 'What the hell,' I mused, 'I'll be out of shape if I stay here long!'

A few days later after the same routine, I feared I was in danger of losing my combat edge that I built up over the past nine months. Similarly, I felt extremely uncomfortable living now in a safer environment. I wanted to get back to the bush.

The next day, all transfers from 1/26 went to resupply to draw new jungle utilities, boots, and other needed new gear. I was fitted with a new pair of boots—the first for me in the last ten months. In addition, I received a few sets of utilities. Hell, I didn't want new clothes, those clothes would make me look like a FNG.

I went to church the first Sunday in Phu Bai. After mass I met Father Bede, a missionary of the Holy Trinity Order, the same order that my brother chose to study to become a priest. Father Bede even recognized my brother Steve's name—what a coincidence! I asked him if he said any masses outside of Phu Bai and he replied, "I have one in an hour, less than six miles south of Bhu Bai at a Marine Combined Action Platoon Base." I quickly asked him if he had a shotgun rider, and he said no.

I jumped at the opportunity and explained how I rode shotgun while on Hill 55. "I can be ready in 15 minutes."

Father said, "That's great, the jeep driver will be here in 15 minutes."

I ran back to the platoon building, grabbed my rifle from under the cot, secured an M-79 from Jim Jones, and slammed on my web belt, complete with six magazines of ammo. Damn, I was happy. I finally escaped from the base where I felt like a caged Asian tiger.

Twenty minutes later, Father Bede, the driver, and I were speeding south. The countryside east and west along the road had golden rice paddies, and the mountains rose out of the landscape to the west. Although the landscape appeared peaceful and serene, I knew to remain vigilant, scanning with my eyes and binoculars.

We pulled into the CAP area unscathed—not even one sniper round fired.

CAP, Combined Action Platoons, was a program started by Marines in Vietnam. The theory behind CAP was that a Marine unit in a village worked with the local Vietnamese militia, and together the Marines and the militia could monitor the Viet Cong's control over the people. In fact, the program appeared to be a success because the Cong didn't bother most CAP villages.

After Father Bede finished the mass, the driver, Father, and I bumped north on the pot-holed national highway, Route 1. Rioux met me back at the platoon hut. He slapped me on the shoulder and proclaimed, "Are you ready to play baseball?"

I quickly growled, "What the hell are you blabbing about, we're in a war zone." The baseball game was actually fun and competitive. We slid into bases while others shouted encouragement. It was two hours that we all could escape the war's hardships.

Reality set in an hour later when India Company was placed on Sparrow Hawk. We had to stay in the hut and be ready to fly out in choppers with five minutes' notice. Standbys were always tense as we waited for choppers to drop us miles away in some slimy rice paddy, swamp, or jungle. We spent the tense thirty-six hours smoking cigarettes and writing our 'last' letters home, wondering when the bell would clang to depart for our next trip. But then, happy days! The company standby was cancelled—no helicopter ride this time.

Two days later, Sergeant Klindenst walked into our hooch and informed us that the squad would be moving out the next day for an operation; however, he didn't have much information about the mission. Regardless, I prepared my fireteam and myself. In my team I had Ramirez from Texas, Lommer from Buffalo, New

York, and Freddie Johnson from the hills of West Virginia. All three were good men; however, I knew Lommer and Johnson had not been shot at yet. 'Yet' was the magic word in Nam for a grunt. If a trooper was assigned to a line company, sooner rather than later, that trooper would collide with a Viet Cong unit or a North Vietnamese unit. Then, that trooper became combat tested in seconds.

At 0800h the next morning, the platoon scrambled aboard waiting trucks. After bumping south on Route 1, we jumped out in open country with rice paddies on both sides of the road. To the west, the terrain rose into small hills, but the small number of large bushes and trees in the area indicated to me that the Charlies and NVA had few hiding places.

The platoon slowly moved west towards the hills until around noon when we set up a defensive position on a small hill. Defensive positions required foxholes and the 100-degree heat brought out the bitching: "God damn, this is hard red earth!" From another Marine, "Dig in or die!" and "Welcome to the bush." And from another trooper, "If I die here tonight, at least you'll have a hole to throw me into!"

Later that afternoon, after getting comfortable in our holes, Sergeant Klindenst came to my hole and knelt down. "Hey Stein, our squad has the ambush tonight."

"No big deal, Kenny. I'll prepare the fireteam, and I'll be up on point."

He said, "Okay, we'll discuss the patrol plan and route later."

Sergeant Klindenst came by later and we talked about the ambush site. Kenny pointed about 500 yards and said, "Well be setting up on the hill just north of that small gap between the next hill south. That ambush site was chosen to catch any Viet Cong units sneaking in from the west."

"Sounds great to me, Kenny. What time do we push out?"

Kenny replied, "After dark, about 2100 hours; we'll be out about five hours."

I stepped forward into unfamiliar country at 2100 hours and the patrol was my first since leaving 1/26 two weeks ago. However, I preferred night time missions because darkness covered our movements. I snuck into the ambush site twenty-five minutes later and huddled down with Freddie Johnson as my partner. Each two-man team set in to my left. No one would sleep—we were on one hundred percent alert, staring out into the darkness waiting for living prey to stumble by. By early May 1967, I'd been living a warrior's life for almost 11 months, but I felt as if I had been sitting ambushes my entire life. A recurring thought kept nagging at me... could I ever go back to the 'World?'

After sitting motionless for five hours, Rioux tapped me on the shoulder as a signal to start creeping back to the perimeter. That night I was the rear man, or last in file going back. Thirty-five minutes later, our patrol entered the platoon perimeter back on the hill. Then I slipped down into our cozy foxhole and told Johnson to get some Zs and that I would take the first watch. In general, my one-hour watch was quiet except for illumination flares popping around Phu Bai. I heard artillery fire in the distance, near the mountain valleys. 'Yes,' I thought, 'the war continues in other locations.' But where I sat, the war had taken a break, and that break continued to unnerve me.

The never-ending blistering sun popped up to the east over the South China Sea and forty men in holes stirred. Cigarettes were lit; gourmet breakfasts were eaten. Ham and limas, beans and franks, boned chicken, and instant coffee were warmed over improvised can stoves by a little blue heat tab about the size of a silver dollar. Forty men were simply living the moment, feeding their bodies. None of us cared what excitement might occur that day.

A bit later, word came down from Lieutenant Johnson that the platoon was moving east towards Route 1, then back to Phu Bai. This operation was nothing more than a training mission for the new troops. In preparation for the move back to the road, the usual annoying tasks were tackled by bitching Marines. We buried our cans and covered our foxholes and policed up any cigarettes strewn about. We left the country's landscape as we found it.

Following the cleanup, the platoon moved east. Our squad had the rear until 1300 hours when we halted along a clear river. Kenny Klindenst passed the word down, "After we eat, the Lieutenant said we could take a swim to cool off." Young men frolicked in the cool water stripped to the waist like a group of boy scouts—the scene reminded me of the carefree days with neighborhood friends on the Susquehanna River, swimming and diving off our three-barrel raft. After soaking in the cool water, I swam to shore to relieve the Marine standing on the river bank providing security for those swimming. As I slipped on my boots, I had my rifle on my lap and was on full alert, feeling like a sitting duck in the water.

A bit later Lieutenant Johnson ordered everyone to 'saddle up' for movement to the pickup location at the road. After reaching the narrow Route 1, the platoon sat under the sweltering sun another hour before the trucks arrived from Phu Bai. We were back in our platoon hut twenty minutes later. I had just completed another quiet operation, not even one sniper round.

* * *

Two days after the short operation, we received word of a movement south to relieve a platoon in the same village where

Father Bede celebrated mass every Sunday. In general, the platoon would be working as a Combined Action Platoon. Our platoon would provide security for the village and run patrols and ambushes. For myself, the mission meant getting out of Phu Bai and maybe doing some good for those Vietnamese in that small ville near the South China Sea.

Our platoon settled into a strange routine at the ville. Two squads manned the four-tall sandbag bunkers on each corner of the village. The rest of the men were dug in on a small hill, less than seventy-five yards northwest. We had free movement all day to visit the farm market by the water. The market had many luscious choices of vegetables and fish. I noted beans, melons, sugar cane, hot and sweet peppers, exotic squash and root vegetables that I couldn't identify. We carried Vietnamese currency, so I bought some pretty red Thai peppers and a melon for the fireteam to feast on that first night. What a vacation!

Sunday, April 30
Dearest Diane,

Hello! Honey! The paper is unreal, but I am 20 miles south of Phu Bai working with CAC units (Combined Action Companies). Our platoon is running many ambushes out of this area. We practically live with the people. It's right near the ocean and the sun rise was so beautiful today. Diane, I am here with no writing gear and it's been 9 days since I wrote you. I'll find an envelope somewhere!

I received two great letters from you. The one with the pictures came also. Thanks much. I liked the pictures. Boy! That must have been a wild birthday party! Huh? I liked the picture of you in York especially. I can hardly wait to see you again.

Yes! I know Tod Beck. He's my second cousin on my Mom's side. I'll send you those pictures as soon as we get back to Phu Bai, okay! And-I have to throw away my letters over here after about a week. Too much gear to keep track of. Soon I'll be with you and I won't have to write! You'll graduate, don't worry. Phu Bai was mortared the last two nights but don't worry, I wasn't there.

I'll go now and I'll try to write soon. Please keep praying Darling.

I love you very much,
Wally

P.S., I miss You!

Interesting activity centered around a combination beer hooch and red-light house. In the morning a few prostitutes came by bus from Hue to ply their trade in a room off the beer house. On most afternoons we'd gather in the beer house and slop down Vietnamese Tiger Beer, served warm or on ice. Only a few brave Marines went in the adjoining room to get their rocks off for five minutes for five dollars. Although we all salivated at the mouth for sex, the potential consequences outweighed the anticipated pleasure. WWII vets talked about some far east Black Syphilis that, if contracted, the Corpsman would lay a soldier's penis on a stump and pound out the pus! If one contracted a modern-day venereal disease, the infected trooper might be barred from entering the United States. Fact or fiction, who the hell knew? Regardless, the quaint little beer hut provided a special escape from the war for us.

Marines kept their weapons ready and close at hand

After a week, half the platoon, our squad included, rotated out to the hot perimeter, seventy-five yards from the ville. The foxholes we manned sat on a small rise; however, no trees grew on the spot to provide relief from the relentless sun. Nevertheless, we quickly cut some nearby bamboo and stretched our poncho liners over the holes, with the bamboo serving as tent poles. Though we had few luxuries, we always managed to seek little 'bennies' like the shaded foxholes.

At the new perimeter we settled into the same boring routines of perimeter watch in the hot hole during the day and night. At night I didn't sleep well, because a few 'boots' in the squad kept dozing off while on watch. I would sneak up on them and bang their heads lightly with my rifle and whisper in their ears: "You just got your throat cut by a roving Charlie!" Hell, I knew all they needed was a vicious firefight with Charlie to get their attention.

The fourth day out on the perimeter Kenny Klindenst came back from a meeting with the Lieutenant. "Stein, we have a two-squad ambush tonight, east towards the South China Sea. Sergeant Bailey is commanding the patrol." In preparation, our squad ran a short patrol out northeast of the ville to check out a secure location to set in for the night. Kenny and I observed a rice paddy dike running northeast past the small ville, close to the sea. We'd use that dike to get near the ville, and then we would set up the ambush forty yards north of the hooches.

At sunset, twenty men gathered around Sergeant Bailey for the final briefing. Bailey had his shit together, as he had a few years in the Marines. Furthermore, he saw heavy combat when 3/26 was a landing Battalion a few months back. He was a likeable, soft-spoken, religious man. I thought then, 'Maybe God will be with us when we're with Sergeant Bailey.'

After the briefing, we silently moved towards the dike with my fireteam on point. While moving down the dike, I kept contact behind me to make sure the patrol followed close behind. The ambush was good medicine for me, because I needed activity to maintain a combat edge. I hadn't been shot at since landing in Phu Bai!

I moved into position, 600 meters out, and our squad faced the ville while the other half of the patrol set in at a 90-degree angle— north and south to create an L-shaped ambush. We broke into two man teams—one on watch, the other at rest. I was with Private Johnson. I took the first watch, staring down towards a path.

About 2300 hours, I woke Freddie for the next watch. I was only half asleep about a half hour later, when Freddie shook me and whispered, "Stein, Stein, someone's out on the trail!"

I strained to focus my eyes on the trail. About fifty yards north, there appeared to be two men on the trail walking away from my position, but then they disappeared. I grabbed Freddie's arm and whispered, "It's okay, Fred. We can't spring an ambush on the tail end of a patrol, if in fact it was a patrol. We need the Charlie's full patrol to our front before opening up."

After calming Freddie, my eyes strained to spot anyone in the distance—nothing moved. I decided to stay on watch until morning. Control and discipline equaled survival. It would have been insanity to rip wild shots down the trail at two shadows. I had not lost my combat edge.

By 0530h we started west towards the perimeter. We needed to be out of the open rice paddies before sunrise. Back inside the perimeter, the first order of business for the squad was chow. The blue heat tabs soon blazed away, heating instant coffee and hot chocolate. Then cans of C-rats were heated and devoured. The simple act of eating was a luxury in the bush. After chow down, Sergeant Klindenst stopped by our hole to announce the latest word. "Hey Stein, the platoon is moving out later this morning back to Phu Bai!"

"Great news, Kenny. Back to that stateside, boring Phu Bai. At least out here we had the beer hut, the market down by the water, and the young Vietnamese boys selling us luscious frozen rice pops every afternoon!" I wasn't surprised, as the word always came swiftly concerning our next move. Nevertheless, my patience became paper thin, as revealed in a letter written home while out in the ville near the South China Sea:

Tuesday, May 16, 1967
Dear Mom & Dad,

Received a wonderful letter from you today. I am in a Ville right with a CAC unit. We will probably go back out to our patrol base tonight or tomorrow morning. I also received letters from Aunt Elinor, Steve & Aunt Vivi. Very seldom we get mail when I don't get letters. Soon I'll be able to see all you great people. I really don't have that many days left in the field, but the nights get 'longer and longer' sitting in a foxhole waiting, or out on an ambush. Seems like only yesterday I was in my first foxhole last August and I am still doing it 10 months later.

Somehow, this 'nightmare' will end soon and I'll come home. Too bad the war isn't going to end before I leave, but we Americans have still a long struggle ahead, barring miracles.

How is the garden coming? Soon you'll be going to Steve's graduation. He wrote me a real nice letter. I'll go now so as ever, thanks for the many prayers & letters.

Your loving son,

Wally

* * *

Later that afternoon while writing a letter home, Rioux handed me a copy of *Stars and Stripes*. An article about the hill fights at Khe Sanh popped out of the paper just like a shrieking round past my ringing ears. The headline named battalions, including the 1/9, 3/3, and 2/3, that encountered strong North Vietnamese units on Hills 861, 881 south, and 881 north. Those hills were west of Khe Sanh Combat base. Another operation in the Que Son Valley involved Landing Team SLF Alpha, 1/3, and HMM-263. Still another headline—North Vietnamese forces attack Con Thien near the DMZ.

Then another headline caught my full attention: "2/26, 2/9, 3/9, 2/3, and 3/4 are engaged with the North Vietnamese near the DMZ." Dear God, Gary was with 3/9; I had not heard from him for almost a month. No wonder, he was in a world of shit! I could not help Gary while sitting there. Moreover, I knew that casualties had to be high, considering the number of Marine battalions engaged along the DMZ.

Later that night Rioux and I headed to the 'slop chute' to down some beers. The club was packed, standing room only. I spotted Marines from 1/26—what the hell are they doing in Phu Bai? Then I saw Falone and pushed my way through the club until I grasped his hand. "What the hell's up, Falone?"

"Stein, 1/26 is moving to Khe Sanh tomorrow. The word is that the entire regiment will be at Khe Sanh within three weeks." Then he poked me and said, "Phu Bai is like stateside duty, Stein."

I countered, "I know, Falone. I haven't hit any shit the past weeks—the war forgot about Phu Bai!" Then we talked about the savage 'hill fights' and we both agreed: Khe Sanh was a 'spooky' zone to end our tour in six weeks. After talking to Falone, Rioux and I circulated through the crowd, tipping drinks with old salts from 1/26.

The next morning, I quickly forgot about the celebration at the club the evening before because the platoon was on standby. Same old shit. Fully packed, rifle ready, and ready to board choppers with five minutes' notice.

Nevertheless, after twenty-five cigarettes smoked, four letters written, six C-rat meals eaten in the hut, surprise!—the standby was cancelled. But, later that afternoon, Sergeant Klindenst came back from a briefing with the Lieutenant and announced, "Stein, the company is flying out on a big operation tomorrow."

"I'm not surprised, Sarge!"

Photograph of Diane Weston carried in Walter's wallet

May 28, 1967
Dear Diane,

I am just lying here 'rotting away' in the hot sun so I'll try to occupy myself by writing you. We have a shelter but the sun beats through. When I can't find anything to do I take out my wallet and look at your pictures and wish I could see and touch you in person. Days drag by as I get closer but really, time is time, it just works on your mind more than ever. Diane! All kinds of thoughts go through one's mind over here. I can better explain myself when I come home. We'll have plenty of things to talk about and it will be a very fulfilling time in my life. I find myself thinking of you and home while on a small mission and it's quite a fight to get my mind on my job. Don't worry though, I do manage to 'keep on my toes' just like always. Tonight our squad will have the ambush!

Many times it feels I've been over here for a lifetime living with the sounds and dangers of war, but I remember that once I had life great and now I'm sort of paying for what I had easy in the States. Believe me, there is no place in the vast world like the U.S.A. I am not feeling sorry for myself, I am just telling you, someone I am 'close' to, how it is over in the Nam. I'll tell you a lot more in about ten weeks.

By the way, are you still planning on going to California this summer?? Probably, if you and Jackie get a job you won't be able to go, right? It takes a lot of money to go that far. I'll probably never be able to take you to a place like California but we sure can have a wonderful time around the beautiful mountains, rivers, lakes and valleys of Pennsylvania. Are you going to have to buy another car? Incidentally, how does my car run any more. Mom told me you drove it to school once. I am glad you could do that, after all, Jackie drove it already.

Boy! My brother will be home before you receive this letter. You'll get to talk to him most likely. As you know Steve and I are very close and I can't wait to see him also. I guess Stan is quitting the Seminary this year. He's talking about coming in the Marines if he does. What can I say?! It's no glorious picnic, that's for sure!

I am sure you'll do ok getting a job Diane. You might get turned down a couple of times, that's how it happens in Williamsport. Remember me? I looked all summer and finally started to work in September. You have a good background in business courses at South Side and from what I hear South Side girls get jobs okay. You'll be working long before I arrive on scene. I'll pray for you as always.

Again, thanks for the pictures and remember I love and miss more than ever,

> *My love to you,*
> *Wally*

P.S. over

May 29, 1967
Hello! Honey,

I broke the letter out of the envelope because I received a letter from you. I am back in Phu Bai, and to send those pictures.

I am not sure if that's all of them but that's all I have. Doesn't seem like long ago we took them, over 13 ½ months.

Diane, I am going North!! Yes, by the time you get this I'll be about 10 miles south of the DMZ, at a camp called Khe Sanh. Not sure what we'll do up there but the 1st week of July I'll be getting out of COMBAT ZONE & boarding ships. Keep praying dear one, and I'll see you soon, God's will be done!

> *You mean a lot to me Diane,*
> *I love you, Wally*

The next morning we received mail, including a letter from Mom. She wrote that Gary was wounded, but according to the Western Union Telegram sent to the Lorsons, he was not in critical condition and would be in the States soon. A heavy burden lifted off of me—Gary made it! 'Hope to see you soon buddy! Get the beer cold!'

As I thought that, I knew it was bullshit, because soon I would be in the jungles and mountains along the North Vietnamese border. Then, Sergeant Klindenst shouted out, "We're boarding choppers in 20 minutes!" I threw the letter in the rubber waterproof bag under the bed and passed the word to my fireteam to saddle up.

We boarded choppers on the dusty Phu Bai airfield fifteen minutes later. One-by-one the birds lifted up, circled, and set in formation. 170 young men were hell-bent for some location southwest of Phu Bai. My chopper swooped down just ten minutes later, and I jumped into deep, sharp elephant grass. Next, we humped west for 400 yards and set up on a small hill. Under the stifling sun, the digging began in earnest to get below ground level.

We dug in, cleared fields of fire, and chowed down as the hot sun set over the western mountains. Night blackness followed and another long night of peering out from our holes, waiting, watching for 'Sir Charles' to sneak in. Thankfully, another night passed without any action, and for the next six days, the company trudged west until reaching thick jungles and steep mountains. Still, we didn't find the NVA army, nor did they find us.

On the ninth day the 'angels from the sky' flew us back to Phu Bai. I wrote about the hellish operation, and the coming move, to the dangerous zone at Khe Sanh.

June 11, 1967, 8 p.m.
Dear Mom, Dad & Family,

Here I am trying to write home. Just spent a hectic eight days in the 'docks.' We were in the mountains the last three days walking and walking. God only knows what keeps me dragging on. I guess because the end is within sight. I am in Phu Bai and tomorrow morning we are moving to Khe Sanh, where I mentioned before a big operation will take place the last two weeks of June.

What can I now say??! Why does a guy have to 'sweat it out' right down to the last day. Our ship is leaving on July 3. It just has to be true! Coming home is still a big dream. I think how great it will be then. I remember I am not out of here yet. Being short is the most worse time I've spent over here! I must try to trust in God's will.

I still can't believe you actually saw Gary. I guess I'll have to dream on.

I am glad you all had a nice trip to Virginia. What is Steve going to do this summer?

I'll go now, hoping I'll get chance to write soon again. Thanks for the two great letters and for yours also, Bernadette!

Your loving son & brother,
Wally

June 11

Dear Diane,

I received your letter today and was glad to hear from you after a little while.

Well! Diane! Tomorrow I start on the 'last leg' of my long trip over here. We're going north!! It's going to be scarry and I'll be sweating it out. It's only 19 days till July 1st and the ship is still leaving the 3rd! I can't believe Gary is home and out of here. How does he look or didn't you get to see him? I am still dreaming and hoping it's God's will I make it out of here. Diane, I am so close, close. What can I say?

I am glad you got a job. You'll do okay.

Well! I am short of words and soon I'll be with you. I don't even count days any more. It's doesn't help. I am not sure how many more letters I'll be able to write. Wait until you get the one saying I am on a ship.

My love for you,

Wally

* * *

The early morning hours of June 10th, 3rd battalion, 26th Marines prepared for the long, dangerous trip on a truck convoy to Khe Sanh. After clamoring on board at 0900h, our squad, in a six-by-six truck, started rolling north in a cloud of dust. The convoy stretched out for a mile, and a bit later we passed the 'Jewel of the Orient'—the beautiful city of Hue!

The colorful buildings and the clean, orderly streets, complete with streetlights, amazed me. The city and the people on the sidewalks and streets appeared far removed from any war activity. However, thirty minutes later, while passing the large Marine base near the DMZ, Dong Ha, I quickly realized how massive the war had become in the past nine months. Many C-123s, C-130s, and helicopters were buzzing in and out of the air field. Dong Ha now was a sprawling base, much larger than I had viewed the previous September when we flew in to get the tanks.

From Dong Ha, the convoy rumbled west, and I noticed hills, then taller mountains visible in the near horizon. It was a great place for the NVAs to ambush us. Surprisingly, we didn't even draw any sniper fire. At 1600 hours the convoy stopped east of Camp Carroll, and fifteen minutes later, word came down that the North Vietnamese blew a bridge one mile west of the convoy! Soon we were directed to off-board the trucks. India Company and the entire battalion would not reach Khe Sanh before dark. Instead, choppers would have to lift us to Khe Sanh the next morning. "God damn this, God damn that, fuck this, fuck that," came the bitching from the Marines. "It don't mean a thing!" The troops hated lightning-fast change of missions.

Regardless, after humping 100 yards up a steep, tangled, heavily vegetated hill, we started digging in for our one-night stand. Then, right after chomping down a cold C-rat meal, the clouds opened up with a fifteen-minute deluge. That meant soaked, cold, and miserable Marines that night, watching out into the dark, thick jungle waiting for the boogeyman to appear. The NVA stayed away that night, but I didn't sleep well because flares popped around Camp Carroll all night and the big artillery pieces at the camp blasted away in support of some Marines, somewhere out in the rugged mountains.

The sun from the east was a welcome and warm relief from the cold night. Word came down to prepare to move in an hour to board choppers. In preparation, I choked down a can of cold beans and wieners and threw the can in the foxhole before covering it with the rocky, red earth. Soon we were heading down the road. A bit later, I heard the familiar and welcome chattering of choppers approaching. Just above, giant CH-53 Sea Stallion choppers (a new helicopter in Vietnam) circled to land near the road. Our entire platoon clambered on board, the pilot powered up, and soon the great new machine whizzed above the lush mountains.

Following a short flight, the choppers dropped down on the landing strip at the old French fortress—Khe Sanh. As soon as I walked down the ramp, my eyes nearly popped out at the sight of the base and the high mountains surrounding the perimeter. Giant sand-bagged bunkers and thick strands of concertina wire stretched to the edge of the jungle. In general, the rugged base and surrounding hills looked like a spooky area to spend my last days in Vietnam.

As soon as we walked off the tarmac, we headed to a rugged mess hall. Sandbags were stacked high around the walls, unlike the neat mess hall in Phu Bai. Outside the mess hall, I spotted Lieutenant Kilhenny waiting in line with other men from my platoon at Hill 55. I grabbed his hand, and he was happy to see his former salty radio man and squad leader. He looked older and worn, compared to that fresh, clean man I met in January. His appearance was typical after months in the bush—it turned young men into old men. Regardless, after we small-talked a few minutes, I entered the crowded mess hall and enjoyed some beef, green beans (from a can), and some real bread.

After the meal, more surprises awaited the company. We learned our position would be outside the main wire facing west. Ten minutes later, the platoon dug holes and set trip flares in the low brush forty feet to our front. We settled into the familiar routine of watching and waiting.

June 14 (Weds.)

My Dear Diane,

Well! Here I am at Khe Sanh near the DMZ & Laos border. We're just outside the perimeter and we'll probably be moving out in the mountains soon. What can I say?? Seems like I'll never get out of the field! Just pray and hope it's soon. They won't even tell us for sure when we're going stateside. I wish I could tell you when.

As you noticed, enclosed was a roll of 12 pictures. I can't get them developed over here. Not sure even if they're worth sending? Just a bunch of pictures I took today of guys in the squad. At least you can see for yourself when they get developed. I'll pay you back with a wonderful time when I get home.

How is your job coming? I hope good! Anything new happening around home. Gary told me everyone is either married or in the service. I don't know how it's going to be to live and be back there. Still a big dream since I am not even out of the field yet. I am sick of the service and this war!

Well, I'll end this short letter saying I miss you so much and God willing I'll be with you in 54 days. Please keep praying honey!

I love you,

Wally

After four days in our position, Sergeant Klindenst delivered news about a platoon operation that was to start in the morning. The platoon moved out at 0900 hours the next morning and headed northwest across the valley towards some small rolling hills. Hill 950 loomed ahead a few miles north, overlooking the valley that the base rested on. On the many hills that surrounded Khe Sanh, I was sure one or more North Vietnamese soldiers were perched in trees with binoculars watching us as we moved out from our positions.

After slowly moving through the thick jungle, we stopped along a pristine mountain stream rushing down the gap north of Khe Sanh. Damn, that stream reminded me of Big Run, a stream I fished, five miles west of my home on Bald Eagle Mountain. But Big Run remained in another world. This stream bed location appeared to be a great place for the NVA to strike us from higher ground. My grip tightened on my rifle—it was lunchtime, but I didn't want to fiddle with any cans of food. However, the NVA didn't show up for lunch. I was spooked because I knew that in the surrounding jungles the North Vietnamese Army had to be present in large numbers. Laos and the Ho Chi Minh Trail were only four miles west, and the DMZ was only fifteen miles north.

After humping around in the valley northwest of Khe Sanh for two more days, we failed to make contact with the North Vietnamese. After C-rats on the third morning, we returned to our foxholes on the western end of the combat base. That afternoon, Rioux and I checked all the trip flares to our front and added some more greenery to our foxhole to settle in, ready for another long night.

Two hours before dark, the platoon site received mail. Mail was always a welcome distraction from our daily routine. Reading words from loved ones back home provided me with a thread of sanity from another world—a world that no longer existed for me, maybe lost forever? Sadly, I didn't receive any recent letters from Diane. Hell, maybe it was 'Dear John' time. After all, I told her to date. Moreover, how could I expect her to give up living, waiting for me, possibly a dead man? 'It didn't mean nothin.' I still had to crawl out of this hell hole without getting chewed up.

The next two days we spent idle time near our holes. In fact, I had time to take some pictures of squad members and they took pictures of me, all looking west, one mile towards Hills 881 North and South and 861. Scores of Marines died and hundreds were wounded in vicious battles with the North Vietnamese Army on those steep slopes during April and May.

Walter with Sergeant Klindenst near Khe Sanh

The two slack days provided time for us to discuss the fate of 'short' Marines in the platoon, including me. Most troops of 3/26 thought 'short' Marines from 1/26 should not venture beyond the perimeter. On the other hand, Lieutenant Johnson argued, "Other past wars didn't have a tour of duty. All troops stayed until the war ended." He was partly right; nevertheless, our mindset focused solely on the number of 'magic days' left in country. Though I wanted out of the field, I knew I had to play out the hand of cards dealt me to the bitter end. Because I loved all the men in the platoon, I had to stay with them and end my tour up front, on point.

When we clambered out of our foxholes the third day, word passed down to make preparations for another operation. Hell, we were always prepared to move on five minutes' notice. As usual, I had already stashed three days of C-rats in the dirty pack, six magazines of ammo, and two canteens of water.

Later that morning around 1100h, Marines came out to fill in our positions as the platoon moved out and headed northwest into the dark forest. Our squad filled out in the rear. I felt uneasy. Was someone cutting me some slack, because I was a short timer? I quickly put that thought to rest, because I knew covering the rear of a patrol was also a critical job. The NVA and the Viet Cong often hit the rear because they knew the remaining column could not bring them under fire in the thick jungle.

After cutting our path through thick brush and bamboo for four hours, we set up on a high hill. We then dug foxholes, which meant that hill would be home for at least a night. As soon as Rioux and I dressed up the hole with greenery, we settled in and broke open C-rats for a gourmet lunch. After the platoon dug in, outposts were sent out to watch for any surprise assault by NVA troops. The afternoon passed quietly and when the sun set behind the steep mountains, the platoon pulled in the outpost men and we settled in at full alert.

Before midnight, loud explosions broke the silence. I bumped Rioux, "What the frig is going on? Those explosions had to be near Sergeant Klindenst's foxhole." A bit later, word filtered down to our hole that Kenny was wounded but could not be medevacked until morning. Kenny was down—instantly I became a squad leader again; but that was no big deal, because I had been a squad leader or assistant leader for the past five months. Still, I had to stay in place; I could not move to check on Sergeant Klindenst's condition.

After the sun brightened the black night, a chopper came into a clearing not far from our holes and lifted Kenny out. He was a great leader, and I never got to say goodbye. Here today, gone tomorrow—the law of the bush. And, I never learned where the blasts came from—mortars? Hand grenades?

After choking down some more cold C-rats, the platoon continued moving, seeking the North Vietnamese Army. Yet after two more days of sneaking around the thick growth of bamboo, trees, and vines, we still hadn't bumped into the NVA.

While heading south in the morning, we encountered some Montagnard people working in a coffee plantation near their village. In fact, those 'mountain people' reminded me of Native Americans. Their clothes were brightly colored in black and red, and the men wore scarves tied around their heads. The women carried babies in sacks on their backs. Their sturdy huts were built of bamboo with thatch-covered roofs and the homes were elevated four feet above ground level by large bamboo poles. Those same people (known as Yards) served as scouts for American troops in Vietnam, and they proved to be loyal, fearless, and fierce fighters. As a result, they were hated by most Vietnamese people. Still, I thought they were amazing members of the human race.

After turning east for about one klick, we sauntered back into our perimeter, where we hung around for a few days. Those idle days near the foxhole gave me too much time to think. Unanswered questions were numerous: When in hell would the 1/26 Marines depart Vietnam? And, when and where would the next operation commence?

Walter waiting for next mission, Khe Sanh, June 1967

June 22nd

Dear Mom and Dad,

Well! Time is going by but I am still waiting, hoping and praying!

Our unit is manning the outer perimeter of Khe Sanh while two companies are in the mountains. I hope they don't hit nothing! Another thing, my orders are in! I don't have them on me but my platoon sergeant gave me the word my next duty station is Quantico, Virginia. Straight word, I am leery still, even though most likely we were told we won't have to go to the field anymore. I am counting on a few ambushes yet! It is a 'step in the right direction' though, right?

I talked to Father Bede and he said three ships are leaving, one the 3rd, 15th and 28th. No later than the 15th Mom & Dad, because 2/26 will be on the last one. 1/26 came over three weeks before them. So much for all this scoop! I told you everything I know, maybe it will help relieve you all! Very soon I'll be taking a plane to Da Nang and a happy guy will board a ship for Okinawa & the States. Everything back home okay? I sure hope so! I wrote just about everyone my last letter so please tell everyone I probably won't write again 'till I see them.

I'll end this letter in better spirits so please keep praying and Ole Stein be home soon.

Your loving son,

Wally

June 23

My Dear Diane,

I haven't written you for a while but really haven't had the time. We came in off an operation in the mountains just a few days ago.

Right now our unit is manning the outer perimeter of Khe Sanh. We're supposed to be here a couple of weeks. Another thing, My orders for stateside duty are in, but I don't have them on me yet. My next duty station will be Quantico, Virginia. Really, I am not out of here yet so it didn't excite me that much. Two ships are leaving, one the 3rd and one the 15th of July. I think I'll be on the one the 15th. This means a very maximum of 21 days left in Nam. We were told that we might never go to the field again, but I am leery of that. These fools have a lot of guys who are going home with me out in the jungles now. Tomorrow night I'll probably get an ambush so you know I'll be sweating the next few days. I am praying I never have to go on another operation. I am so close now I wish I was in the far rear, but they aren't going to leave us go until about 5 days before the ship leaves. So much for all this.

How's your job coming? Is the work tiring or better than your job you once had? Are you getting a car? It won't be long, but time is dragging worse than ever. I am in suspense wondering what will happen the next few days, etc.

Well! Please write me soon Diane! Did you get that film yet? I'll bet some of the pictures are wild, huh? I've lost a lot of weight and look older I guess.

        Keep praying, okay! Love ya,

        Wally

Just after mailing that letter, I received a letter from Diane. She said a new boyfriend was part of her life. I wasn't surprised. I hadn't had a letter from her for days. I was shaken at first, but I told Diane to enjoy life and date while I was absent. If I got out of there alive, maybe I'd be able to win her back!

The same day I had another bit of crazy news. Lieutenant Johnson told me that I would probably be training 'boot' lieutenants for jungle warfare at my next duty station in Quantico, Virginia. I thought, 'Why give orders to a dead man?' I was still in a combat zone.

> *June 25th*
>
> *Dear Mom, Dad & Family,*
>
> *Just some more words home. I try to write every day while I am back near the perimeter.*
>
> *Well! The summer must be rolling along back home! Everything about normal? My dream is getting closer every day. Time has gone by fast since I was transferred in April, but now it seems to be dragging.*
>
> *Situation report! All us guys that came over with 1/26 are still in the 'field.' 1/26 is short of men and these guys in 3/26 are waiting for replacements just like 1/26. Word is they will start to come in around the end of June. A maximum of 13 days & I wake up and I should be boarding a plane for Da Nang to board the ship the 15th. It's quite definite and I am praying. What more can I say?? Makes us guys sick to see guys back in the rear 'skating,' when we're two weeks from getting out of here. Oh well, being 'short' is hell also! Can't think of much more so I'll write soon again.*
>
> *Your loving son & brother, Wally*

The next morning, June 26th, the squad was ordered to prepare for a movement late that afternoon. A light rain started falling, which meant the platoon would be wet and miserable before moving later that afternoon. At 1300 hours, Jack Phillips briefed the squad. "Our squad has the point and we will head southwest towards that tall mountain in the distance." That mountain appeared to be about two klicks from where I stood. We had not operated in that area before, but I was prepared—what was another operation?

* * *

At 1600 hours, 1st Platoon prepared to move—full pack, extra ammo, and two canteens of water. As soon as I stepped into the low bushes beyond the perimeter, my brain immediately switched to a high state of alertness, because I had not patrolled the land beyond before. I moved slowly, because I looked for details such as well-used paths, smoke, or anything to indicate the presence of the North Vietnamese Army.

Two hours later, after crossing a small stream in the thick jungle, I noticed a small cliff at the base of the mountain. It was well-concealed at the top by tangled vines and bushes. I quickly slipped back to Rioux and signaled for him to follow me on a change of direction northwest in order to get the platoon away from the cliff. I took a deep breath—that cliff area appeared to be a prime ambush site for the NVA. I knew they were somewhere close to us in that thick maze, because we were not out there for exercise—the platoon was sent out to hunt and make contact with the North Vietnamese Army.

After sneaking another seventy-five yards, through dense trees, bamboo, and brush, I turned and saw Sergeant Bailey coming from behind. "What's up Sarge?" I whispered.

"Stein, we have to relieve your fireteam from the point."

I quickly protested, "What bullshit am I hearing? It's because I'm *short*, I know."

Sergeant Bailey was an outstanding platoon sergeant. He knew we had to get our nighttime defensive perimeter set up soon, and we needed to move more quickly. I relented and told him to bring up another fireteam. As soon as the other fireteam came up, they cautiously worked their way another 100 yards to a semi-clearing, surrounded by tall trees. Next, we set in with two men to a position and formed a circle. Unfortunately, darkness set in and digging foxholes was now out of the question, since the noise might give away our location. Rioux and I prepared for another hairy night without a foxhole. The rain had stopped, but the night air was hot and sticky. I slipped off my flak jacket and hunkered down, resting my head on the jacket with my rifle clutched on top of my stomach while Rioux took the first watch.

Around midnight, while staring into the bleak blackness, I heard a distinct hollow noise, *womp, womp, womp,* in the direction of that high mountain to our southwest. That noise came from mortar rounds piping out of mortar tubes, and I knew Marines did not occupy that mountain top! Then I heard the impact, two klicks east on Khe Sanh. More rockets and more blasts on the base. Khe Sanh was getting plastered by North Vietnamese mortar rounds. That deadly barrage from the mountain sent a cold shiver down my spine. I knew in the morning we would be pushing up that steep, jungle mountain to make contact with those NVAs.

I said to Rioux, "Frig this shit—so much for being short!"

Rioux smacked my arm; "We're fucked, Stein. I'm betting that mountain top has a shitload of gooks dug in deep!"

To my left across the perimeter, I heard the Lieutenant and Sergeant Phillips call for an artillery mission towards the mountain. I was wired, 220 volts, gripping my rifle, wondering if the North Vietnamese would find us. I thought about when we left Khe Sanh eight hours earlier; the mountain the NVA now occupied had been fogged in then, so maybe they didn't spy us leaving on patrol.

Seconds later, an eerie sound from above pierced my ears. My God! Incoming mortars! Deafening explosions lifted my body from the gravity that glued me to the earth. I slammed down, and smoke and the smell of cordite enveloped the air. As soon as I hit the ground, I felt a sharp sting down my right ankle. Also, I felt something pouring down on the right side of my back. I reached down to make sure my right foot was still intact—it was. Next out of my mouth, "Rioux, I'm hit, I'm hit. I'm going home!"

"Stein, I'm hit too, and I hear other men moaning to our right and left. Too many for the Corpsman to treat!"

I unbuckled my pack and yanked out some extra-large battle dressings I carried. "Rioux, where are you hit?"

"I have blood dripping from my right side, but I think I'll live," he said. I pulled up his bloody shirt and tied a dressing on his side. Rioux then pushed me over, checked my side wound, and slowed the blood flow by packing on a dressing.

Another Marine in our squad crawled to me. "Shit, Rioux, he's got a lot of blood gushing from a head wound." I wiped his head with my bloody shirt and carefully applied another large bandage. "You'll be okay guy. We're all going to make it out of here," I reassured him.

To the right of me at the base of a large tree, a Corpsman treated another wounded man. I crawled around the tree and I found Doc Stephens working feverishly on a badly-wounded kid. "Can I help Doc?"

"Stein, he's lost a lot of blood and his body is ripped up bad—he might not make it." I crawled back around to check on Rioux and Ramirez, realizing that if that shell would have exploded on my side of the tree, I would have been ripped to pieces.

When I bumped into Rioux, I suddenly felt extreme pain and a swelling under my right boot. Adrenaline must have masked the pain until that moment. My boot had to be removed before the swelling made it impossible. Quickly, I unsheathed my sharp Ka-Bar and cut the shoe strings and the leather off the side of the boot, pulling my throbbing foot free. My hand revealed a lump the size of a football! However, I did not want a shot of morphine for the pain, because I needed to be focused and able to fight if we were attacked again.

A minute later I heard, *womp, womp*—the sound of a CH-34 approaching from the east. Those fearless, daring pilots and crew members were ignoring the blackness and tight jungle landing zone to assist us grunts on the ground. Seconds later, just above, like an angel from heaven, the chopper slowly started dropping towards us, the blade cutting tree limbs until touching down.

I limped, rifle clutched in my hand, dragging all my clips. Along with eight other bloody Marines, we scrambled into the vibrating machine. The machine gunner shouted to the pilots "We're loaded," and the screaming engine labored as the pilots powered the chopper straight up, tearing at the trees. They turned south, but the CH-34 was still not gaining altitude. Was that rifle fire I heard over the roaring engine? Seconds later, we lost altitude, and I heard the blades chewing up trees—the limbs smashing against the cabin. My life flashed before my eyes. 'Shit, we're not going to make it!' The chopper began spinning wildly towards the jungle floor. When we hit the ground, the bird shuddered to a stop, and we were on our side, leaning on bent blades. Out of the darkness, from up front, the pilot shouted, "We have to get out because this smoking bird could still ignite!"

Quickly, I snapped on my clutch belt and slid down to the door and jumped out. As soon as we were free, we formed a perimeter in the thick bush. Unfortunately, now we were much closer to the NVAs on the mountain. While I sat watching into the darkness, I noticed we landed a few feet from a large rock formation that could have ripped the chopper up and caused an aviation fuel fire and roasted eleven men.

A bit later, we heard human movement coming from the original perimeter. Then we heard Sergeant Bailey's voice. He had organized a search patrol to locate the downed chopper and survivors. He quickly had us moving towards the perimeter, about 100 yards south. Behind the lead point, I hopped along, one boot on and one off, my adrenaline still peaked. I clearly remember Novinger behind me remarking, "That crazy Stein is pushing through the bush like a man possessed."

Fifteen minutes later, the wounded, battered patrol limped and stumbled back into the perimeter. As soon as I dropped on the ground, Sarge Bailey told us, "Choppers may attempt again to medevac the wounded men." A few minutes later, I heard two 'birds' flying in our direction and wondered, 'How in the hell can they snatch us from the same tight landing zone?' Regardless, just above, those brave men slowly lowered down and settled on the ground.

Holding my helmet tight, rifle still in my hand, I clawed my way into the vibrating machine, while holding my other hand out for Rioux. When we were secured inside, the machine gunner shouted, "Take her up!" Again, I heard the blades slashing at trees, but the pilot kept hammering the CH-34 and I felt the bird tilting towards the north, then turning east. That gutsy pilot and crew had us flying towards Khe Sanh in total darkness.

When we set down on the steel tarmac, Marines were waiting to help the wounded get to the crude field hospital tent one hundred feet south. When I reached the tent, the man holding me up said, "You won't need your rifle and clips anymore; I'll take them from you."

"What?" I shouted, tightening my hold on the rifle. I was extremely frightened to give up this object that had become a third arm. It was my 'life blood' for a year, and I felt helpless without it. However, I recovered from my fear and gave him the rifle and clips.

As soon as I found a cot to lay on, a Corpsman came in and started assessing the severity of the wounded men. After checking me, he smiled and said, "Marine, that puffed up right ankle and foot will get you on a freedom flight soon!" Freedom flight was the term we relished—a plane that took us out of Vietnam and back to the 'World.' He gave me a shot of penicillin to prevent infection and moved on to the next wounded man.

A bit later, a Marine came in with tuna fish sandwiches. Hell, we were all famished, and that sandwich tasted like heaven compared to C-rations. After that, Rioux went to the surgical tent to check on the other casualties from the mortar attack on the base. When he came back he said, "A mortar hit the tent of our buddies from A Company. Stein, a lot of old timers are fucked up bad, including Stone Mountain. The surgeons were working on a bad chest wound on him!"

"What the hell," I shouted, "he only had a few days left, the same as us!"

Before that thought registered, a Marine burst through the canvas flaps screaming, "Incoming, incoming, the gooks are mortaring us again!"

Total insanity erupted in that tent packed with damaged bodies. Men were stumbling, crawling, and limping to escape that possible death trap—the open tent. After everyone else escaped, somehow on one leg, I jumped off the cot and scrambled outside. My God, rounds were exploding close to me on the airfield tarmac, showering out bright red sparks. My ears rang from the loud explosions and the zipping steel flying past me. Then, to my right, someone screamed, "In here, in here!" As soon as I heard the scream, I stumbled towards the voice, finding an outstretched arm. A second later, I slid and was pulled into a black hole.

"You're safe now Marine, you're in an underground bunker covered by many layers of sandbags." Next to me, men crowded together in total blackness to escape the carnage above us. A short time later I heard our 105s blasting artillery towards Hill 689 to silence those mortars. As I sat in the darkness, I thought about the squad and the remaining platoon that was still out in the jungle. I felt guilty because I couldn't help them anymore. Nor could I help my friends hit by the mortar attack on Khe Sanh. I pondered about the brave surgeons just above with only a canvas roof for protection, operating on critically injured men.

As exhaustion and the thumping in my right ankle and foot set in, I fell asleep. When I woke, the shelling had ceased. Later, a Marine plopped down into the bunker, announcing that dawn was breaking, making it possible to medevac the seriously wounded out in Chinooks. He indicated that the other wounded would be medevacked in C-123s. I needed surgery; therefore, if the North Vietnamese mortars stayed quiet, I would be headed south to Phu Bai.

Ten minutes later, we climbed out of that dark bunker and immediately heard the rattle of small arms fire out near the mountain. Instantly I thought again, 'I should be out in that jungle with those men!' However, what good was I now, stumbling around on one leg? My attention was directed back to the tarmac, where I saw Marines loading wounded men on a waiting Chinook, bound for Phu Bai.

A C-123 lumbered down the runway a bit later and stopped ninety feet from our group of bandaged men huddled together. It was imperative that we load that running plane quickly, because it was a juicy target for mortars sitting on the tarmac. Stretcher bearers began running to the plane, but I refused to be carried. I shook Rioux's hand since he was staying at Khe Sanh. I told him to keep his head down and then I hobbled toward the C-123. Before tripping up the ramp, I saw a streaking F-4 Phantom making a bombing run on 689. "It don't mean a thing."

Chapter 9:

Freedom Birds and Angels

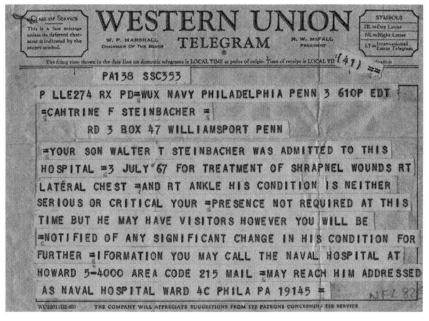

Western Union telegram sent to Walter's family, July 1967

INSIDE THE PLANE, I strapped myself to some netting attached to the bulkhead. Soon the ramp went up and the pilots had the beast rumbling down the short runway, barely clearing the tree tops. Thankfully, we made it without getting blasted from the sky. An hour later the C-123 delivered its cargo of wounded men to Phu Bai. Marines hurried into the plane to carry us all to the field hospital. Although I protested, the stretcher bearer growled, "Marine, you will be carried in!" Minutes later I was placed in a 24x30 foot hut which was soon packed with blood-soaked bodies, awaiting surgery.

Although my right ankle was thumping like a jack hammer, I kept telling myself, 'You're alive Stein, screw the pain!' I was taken into the next room about an hour later and immediately given a spinal block and a shot in the leg to numb that area. The surgeon soon began digging for steel, and then started cutting open my ankle. He bent over me, placed the steel in a bag with my wallet, then moved on to the next operation. Later I was carried to another C-123 waiting to take a planeload of patched-up men to Da Nang.

While flying to Da Nang, the anesthesia finally sent me into a deep rest. The next thing I recalled was a pretty American nurse standing by my bed. I gasped, thinking I had gone to heaven, because it wasn't possible to see an American woman in Vietnam. However, I soon realized she was not an illusion. I felt her soft hand holding my shaking hand. "Marine, you're okay. You're in the Da Nang field hospital, and if your condition remains stable, you will be on a plane tomorrow for Clarks Air Force Base in the Philippines."

Hearing that, I felt a healing rush through my body. I wondered, 'What passion drove that angel to come to this extremely dangerous land?' In fact, I already knew the answer. She wanted to make a difference for humanity—to heal damaged bodies. I recall tears rolling down my cheeks. How in hell would I be able to thank her and all the others responsible for my being here, still breathing? That list was long. It included my buddies in the platoons covering my backside every day, brave forward observers who called for naval gun fire, jet airplane and helicopter pilots, artillery and mortar crews, Seabees who built safe bridges and roads, tank-Amtrac crews, Navy men on the ships, and surgeons and nurses. The simple answer: I'd be forever indebted to all those people.

Later that afternoon, a man appeared by my bedside, squeezed my hand and spoke softly, "Marine, get well soon!" Surprised, I looked up—another angel! Standing there was Floyd Patterson, the former world heavyweight champion boxer. I was still woozy from anesthesia, but I did blurt out a 'hello' and 'thank you.' Another human in a dangerous place, giving solace to wounded men.

Just before dark, more wounded men were wheeled in from Khe Sanh. There beside my bed, Sergeant Bailey stopped the Marine pushing him. In a faint voice I heard, "Stein, I'm screwed up bad, shot three times. But also, we lost dead and wounded, and I had to crawl alone off that steep slope on Hill 689!"

I threw my hand over to touch his arm as they wheeled him away and I hollered, "You're going home to Virginia Sarge; you'll be OK." I never saw him again.

June 27 6:30 pm (on American National Red Cross stationary)
Dear Mom & Dad,

What can I say?? Last night near Khe Sanh I was hit by shrapnel in the right ankle, and a slight wound on my right side. My foot is in pain, but I am very much alive. It was 'hell'! The Cong did us a job with mortars and rockets. I should be in the States soon. I'll let you know soon. I'll be laid up maybe 3 to 6 weeks!

I'll be glad when the pain goes away! I knew I was pushing my luck. I told the Marine Corps not to contact my next of kin. My decision so please understand.

I'll end so remember I am a lucky guy, no loss of limbs etc. just pain.

I love you all,

Wally

P.S. It must all be God's Will. Everything turned out like it did.

Later, my 'angel' nurse came by to check my vital signs and she gave me a pill for pain. After pulling the warm blanket to my chin, I must have slept through the remaining few hours of that incredible day in my life—June 27, 1967.

The next morning, the same sweet nurse brought me some food and smiled, "Marine, you'll be on a flight to the Philippines within the hour; good luck." She squeezed my arm and disappeared into another room.

June 28th

Dear Mary,

Yes! The writing gear is different. June 27th at 1 a.m. in the morning I was wounded in the right ankle and right side on my chest by shrapnel! It all happened when the Khe Sanh was mortared. Mary, I am lucky! No broken bones, loss of limbs, etc. Many of my buddies didn't make out as good. I don't even want to talk about it. It was hell! And Khe Sanh was erupting with action today.

I am at Da Nang in a decent hospital waiting to be sent stateside, maybe tomorrow morning. What else can I say. I won't be able to walk on my foot for a few weeks to come, but God's Will be done.

Oh! Yes! The 1st medevac chopper I got on crashed in the jungle at 1:30 in the morning. Yes! All this in one night plus more. Wounded and all, we walked through the jungle 400 meters to our original landing zone. So much for all this. See you very soon,

Love,

Wally

P.S. Mom already let you know, I'll bet!

June 28th

Dear Mom & Dad,

This may be my last letter from the Nam. Yes! I am in Da Nang waiting for a jet stateside. I am under good care so try not to worry. I hope my letter I sent yesterday got home. If not I'll repeat I was wounded by shrapnel in right ankle and right side of my chest. A Navy doctor took pieces out of my ankle but no broken bones. Probably be a couple of weeks before I can walk but I am very lucky as I said before. 'Hell' was erupting up at Khe Sanh after I left and today also.

Please stay 'cool' at home and I'll see all of you soon. I'll go to Philly Naval Hospital.

Your loving son,

Wally

A short while later, stretcher bearers began moving us to a waiting C-130 on Da Nang's runway. Soon after I was strapped down, I heard the ramp close and the four powerful engines revved—we were moving down the runway gaining speed for liftoff. As soon as the plane cleared the tarmac, a cheer erupted from elated, wounded men. In fact, that triumphant moment defies description! I had made it out—alive, on my freedom flight.

The flight to Clark was smooth. The C-130 floated like a feather through the air, unlike the dependable, but bumpy C-123.

When I arrived at my new bed, a sweet nurse greeted me—the 'angels' kept descending to my aid. As soon as she discovered I was covered with only a white sheet, she hurried out and came back with a set of soft cotton pajamas and a soft, warm pair of booties. Later I received a tray of food—cooked meat, potatoes, and a vegetable—what a luxury compared to months of C-rats. Maybe with a better diet, I would put some pounds on my gaunt body. Gaunt bodies were common among grunts because of the harsh conditions in Vietnam, including poor diet and intense heat. I was pampered by the nurses and slept well over the next two days in the hospital.

> *June 29*
> *Dear Steve,*
>
> *Just your 'ole brother. Please let everyone read this next line. I am at Clark Air Force Base in the Philippines. No more jungles, rifles etc., etc. Tomorrow morning I leave by jet for the States! What can I say?*
>
> *I am stiff and can't walk but I am a lucky guy. I should be in the Philly Hospital by the time you receive this letter.*

Soon I hope to be able to come home! Take care!
As always,

Wally
Tell everyone I'll try to call home as soon as possible!

Then, on June 30th, the nurse stopped at my bed and patted my arm, "Marine, you will fly to Japan today, then to Anchorage, Alaska, and finally to Andrews Air Force Base on the east coast. Your freedom bird will be a C-141." Later that morning, many wounded men were loaded on the giant jet. I was on my back, strapped tightly to a bunk above another wounded man. There were many rows of bunks with wounded men, many of whom were busted up worse than me and required constant monitoring by the doctors and nurses.

As soon as we lifted off, a nurse said hello. She told me, "Every day seventeen C-141s fly to the states and seventeen return to Vietnam." On the short flight to Japan I relaxed and fell asleep until the great jet landed. When my new angel stopped by my side, her words were music to my ears, "Next stop, Alaska, USA!"

Later, as we were departing Anchorage, we were informed our flight would be non-stop to Andrews Air Force Base. Flying towards Andrews, still flat on my back, I had ample time to think, especially about escaping Vietnam alive. While there, I didn't actually think I would ever fulfill the dream of returning home.

I slept many hours during the flight, before I felt and heard the screeching wheels of the C-141 as it touched down at Andrews. Not much later, I was wheeled into a large ward filled with evacuees. A nurse checked my blood pressure and heart and informed me I would be at Andrews one night before departing for the Naval Hospital in South Philadelphia. Then she offered to get me a phone so I could call home.

I heard those words and I started to sweat. July 8th, 1966 was the last time I called home, and I only talked for three minutes. I wondered what I would say, considering I felt I had lived a full lifetime over the past fourteen months. But, of course I would call! Not long after, the nurse came back and plugged a phone in for me to use. As I started dialing our home phone number, my hand was shaking and sweat dripped from my face.

Mom answered, and I hesitated, attempting to find words. Then I finally managed, "Mom, I'm in a hospital at Andrews Air Force Base, and the nurses are watching over me."

"It's good to hear your voice son," she said.

I told her, "I will soon be sent to the Naval Hospital in Philadelphia and I'd love to see you all soon. When I get there I'll call again." Then Dad got on the phone and asked me how I was doing. I also talked briefly to Bernadette.

I hung up and quickly lit a cigarette, still sweating and shaking. Hell, what did I expect from myself—I was barely five days removed from the lifestyle of a combat warrior!

* * *

When I was wheeled into a large ward on the fourth floor of the Naval hospital the next day, I breathed a sigh of relief. The last five days I had been in and out of two helicopters, three planes, one jet, and three buses. I now wanted to be grounded in one location.

Soon after getting settled into a soft bed, a nurse and doctor stopped by to unwrap and check my wounds. I glanced down at the four-inch gash on my ankle. As the nurse commenced dabbing on hydrogen peroxide to clean it, intense pain shot through my whole leg. At that moment, I had doubts about my ability to ever walk on that leg again.

The next few days I settled into a simple routine with four painful peroxide cleansing treatments per day. I had a wheelchair for mobility, and I buzzed around the ward conversing with the other patients. Although the shooting war was 11,000 miles away, our conversations always led back to Vietnam. One Marine five beds down from me had a large hole shot through his upper arm. He was wounded at Con Thien, a base east of Khe Sanh where the North Vietnamese shelled from their safe haven across the border. He said that many Marines died or were butchered on that suicide base. Similarly, other Marines told stories of battles along the border with North Vietnam. However, we tried not to dwell on the war, because we all thought maybe we could forget the past months and move forward.

One early afternoon, about a week after arriving at the hospital, I was suddenly roused from a deep sleep by the presence of people nearby. I thought I was dreaming—at my bedside were Uncle Jim, Aunt Margaret, my cousin Joe, and his wife Vickie. I immediately began to sweat. I quickly reached for a Benson and Hedges and managed somehow to strike a match to light up. Although visually shaken, I was overjoyed to finally see some loved ones. I had not seen any relatives from the 'World' since April 1966. I saw their tears, but quickly reassured those beautiful people that I was a lucky man compared to so many other men caught in the chaos of June 27th. Other than those words, I didn't talk much while they visited, but their visit was a starting point for me. I realized that I would soon have to relearn how to talk to people other than Marines.

A few days later, the day shift nurse came by and smiled. "Stein, you have some visitors." I intently waited and in the doorway stood Mom, Dad, Pauline, and Theresa. My God, Theresa had grown up—she was sporting nylon stockings and wore red lipstick. I guess I was gone a long time! Eleven-year-old Pauline, Mom, and Dad all looked well. Seeing them cemented a crucial fact for me: in that moment, my dream of ever coming back had become a reality.

As they approached I sat up and hugged each of them, holding back tears as I told Mom and Dad that I was receiving outstanding care. I noticed my little sisters standing quietly, appearing frightened. I felt helpless, because they were surrounded by fifty damaged young men in that ward, and I couldn't explain how or why. I was thrilled to see the loved ones I had been writing the past months. Although visiting with them was still difficult for me, until they left my bedside I remained brave and reassured them I'd be home soon.

A few days later, I encountered my Navy doctor in an elevator. He noticed me sitting in a wheelchair. He admonished me, "Steinbacher, if you want to walk again, you must start stretching those stiff muscles on your right leg and ankle." While I didn't say anything, I took his challenge to heart, and after that day I started limping around, forcing some pressure on that extremely sore lower leg.

My non-productive existence continued in the hospital. My daily routine began with a hearty breakfast, followed by wound cleaning, a cigarette, lunch, dinner, and ended each day in a small television room connected to the ward. I was bored, restless, and wanted to go home to the mountain!

Late that week, while another Marine and I were having our wounds treated in the medical room, another Marine limped in. "Hey," he shouted, "there is a blonde and a brunette outside who want to see you guys."

My heart jumped ten beats—maybe it was Diane and my cousin Jackie! "Send them in," I shot back.

When they entered the little room, I gazed at a pretty blonde and a stylish brunette—not Diane, the girl whom I had been writing 'love letters' to the past fourteen months, but two women who wanted to visit wounded Marines. After they introduced themselves to us, I muttered a weak hello. Hell, I still was not functional enough to interact with young women because I was out of circulation much too long.

Regardless, I enjoyed their visit and I asked for the blonde girl's address—Sherie Buss—I still remember her name. She lived close to the hospital. About a month later I called her for a date; however, she was busy that night, and I never called back.

The first week of August 1967, a Navy doctor told me I could go home on convalescent leave, as long as I would treat my own wounds with peroxide while I was at home. He also gave me a list of five departments around the hospital that I had to contact for signatures to get permission for the leave. Then he stated: "Get the forms signed by Thursday night, and I'll release you on Friday." I agreed and spent the next day hopping around the giant hospital collecting all the signatures. That afternoon, when I was finished, my ankle was puffed and sore, but who cared, I was going home!

* * *

Thursday night I called Gary, who was stationed at the Philadelphia Naval Base. I informed him I was granted leave for Friday morning. I also told him I didn't have a clue how to get to center city Philadelphia to catch a bus home. Gary responded, "Steinbacher, I'll meet you at the main gate and we'll take the subway uptown to the bus terminal."

The next morning, I was given a small medical bag containing peroxide, large bandages, and cotton swabs: all the items I needed to treat my open wounds. I put on a shirt, pants, a shoe on my left foot, and a bootie on my right. I limped around to all the Marines in my ward and bid them goodbye. A bit later the nurse told me to walk across the hospital park outside to reach the main gate, which was about a quarter of a mile away.

When I stepped outside of the hospital, it was the first time since June 8, 1966 that I stood on American land. Furthermore, I was alone with no Marines covering my ass. I stumbled 100 feet into the park when I spotted a man with two large German shepherds on the sidewalk about seventy-five feet ahead. I froze, and my mind switched into survival mode. 'My God, I'm going to be killed by two large dogs and never make it home.' My right arm automatically reached down for my M-16. Damn, it wasn't there—I needed my life blood; however, my 'third arm' no longer existed. Then to my left, I spotted a police paddy wagon cruising slowly through the park. I quickly moved to the left off the sidewalk and screamed, "Hey, stop," and the cop slammed on his brakes. I stuck my head in the open door and asked, "Can you take me to the main gate?"

He replied, "I usually don't pick up anyone."

Firmly, I demanded, "I need a ride to the main gate."

"Hop in, I'll take you across the park."

When I stepped out of the paddy wagon, Gary was waiting by the Marine guard. What a relief—bailed out by a cop and my old friend!

Six hours later, after making 'milk stops' in many towns on the way to Williamsport, the bus passed through the gap on the Bald Eagle Mountain. There before my eyes as I looked down, I saw the blue water of the Susquehanna River flowing south through the West Branch Valley. I knew at that moment that I had made it back to my dream valley!

W. T. STEINBACHER
. . . Marine corporal

Marine Home To Convalesce

Cpl. Walter T. Steinbacher, son of Mr. and Mrs. Walter J. Steinbacher, Williamsport RD 3, is spending a convalescent leave at his home.

He was on patrol duty on Hill 881 in Vietnam when he was wounded in the ankle and chest on June 27.

Cpl. Steinbacher was with a Marine unit that smashed a Viet Cong force that sneaked back onto the Vietnam war's bloodiest battlefield on June 27. The company of L e a t h e r n e c k s jumped on North Vietnamese troops spotted on Hill 881, the strategic mountain just below the North-South Vietnam border.

Williamsport Sun-Gazette announcement of Walter's return home

Minutes later the bus pulled into the Susquehanna Trailways station and Gary pounded my arm. "You made it Steinbacher. I'll call Dad for a ride." A bit later, I was once again standing on the ground across the small stream, gazing at the small, humble, white-trimmed farm house—home at last.

A chill shot down my spine—everything appeared to be the same: peaceful and serene. I crossed the stream on the sturdy concrete bridge, looked up, and saw Bernadette bounding down the mountain stone steps from the house. Tears trailed down her cheeks. "I thought you were killed when Mom called Aunt Mary while I was on vacation in Canada," she cried.

I quickly hugged her and replied, "Well, here I am little sister."

Then, slowly, like I was walking on air, I made my way to the back porch, opened the old wooden screen door, and stepped into the kitchen. A heavenly smell filled the air from sweet baked goods, and there, next to the porcelain sink were two pies, a cherry and a pumpkin. Months ago in a letter, I told Mom if I made it, a pie would be a most welcome homecoming gift.

I turned to Bernadette and told her I wanted to take a walk on the path towards the barn and the pig pen. When I started out the path, I felt as if I were back in Vietnam, looking down for booby traps. I looked up at the thick tree line where the swamp began, and my first thought was whether there could be snipers lurking in the woods beyond the pig pen. I stopped and told myself, 'You've got to force yourself to continue to the swamp.' I took a deep breath of mountain air, conquered my fears, and walked the final steps to the empty pen. Still, I was reassuring myself—'You're safe Stein, it's okay, you're home, at the base of the Bald Eagle Mountain!'

Mom, Dad, Theresa, and Pauline came home a bit later and we enjoyed a piece of Mom's pie. Steve arrived ten minutes later behind the wheel of the Thunderbird. What a surreal experience: the house, the Thunderbird, and my family were still in the same location. However, I wasn't sure where I belonged—at home, or back in the bush with my buddies.

Around sunset, after enjoying everyone's company, Dad called Uncle Dick to set up a coming-home drinks celebration at the VFW. Uncle Dick took a round through his arm when the 1st Marines Division assaulted Saipan during the Second World War. When we arrived, Uncle Dick shook my hand and slammed me on the back, "How're you doing, Jar Head. Let's have a shot."

As I sat down on the barstool, I glanced around at the older veterans at the bar, mostly World War II vets. Immediately, I felt intimidated and jealous of those men. Those resilient souls saved the world from the tyranny of Hitler and the Japanese Empire; each had a sparkle in their eyes revealing the satisfaction of a job well done. On the other hand, although I was extremely proud of myself and the Marines that fought beside me, what the hell did I accomplish during those brutal days in the bush? It was an accident of birth that we ended up fighting in such different wars. Those vets had no choice regarding when they were born; likewise, I could not have picked my birth date, just a few months after the Second World War ended! After a few drinks, I relaxed somewhat and enjoyed Uncle Dick's company before Dad and I departed to return to the homestead.

When I entered the kitchen, Mom and Bernadette were seated at the table talking. I sat down with them and quickly asked the dreaded question—"Where is Diane tonight?" Mom hesitated, then she softly proclaimed, "Diane's engaged to marry her new boyfriend." I instantly reacted by slamming my fists down on the oak table, turning and racing upstairs. I threw myself down on the bed, but I couldn't get one tear to flow. Diane, gone? This was not the tearful and loving homecoming I had dreamed about for fifteen long months.

After adjusting to the shocking news, I jumped off the bed and hopped down the steps and calmly returned to the kitchen. I told Mom and Bernadette I had suspected Diane had a new boyfriend, because I hadn't received many letters during June. "However, Mom, I had planned to win her back when I returned home; but an engagement ring is a powerful symbol. I guess I'll have to move on." After that pronouncement, I went up to the same bed I hadn't slept in for fifteen months.

I rested well that night, but when Mom cracked the door the next morning, I sat straight up on full alert, faster than she could close the door. "Good morning, Wally!"

"Good morning, Mom," I said, sweating some. She didn't say anything more, but she must have recognized a changed son from the one who left home in the spring of 1966.

A few days later, my Uncle Bob and Aunt Hatti came to visit. He had trained to be a fighter pilot during the Second World War, but missed the Pacific war when the Japanese surrendered. I welcomed their company; however, I was uneasy since I couldn't talk about the war and had little to say about any other subject. Instead, I kept my mouth occupied by puffing on cigarettes. Still, their visit took me back to good times when our family used to visit their farm thirty miles southwest of the homestead.

Later that week, Gary and I got together for a few drinks at the Cottage Inn, a bar one mile west in the village of Nisbet. It was dark when we left the bar, and we took on another passenger who sat in the back seat of Gary's Pontiac convertible, Gary Day. He was a few years younger than us, and a year later he would be in Vietnam. A bit later that evening, after racing around the Third and Fourth Street strip in Williamsport, we headed home.

Unfortunately, Gary was blasting through Duboistown too fast; behind us with bright lights and siren blaring, a Duboistown cop was in hot pursuit. Gary did a quick ninety-degree turn north down Cochran Avenue and took another ninety-degree turn east at fifty miles per hour—yes, 50 miles per hour! He then slammed on his brakes and the car violently slid; as he hit the gas hard, we sped another hundred yards and turned quickly in behind the Valley Inn and shut off the lights. Seconds later, Taca, the policeman, cruised by and didn't spot us in the dark alley. Minutes later, Gary hit the lights and I glanced back at the Day boy. He hissed, "I'll never go anywhere with you crazy people again." And, he was right on the crazy part—Gary and I never broke a sweat, because we were still traveling at warp speed due to our tour in the bush.

A few days later my cousin Stan knocked on the kitchen door. When he entered he told me he was joining the Marines with two other guys I knew: Bugs Baier and Frank Stetts. When I heard that shocking news, I bellowed, "Do you know what the hell you're jumping into?"

He smiled at me, "No." My God, what did I start back in '65?

A while later, after we had a drink, Stan asked me if I wanted to take a ride with his girlfriend and her friend. "I'd love to Stan. I'll fire up the Thunderbird," and a while later we met the two girls at a food hangout near Lycoming College. Stan's girlfriend was a cute blonde from Williamsport, and her friend was a brunette with a chic page-boy hair style.

When we sat down in a booth to have a soda, the girls were clearly chomping at the bit to ask me questions about the war. Sue politely asked, "How was it like in Vietnam?"

I slowly stumbled through some answer that actually avoided the question. I said, "Oh, it was a little rough at times." She was gracious and didn't press me any further.

Then, before I had time to recover from one question, I experienced my first taste of anti-Vietnam War sentiment. Betty pointed at a student three booths down and said, "That guy is constantly bad talking about the war." Damn, I was not prepared to hear such talk, because some of my beloved Marines were still in that hell hole.

What the hell was I to do? Go yank the 'slime ball' out of the booth and beat him? On the other hand, I couldn't beat everyone who opposed the war. Beating and killing back here in the 'World' was not legal! Sue and Betty sensed I was growing restless, and Sue said, "Let's get out of here."

Back in the Thunderbird, a while later, I rolled through a stop sign and immediately saw the bright lights of a police car to my rear. I hit the brakes and pulled to the side. When the policeman came up to my window, I told him I didn't have a license yet, because I'd been in Vietnam the past year, but instead I quickly handed him my military ID card. He explained to me how to send for a temporary driver's license and said it was okay to go.

A few days later, I asked Bernadette to intercede for me and ask Diane to meet me at our property line (she lived next door). A bit later, Bernie informed me, "Wait outside on the porch at 4:00 pm. Diane also wants to see you." At 4:05, like a vision coming through the fog, I saw Diane for the first time in sixteen months. She approached, and I quickly closed the distance between us until we stood only four feet apart. Diane's blond hair was neatly cut short, and she appeared older and more mature since we parted in April 1966, but she still looked radiant.

I can't recall my exact words, but I asked her how life was treating her. I got a simple answer, "Oh, alright."

Damn, I was uneasy. This meeting was not my dream from nights in that rat-infested bunker in the bush. I longed to hold

Diane tight, kissing and hugging with tears dripping down my cheeks. I remained calm and asked Diane, "When are you getting married?"

Diane was evasive. She smiled and said, "Oh, I don't know."

After that answer, without touching her, I told Diane, "Take care of yourself," then turned and walked towards the homestead.

Now, I am not able to recall my thoughts and emotions at that moment; however, I am convinced that the cool, calm behavior indicated that I had switched on my survival mode. I simply buried the harsh reality that my dearly loved Diane was no longer an intimate part of my life.

Later that week, I received a call from Joe Gansel who was the head supervisor at Syntex Fabrics. He invited me to a dinner, on him, and said that I could bring a date. I quickly accepted, but the task of finding a date tortured me. I doubted that I still had the skills to interact with a woman, even if I found a date. Regardless, I had to start somewhere. First, I called Cherie, a girl who lived 500 feet up the road. I can't remember if I talked to her, but I gave up and then called a girl at the bank whom I had admired from a distance. I never said anything other than hello when cashing my checks before I joined the Marines. The result: she gracefully turned me down. The third girl I called was now married—'The hell with it, I'll go to dinner alone.'

The next day, Stan stopped at the homestead and I told him I couldn't find a date to take to dinner. Stan smiled and said, "We can fix that, I'll loan you Sue for a night."

I hesitated a moment, but I finally said, "Stan I can't turn the offer down."

Saturday night, while driving to Sue's house, I felt like a teenager on his first date. Serious doubts persisted. What would I talk about? I felt I had been absent from the human race for a long time. An hour later, I began relaxing in the back seat with Sue as we pulled into a classy restaurant parking lot thirty miles south of Williamsport.

Later, on the trip home, I held Sue's hand. The smell of her perfume and her quiet voice were soothing to me, especially compared to two sweaty, stinky Marines in a foxhole reeking from muddy, slimy water. Maybe I could rejoin the 'human race.' While driving along the mountain towards the homestead, I knew that one date would not be enough. I had to see Sue again before reporting back to the hospital in a week.

I couldn't wait any longer, and two days later I dialed Sue's number. To my surprise, she invited me to take a ride on the Susquehanna River on her Dad's boat docked at the Maynard Street bridge. While splashing west on the water, with Sue at the helm, I was in high spirits. The majestic Bald Eagle Mountain rose to the south, and by then I was confident that the thick riverbank tree lines did not hide snipers. After a glorious hour on the river, I took Sue back to her home on the east end of Williamsport. There we sat on the porch swing holding hands, sipping iced tea, and making small talk. Dear God, another angel was sent to me, because she was good medicine for me. Before leaving I dared a light kiss and then told Sue I would write her from the hospital.

A few days later, my dream homecoming with Mom, Dad, brother, and sisters ended, and I was on a bus with Gary speeding back to Philadelphia. Gary had new orders to Camp Lejeune, North Carolina. The only fact I knew for certain was that after the hospital, my next duty station would not be Vietnam.

* * *

On Monday afternoon, I was examined by the Navy doctor and he told me my wounds were healed enough to discharge me to Casual

Company at the Naval Base. I didn't tell him that I still had some pain and stiffness in my right ankle because I wanted to be free of the confining hospital.

Early Wednesday morning, I limped around the ward, shaking hands, telling everyone to "Get well, and get the hell out of here!" Mid-afternoon when I checked into Casual Company, the duty clerk took me to a nearby old barrack, and I grabbed an upper bunk. I moved up to luxury living quarters, compared to that cold, wet, earthen foxhole!

The next morning, after enjoying chow at a clean mess hall, about thirty men fell in outside the barracks for roll call. I looked at the formation and I saw what appeared to be a gathering of orphans. Not many Marines were dressed in full uniform. The rest were decked out in civilian clothes, white shirts for mess duty, sneakers, loafers, and jungle shirts. In fact, the list of combinations was endless. Nevertheless, the group standing in formation was proud and salty and not concerned about any bullshit dress code because our sea-bags were left behind 10,000 miles west of Philadelphia.

After we broke formation, I talked to a Sergeant who was in charge of outside work details. I told him, "I'd prefer an outside detail while at the base." A bit later I reported to him at the maintenance office, and to my surprise, he placed me in charge of a small group of men. I would be a working foreman: mowing grass, trimming shrubs, landscaping, trash removal, and painting. Hell, I was like a kid with a new toy, because those tasks were similar to work back on the homestead.

Over the following days, I settled into a daily routine that kept me busy and content. The days began with chow at 0700h, then reporting to the maintenance building at 0800h. At noon we had lunch which was usually followed by a stop at the 'slop-chute' for a beer, and then we were done at 1600h and had free time. In fact, I soon discovered that the base had a first-class gym for basketball, and a state-of-the-art workout area with Nautilus equipment to help me build up my worn body and right ankle. I even entertained the idea that the Naval Base would be an ideal place to hide from the 'World' for the next eighteen years.

The following week on the base I went to supply to secure a khaki uniform, complete with new black shoes, trousers, shirt, and cover (hat). When liberty started at 1500h on Friday, I was dressed and primed to wear the uniform up town and then on the long bus ride to Williamsport. It wasn't considered 'safe' wearing your uniform in public because many civilians blamed us for the still active war. Regardless, by that time I had developed a belligerent attitude. I had earned those threads and medals through blood, sweat, and tears, and I dared any son of a bitch to spit or say anything negative about me. Six hours later, I arrived home again. Although there were a few stares, not one negative word had been directed towards me running the gauntlet through the Philadelphia bus station or the entire trip to Williamsport.

That weekend I had another pleasant date with Sue, riding in the 'bird, sharing pizza, and lounging on her front porch simply holding hands and talking. Those simple pleasures were enough for me and they began to soften me from my harsh existence in the jungle. Then, Sunday night, I was behind the wheel of the Thunderbird rolling towards Philadelphia. No more long bus trips for me, as I would have transportation to explore Philadelphia's night life.

Thursday night, after a busy week working on the base, four of us decided to check out the night life up town. Later, while racing a GTO between Broad Street's many stop lights, a policeman pulled me over. My God, I was brazened enough to ask him why he didn't pull over the GTO. He simply smiled while checking my Marine ID card and license and told me to "hold it down." How in hell did I deserve that break? Who knew, maybe he was a Marine.

Later the guys and I had a great time at Micky Finns, a speakeasy that served foaming pitchers of beer and peanuts in the shells. The shells were thrown on the old, worn, wooden floor. Later, as we drove south back to the base I showed some restraint, and we were all back in the racks by 0100h.

Friday afternoon I was on the move again, streaking west on the Schuylkill Expressway with two Marines, whom I would drop off near Harrisburg. After getting the toll road ticket at Valley Forge, I pressed the pedal down until the speedometer read eighty. Ten miles west on the turnpike, a Mercury Comet passed the 'bird. The Comet had a big block 390 cubic inch vibrating under the hood. I accelerated past the Comet and a cheer was heard from my passengers. In fact, the passing and cheering continued for the next eighty miles until we slowed for the Camp Hill pay station. Remembering that race west on the turnpike at speeds up to 100 miles per hour left no doubt: life for these three Marine warriors was boring and moving too slowly back in the 'World.' Still, the grim reaper watched with delight during that wild eighty-mile ride.

1 Sept. 67

future Ex Marine

I received your letter yesterday & all the boys say hi or at least whats left of us.

I don't know if you've heard but the day after you were hit we took hill 689. Here's who was killed – D. Allen, S Sgt. Hamilton, DeCeaser, Mullard, David, Walker, Freddy Johnson, Gardineze, Gaddis and a few others I forgot, many were wounded.[†] Out of the 2nd sqd. Cullen, me, Nabinger & Oscar were left. O'brien was wounded but he's back working in the rear.

It was a bad day & lucky you weren't around. Them ass holes put me & Musgrave up for Silver Stars & Bristol & Lindsay up for Bronze stars! I got a Purple Heart for a small leg wound.

Happy to hear you a fine & walking. We threw one hell of a party for Rioux & Bristol when they went home.

I went to Hawaii on R & R & I flew home & spent 4 ½ days there. I brought back all the booze for the party.

We got all kinds of new replacements. They are all boots. 3/26 rotates at the end of Sept. 18 more days and they get out of the field.

We are in the same area! We built bunkers and should be here at Khe Sanh for the Monsoon. K & L Co. went to the DMZ to assist the 9th marines.

There hasn't been any action here lately so we ain't to worried.

Sorry I have to end but today we are security for engineers building a road. It was good to here from you write again

Your Automatic rifleman
Lommer

[†] 2ndLt Dale Charles Allen, SSgt Donald Paul Hamilton, Cpl Anthony Dicesare Jr, LCpl Kenneth Arthur Millard, LCpl Jeffrey Jay David, Cpl Richard Lee Walker, LCpl Freddie Lee Johnson, and LCpl Alejandro Ray Godinez (all died on 27 June 1967).

2 Sept. 67
Dear Stein,

Well I guess I had better tell you now. I am in the first platoon now. And would you believe I am a squad leader now.

In case you don't know second platoon was wiped-out by rockets and mortars one night. Mr. Charles has given up on 60 m.m.'s he is using 120 mm and 82 mm mortars now.

Steve is in second platoon now an I don't see to much of him anymore.

Hell, everyone is either dead, wound or gone home an all that is left here is a mess of boots. Last night my squad got lost on an ambush, a platoon ambush the people we got can't even play follow the leader they are so dumb.

Oh, well enough for that, I am glad to hear you are alright now. An I am sorry to hear about your girl but don't feel bad. I think mine is already married to some other guy.

Well I guess I had better close for now
                Take Care & Good Luck
                    Spenc.

27 September 1967
Wednesday
Dear Walter,

It was real good to hear from you and to know you'll be in good health now. Yes I know Marine Barracks is good duty, I've spent a little time in them myself.

I too was corresponding with "Scotte" and Lommer until Scotte got killed earlier this month. Lommer hasn't answered since I last wrote. I wonder if anything has happened to him.

I have received a letter from Schraff recently and he told me about a few of the fellows getting hit. Oscar Policius, Lindsay and a few others got killed the 7th of Sept.[†] I wish I could go back and help them Walter. They were the best men I have ever worked with. I'm trying to keep up with them as much as possible but its sort of hard to do. Have you heard from Sgt. Klinedist? I was hoping to but I haven't.

Walter if you happen to get orders to Camp Lejeune drop by Ward #9 at the Hospital and see me. I'm trying to contact most of the guys that are coming back to here so we can get them all together and have sort of a party.

I'm out of bed in a wheel chair now. I got out of traction about 2 weeks ago. I still can't use my leg but its getting better all the time. I hope to get on crutches before long so I can go home, I'm so close yet still far away.

As you know I'm suppose to get out of the corp the 20th of Oct. but Doc said I'd be extended a few months. I think he'll let me go around the 1st of the year, hope so anyway.

If you hear any news about the fellows let me know. I have all their home addresses if you want any, just say so.

Well Walter I wish you the very best of luck and success. Hope to see you again before to long. May God richly bless you.

Jim Bailey

[†] LCpl Oscar H. Palacios Jr (died 8 September 1967) and LCpl Gary Wayne Lindsay (died 7 September 1967).

After reading letters from PFC Lommer, Spencer, and Jim Bailey, I was overcome with a dreaded feeling of helplessness and guilt because I was absent when my beloved platoon members were killed and wounded taking that worthless piece of real estate, Hill 689. Thinking logically, I knew my presence on that jungle mountain would not have changed the outcome: the dug-in NVAs would still have inflicted many casualties on us and maybe I, too, would have perished. Nevertheless, losing over 60 percent of my platoon (dead and wounded) hurt me deeply. They had all been healthy when they followed me into the jungle that fateful afternoon. Unable to do anything more to help my platoon, now I was forced to attempt to learn how to live as a survivor—safe back in the World.

During the second week of October, three incredible events occurred for me. First, the news: Wednesday morning I was called from the Sergeant Major's office to report to the duty clerk. The clerk looked up from his desk and smiled, "Corporal, you lucked out. Somehow, we lost your orders to Camp Lejeune. You'll be staying at the Naval Base until your discharge day." I was elated; I enjoyed my ground maintenance daily duties.

The second event happened Thursday night when I took two Marines up town to an Army Depot club. I met a pretty girl with long dark hair and asked her to dance. She was sitting with some friends at a nearby table. While slow-dancing, I learned that she worked at the Depot during the day. After a few more dances, I asked her if she needed a ride home and to my surprise, she replied, "That would be nice." Not too long after the T-bird was cruising south on Broad Street, she was sitting in the front bucket seat and my two buddies were in the back. After I dropped my Marine friends off at the base, she gave me directions to her home on 22nd Street, just west off of Broad Street. Fifteen minutes later,

I parked near her tidy brick row home. Before walking her to her door, I wrote her phone number in my little booklet. Later, while buzzing south on Broad Street, I knew another angel had touched my life that evening—Roseanne!

The third surprise happened that weekend. I was on the move again on Friday, driving toward the mountains and home. I wanted to see my family and to spend some time with Sue. When I called her on Saturday afternoon, she had a date with Stan; however, she said her friend Betty was free for a date. 'Why not,' I thought. I needed adventure, and also some softness in my life. So, a while later I called Betty at her dorm room and was delighted when she agreed to a date. I met her at the visitor's desk at 8:00 p.m. since males were not permitted beyond that point. Betty was a cute brunette with a page-boy hair style, curled under just above the collar. It was a very popular style in 1967. I was immediately at ease in her company; she was bubbly as she talked about her college experiences. Above all, she didn't ask me any questions about the war. After a movie and a short ride in the Thunderbird, I took her back to the dorm in time for the 11:00 p.m. curfew. I gave her a quick kiss and told her I would call the next week when I came home. Yet another sweet girl graced my presence that night—Betty!

Gary was also in town that weekend and we wanted to play 'scrub' football for the first time since 1965. Usually a team would show up at the nearby Nisbet ball field, ready to butt heads with a combination of Nisbet and Nippenose Valley hard-bodies. When Gary strutted across the field to join the team, his blood-shot eyes and face looked as if they had been used for a punching bag.

"Jarhead, who in hell did you tangle with last night?"

"Oh, Bud Thames, one of the baddest brawlers in town, Steinbacher. Don't worry, I got some good shots to his head as well." Gary was fighting a new war; he street-fought anyone who wanted to make a name for themselves by beating up a tough Marine. I often told Gary that we were already tough guys, and we had nothing to prove to any son of a bitch back here in the 'World.'

After two hours of blood and guts tackle football, I limped off the field, bruised, with my jersey ripped off my back. Despite that, I felt invigorated because hard physical activity was good medicine for me at that time. Later that afternoon, I was in the 'bird rolling towards Philadelphia, and Gary was on the road speeding towards Camp Lejeune.

Thursday night I drove to Roseanne's home to see her and meet her family. I immediately felt welcome when introduced to her mother, father, and brother in their warm living room. Later, we watched an Academy-Award winning performance by actor Sidney Poitier in the movie *To Sir with Love*. That film was a powerful story about a teacher mentoring tough students in an inner-city high school. After the movie we went back to Roseanne's street, parked, and enjoyed each other's company, talking for a half hour. I hated leaving her, but I gave her a kiss at her door and told her I'd call next week from the base.

I can't honestly recall my thoughts that night as I drove south on Broad Street; however, looking back, three facts were certain. First, Roseanne was a special woman—reserved and bright. Second, Betty, whom I would see Saturday night was a sweet, fun-loving woman who would have a degree in two years. And third, Sue still held a special place in my heart because she was the first woman who touched my fragile spirit after I returned from the war. Together those sweet women posed a delightful dilemma I couldn't easily solve; I was racing too fast, attempting to make up for lost time.

Saturday night I enjoyed another pleasant date with Betty. We shared a small pizza and then I took her up to Skyline drive, high above the Valley, overlooking the twinkling lights of Williamsport. We talked about many things and kissed for about twenty minutes; the only words I can recall are that I told Betty, "Maybe when I am discharged from the Marines, I'll enroll at Lycoming and try out for the football team." However, I was talking 'dreams' because I had zero plans for my future, other than drifting forward. Regardless, I held that warm, young woman's hand and was damn thankful that I didn't have to flash back twelve months.

A short while later I thanked her for sharing a pleasant evening with me. Then I met Gary at the Susquehanna Hotel where we closed the bar at 2:00 a.m. Afterwards, we drove a few miles north to a late-night food drive-in, the Dog House. Inside there was a large group of about ten to twelve noisy young men who were milling about like a pack of wolves. Gary and I, along with another guy, Jim Wise, quickly slid into a booth and ordered some burgers. We went to the head, and when we returned, four intruders had plopped their asses down in our booth.

I glanced at them and growled, "You punks stole our seats!"

One of them snarled, "So what?"

I quickly grabbed Gary's arm and loudly stated, "We don't have to take this shit, we'll teach you all a lesson, outside!"

Then I headed for the door with Jim, but Gary lingered in the restaurant a few minutes. Jim Wise uttered, "You and Gary are insane, there are too many of them," and he ran to his car.

Gary then strutted out, and I shouted, "What the hell took you so long?"

Gary smiled, "I told those punks if they wanted a piece of me and Steinbacher, they must send out two brats at a time, until they're all beaten, bloody and laying on the pavement." We calmly waited for them to come out and after a bit, Gary slapped me on the back and growled, "They're not coming out. The babies, they must think we're crazy."

As we finally walked towards our cars, I said, "You're right Jarhead, but it would have been fun to teach them a lesson."

The never-ending drama in my life continued Sunday night when I was preparing to drive back to the Naval base as Diane and my sister Bernadette appeared in the kitchen. They were still good friends, but my scrambled brain was not prepared to see Diane at that time. Regardless, she looked foxy and I uttered a weak hello, as she and Bernadette walked by on their way to the living room. Around 10:45 p.m., Mom, Dad, and Bernadette went up to bed, leaving Diane in the living room. Now what?

I unglued myself from the safety of the old wooden chair and slowly entered the small living room, playfully saying, "What's up? I thought you'd be married by now." Diane quickly told me her man had joined the Marines. I did not push her for any further details. I sat down in Dad's rocking chair, and we talked for about an hour—about what, I can't recall. However, I remember Diane telling me she was living near Allentown, helping her Aunt and Uncle with their younger children while they ran a restaurant. I glanced at my watch and told Diane that I had to hit the road, or I would be AWOL when reveille went at 6:00 a.m.

After grabbing my bag and turning off the lights, I gave Diane a kiss and waited until she walked across the narrow field to her parents' home. Seconds later I was in the 'bird speeding east on the narrow road between the river and the Bald Eagle Mountain. I recall my head spinning wildly after that hour with Diane. Had I moved on from losing her, or had I still reserved a corner in my heart for her? Who knew? Regardless, I had to refocus on the mission ahead; I was tired from a lack of sleep and had 180 miles to go before I would reach my rack.

When I reached Interstate 80, I rolled the window down and cranked up the radio. The Beatles, Monkees, Mamas and the Papas, Roy Orbison, Diana Ross, and the Supremes kept me awake. Near Allentown, I must have zoned out and I found myself driving off the wrong exit where a sign read, "North to Lehigh Tunnel." Despite that, at 5:00 a.m., I finally crawled up into my bunk and pulled the warm gray wool blanket over my body.

An hour later, the duty NCO was shouting, "Reveille, reveille, everyone out of those racks!" Who cared? None of us moved first to jump out. It was typical for us, a band of salty, combat grunts.

Later that morning, I was told I would be the duty NCO Saturday and Sunday nights. No big mission for me, because NCOs simply answered incoming calls, held reveille, called formation, held roll call outside, and stood fire watch all night. Later that week, after eating breakfast in the mess hall with three buddies, we stood up to leave when I heard the words "baby killers" slobbering from a Navy man sitting with another squid next to our table. In a flash, I slammed my hand down on their table and they froze. "What the hell would you know about killing babies, you big mouth? You were not in the bush!"

In a split second, I felt six arms reach for me. "Stein, those bastards are not worth it. You're getting out in less than two weeks. You'll be thrown in the brig, maybe for life, if you don't walk away now!" I stilled my rage and allowed those three Marines to guide me to the door. Outside I was still shaking, fearing how I would survive in a few weeks without my Marine buddies to save me from myself.

Friday night I went up town to see Roseanne, and when I entered her living room, her mother invited me to celebrate

Thanksgiving with their family. Quickly I accepted, but I was surprised by the invitation, because I had only met her family four weeks before that night.

When Roseanne and I settled into the Thunderbird, I asked her, "What do you want to do tonight?"

She said, "I have been east and south of Philly to the Jersey Shore, but I've never been west to Valley Forge."

I took her hand, "Soon we'll be cruising west on the Schuylkill."

When we reached Valley Forge, I clearly remember a strong desire stirring in my brain—to get on the Turnpike and take Roseanne home to the mountain to meet my family. However, I knew I had to turn around and take her home and report to the base before 6:00 a.m. or I would be AWOL. Just before midnight we kissed at her door and I told her I'd call after weekend duty.

Saturday night as I listened to music in the office, I wrote Betty a letter. I told her that although I was extremely attracted to her, my future was clouded with uncertainty, while she had a bright future ahead in two years when she graduated from college. It was a bitter pill to choke down, but I had to back away from that bright, young woman.

On Monday morning, I was relieved from weekend NCO duty, but I knew the coming week would be packed full of serious decisions. I had an option to 're-up' for more years and receive a bonus. I heard that a job escorting military prisoners to brigs world-wide could be a possibility for me if I signed on for more active duty. Hell, that possibility was more enticing than going back to the silk mill!

The next night, before my buddies were leaving for the Thanksgiving break, I wanted to take one last bar-hopping excursion up town. Around 8:00 p.m., Jim Kline from Ohio, Fred

Harris and Joe Reed from Harrisburg, and I drove up Broad Street towards center city. Our first stop was the Phone Booth, a quaint little bar, no larger than 18 by 12 feet, complete with a pretty go-go girl dancing in the corner on a tiny platform. At that time, many bars had go-go girls dancing for twenty-five to fifty dollars a night. We slopped down a few beers and then walked a few blocks to Micky Finns, the roaring twenties bar that played live music. We settled in, slammed pitchers of beer, chomped on peanuts, and sang along with the band. It couldn't get any better than that glorious night for four combat Marines blowing off steam for one last night. By half past midnight, we made it back to the barracks, happy and content young men. Nothing more to do but crawl under a warm blanket and sleep.

Thanksgiving morning, I ate a late breakfast at the chow hall, then dressed in civilian clothes and drove to Roseanne's house. When I entered her warm home, my nose immediately caught the sweet aroma of roasting turkey and stuffing. I couldn't wait to eat with her family, but first, Roseanne invited me to a traditional Thanksgiving-day football game at her former alma mater, South Philadelphia High School.

I was impressed with the large crowd that turned out to see the young men playing football on a holiday. But it was also amazing seeing the tall buildings a few miles north that served as a backdrop to the game. In contrast, back home in the valley, mountains served as the backdrop to football games. I cheered with Roseanne and we cuddled to keep warm on that cold, blustery day.

After the exciting game, we drove to Roseanne's home and waited until her Mom put the finishing touches on the meal. When I sat down to eat, the simple, sweet smelling food reminded me of Mom's fresh food back home. Just like home, Roseanne's family prepared the cranberry salad from scratch with fresh berries. The sauce was a perfect blend of sweet mingled with hints of the sour berries. Her mother's fresh-baked buns were wonderfully light and fluffy. The meal was prepared with love, to please Roseanne's guest—me! After I had a tasty piece of pumpkin pie, I recall offering to help clear the table, but Roseanne's mom quickly told me, "You're our guest. I'll take care of it." Over the next few hours, as we talked in their living room, I felt very welcomed. I thanked her family for a great day and for sharing their Thanksgiving holiday with me. I told Roseanne I would call her on Saturday morning.

In the Friday morning at mail call, I received a letter from Betty. I was surprised to get a response from my letter, but anxious to read it. She was congenial, and said we shared some incredible dates together, and she would miss my company. Furthermore, she thanked me for explaining my thoughts so clearly, though I doubted that I deserved that praise. I felt relieved to get a reply from her and knew I would also miss her. On the other hand, I had to make that hard choice, to rein in my whirlwind life.

Later that afternoon after slopping down a few beers at the NCO club, I cleared my mind of another nagging pending decision. I decided to proceed to be discharged on Tuesday morning and attempt to blend into the civilian gauntlet. However, I kept open the possibility of changing from reserve to active duty status, if civilian life became unbearable.

Before dark set in, I phoned Roseanne and invited her out for a dinner date on Saturday night, but only if she picked the restaurant. She quickly accepted the invitation and I told her I would pick her up at 6:00 p.m. Then minutes later I jogged towards the gym, hoping to find enough men for a basketball game.

When I stepped on the court, I found seven other men eager for a game and soon we were running four on four, full court. What a luxury, playing in a warm gym, complete with hardwood floors and fiberglass backboards—I was savoring my dream-come-true life. After an invigorating workout of full court basketball, I stopped at the NCO club for a few beers and camaraderie with other Marines who also would be discharged soon.

Saturday, I visited the PX and purchased a black and burgundy plaid sports coat. I paid forty dollars for the coat that would have cost two-hundred in a civilian store. After stepping out of the PX, I strolled to the waterfront, where workers were refurbishing the battleship *New Jersey*, complete with its giant 16-inch guns. Scuttlebutt indicated that the *New Jersey* was destined for duty by Spring 1968 off the coast of Vietnam.

By 5:30 p.m., I was cruising north on Broad Street, decked out in my new coat and a black turtle-neck shirt. When Roseanne greeted me at her door, she was glowing in her soft, silky knee-length dress with her dark hair cascading over her shoulders. Ten minutes later, we were seated at an intimate local Italian restaurant and bar. The spaghetti was tasty; the restaurant reminded me of the Italian restaurants along the river-front in Williamsport. After a magical candle-lit dinner, I drove Roseanne back to her house where we sat in the car talking for about an hour before I walked her to her door. Before leaving, I recall telling Roseanne I wanted to see her Monday night, before returning to the mountain on Tuesday morning.

Sunday, I was extremely stir-crazy thinking about my fate back in civilian life, so I kept busy in order to bury that boogeyman. For instance, I checked my winter green uniform that I would wear Tuesday morning and shined my shoes. I took a long walk around the Naval Base and then had chow. Afterwards I went back to the barracks and talked with some of the Marines that were getting discharged alongside me. I discovered, like me, they had no long-range plans for their lives. After that busy day, I slept well.

I had an appointment with a Navy doctor on Monday morning for a required physical before discharge. After quickly checking my teeth, eyes, blood pressure, and heart, he scribbled something on a form and said, "You're free to go Marine." The remainder of the day I killed time by walking and talking to the bartender and other Marines at the NCO club.

When the clock struck 6:00 p.m., I fired up the 'bird and soon was cruising north on Broad Street to see Roseanne. When she opened the door, she greeted me with a pleasant smile, and from the living room, the rest of her family said hello. As I can recall, I was feeling strong pangs of guilt because I knew they were aware I was leaving the next day, and she and I had not talked about our future together.

Minutes later, I drove us to a small, green-trimmed brick restaurant on Broad Street. Roseanne and I decided to share a simple evening together, sipping coffee, and eating a tasty bun. Later we drove back to her street and I parked close to her door. I dreaded the thought of walking her to the door that night, because I wanted the night to last forever. Although most of our conversation that cold night in the Thunderbird was a blur, I clearly remember Roseanne's last words to me: "Please don't tell me you'll see me again if it's not true."

I did not give her a response. What the hell was wrong with me? Why couldn't I commit to that sweet woman? Would I run from intimate relationships the rest of my life? I am convinced that multiple degrees in Psychology could not have explained my mindset in late November 1967. I walked her slowly to her door, kissed her and said, "Take care." That's how that cold, November night ended with Roseanne. Minutes later I stopped at a local bar on 22nd Street and ordered a double shot of Johnny Walker Red and soda. I quickly gulped down that drink and another before driving back to the base.

When I got to my bunk, I checked my uniform one more time. Every detail had to be in order: medals, the eagle, globe, and anchor emblems had to be square. Once that was accomplished, I climbed into the top bunk and pulled the warm grey wool blanket over myself for the last time thinking, 'Tomorrow night I will be alone, back in my tiny bedroom at the homestead.'

The scotch must have kicked in then, since the next thing I knew, the duty NCO was yelling, "Reveille, reveille, everyone out of those racks." It was 6:00 a.m. and I needed to get dressed and get to the chow hall before my appointment with the Sergeant Major at nine.

After breakfast of 'shit on the shingles,' accompanied by some orange juice and coffee, I walked to the maintenance office and bid everyone a "Semper Fi" and shook hands. I swiftly walked to company headquarters and reported to Sergeant Major Stroble. I sat down across from him at his desk as he reviewed my records. He looked at me, smiled, and proclaimed, "Corporal, your record is immaculate. Why are you choosing a discharge this morning?"

I smiled back at him and said, "I don't have a concrete answer to that question—only time will tell if I can be a 'scum-bag civilian' again." He didn't press me further. In fact, I had talked to him before and I sensed he wouldn't attempt that morning to push me to sign on for more active duty.

Following that meeting, I strolled down the hall and had my reserve ID picture taken (which I still carry for good luck). That task completed, I walked briskly towards the main gate where I was meeting Gary. He had been discharged on November 28th because he was granted one day's travel time from Camp Lejeune.

As I approached the main gate, I spotted Gary, standing tall in his winter green dress uniform. My God, how fitting—two close buddies since the age of six were now two men, twenty-one years old, who had run the gauntlet of death, destruction, and maiming in the bush. And, somehow, they were going home together on that cold November morning.

A few minutes later I fired up the Thunderbird and drove off, out of the safety of the Naval Base into the 'World' that I was not yet prepared to embrace.

* * *

Gary and I were silent until we were speeding west on the Schuylkill Expressway. Gary slapped my arm and said, "Well, Steinbacher, we made it. Sure as hell, this morning feels better than two years ago when we came south on that bus."

"Roger that, Jar-head," I said.

"You son-of-a-bitch, you sound like a damn Marine radio man."

I looked over at Gary with a sly smile, "You should know Jar-head, you humped a radio in the bush, same as me."

Three hours later, we crossed through the gap in the Bald Eagle Mountain overlooking Williamsport. A short while later, we stopped at the J &L, a small, quaint bar three miles from the homestead. Gary and I needed some food and some drinks to begin celebrating our discharge. We devoured large juicy burgers, slammed down a few beers, and shot two games of pool before heading towards our homes. A half mile from my home I dropped Gary off, and in no time I entered our warm kitchen to find Mom busy preparing a beef roast with potatoes and carrots for supper.

Mom greeted me with a warm hello. "I am happy you're home safe, we'll have a nice homecoming meal tonight."

I said hello. Then I removed my Marine cover, sat down on a chair, placed my head in my hands, elbows on the wooden table, and proclaimed, "It's over Mom, the Marines, Vietnam—I should be happy; however, what is there left to do in my life?"

Mom looked up from the roasting pan and said, "Son, you'll have to be patient. Something good will come for you in the future."

Without answering, I went upstairs and slowly changed from my neat uniform into civilian clothes. I covered my uniform with plastic and hung it neatly in the small hall closet. It was official—I was a civilian again, but by name only. As if I were looking through a kaleidoscope, I saw a different world than the population at large.

Over the next hour I kept the fire blazing in the large coal and wood furnace in the cellar. Soon Bernadette, Theresa, and Pauline came bursting in the house from school. An hour later Dad followed, and we found ourselves seated together at that old wooden table in the warm kitchen enjoying Mom's luscious beef dinner. No more mess hall food served on a tin plate for me!

I was on the move again a while later and joined Gary at the Cottage Inn to continue our celebration. Around 10:00 p.m., after more beers and pool games than I could count, Gary and I started pounding down shots of Four Queens—a nasty 101 proof whiskey that burned all the way down to my gut. Not much later, I told Gary I was cutting out and told him, "Get your ass home!"

"Yeah, Steinbacher," he dismissed me, waving his big arm. "I'll be right on your tail."

As I was driving that short mile ride home, I recall my head was spinning wildly out of control. I attempted to compose myself when I stumbled into the homestead, since my sisters had not retired to bed yet. I clearly remember saying good night to them, before I plopped down on the long sofa and went to 'la-la land.'

My next memory was at 7:45 a.m., when Mom shook me awake. "Wally, Ron is in the kitchen and he wants you to go hunting with him."

When I sat up, my head was gyrating like a spinning top. Regardless of my discomfort, I knew I had to force myself to hunt deer with my trusted friend and hunting companion since childhood. Ron was an uncannily skillful hunter. On his first venture stalking deer with a bow, he bagged a deer on the first morning of archery season. Most impressive, he downed that six-point buck with a bow and three arrows that he scrounged for five dollars, just eighteen hours before the season began!

I slowly rose from the sofa and stumbled out to the kitchen, holding out my hand. "How the hell are you, Ron?"

We slapped each other on the shoulder and he exclaimed, "Let's go get some meat, Clyde." He called me 'Clyde,' after the camel on the packs of cigarettes I smoked at the time.

"Give me five, Ron," I replied.

I climbed the stairs, threw on my old red sweatshirt, and grabbed the vintage .30-06 Springfield from the closet. Downstairs, I quickly choked down some hot coffee and a piece of toast as we headed out the door. When I stepped out into the brisk air, the whiskey from the night before slammed me again and I began to shiver. Moreover, the last nasty blood-thinning shot that I received in the 'bush' had not worn off completely. After walking for a few minutes, the cold air felt refreshing compared to Vietnam's 115-degree humid sweat box.

Later, after humping up the slope on the old logging road, Ron grabbed my arm and whispered, "I'll sneak west and circle back toward you. Maybe I'll kick some deer your way." Sure enough, as I worked my way to set up on the first mountain bench, three white tails flared out of thick laurel. Quickly, I put the rifle to my shoulder and I spotted horns; however, in that split second, I didn't pull the trigger. Hell, I was always quick to get a shot off on moving game. Could it have been that I detested the act of gutting and feeling blood on my hands, especially on that cold morning? I knew Ron would have put that deer on the ground. I would not tell him that I screwed up.

I sat down on a cold rock, lit a cigarette, and took a deep drag. I shivered as the cold wind whistled through the hemlock trees. Damn, it was invigorating to be back on the mountain; I had not hunted on that rocky, steep slope since 1964. Then I heard a shrill diesel horn blowing a warning at a train crossing, just east of the homestead. Seconds later as I perched on the bench, I spotted the diesel engine pulling a load of many box cars. That moment, my mind drifted back to my youth. It had always been a mystery to me where all those trains were headed, carrying passengers and products. In fact, that morning sitting on that cold mountain, I realized that now I had some answers to my youthful curiosity. Just twenty months ago, I was a passenger on a train and I passed through many cities en route to California. Then three months later, a ship took me to my final destination—Vietnam, a country I didn't even know existed during my childhood.

I felt content that morning, knowing I did not have to be on that train. I was back home, protected by the broad shadow of the Bald Eagle Mountain. I came out of my day dream as Ron pushed through the thick laurel to my left and whispered, "Hey Clyde, did you see anything?"

I whispered back, "Yeah, I saw three tails, but I couldn't put horns on any of them. Think I'll head down to the homestead to get warm."

When I started moving down off those slippery rocks, I heard the diesel horn echoing through the valley in the distance. Once again that shrill sound snapped me back to memories of my youth and my incredible journey over the past months. It also made me ponder my extremely cloudy future. I knew that in my spirit I possessed a strength acquired in the 'bush' that money couldn't buy. At the same time, I knew that somehow, sometime in the future, I would have to improvise, adapt, and overcome the defenses I built to survive.

Semper Fi.

Chapter 10:
Life as a Country Gentleman

Walter bringing in the tomato harvest

268 • Point Man Up

AFTER MY DISCHARGE I hit the pavement running, most of the time with Gary. We thought we were invincible when we encountered hostile civilians. I'll only 'bore' you, the reader, with one example, because there were many encounters that cold homecoming winter of '68.

Gary, his brother Leo, and I stopped for a late-night drink at Mom & Pops, a bar in South Williamsport. I was asked for an ID card. When I handed the bartender my Marine ID, he threw it back at me and scowled, "I don't want to see that card; I am not serving you!"

Immediately, I reached my fist across the bar and shouted: "You son of a bitch, you better respect that card." As he cowered against the back bar, I continued ranting: "You come out from behind that bar and I'll put you out of your fucking misery."

The people at the crowded bar scrambled away and huddled in the far corner. Then 'Mom' started screaming at me, "I am calling the cops," as she dialed the telephone hanging on the wall.

I shouted back at her, "Oh shut up, sweetheart!"

I felt Gary's big arm grab my shoulder. "Steinbacher, the cops are coming. We have to get the hell out of here."

Seconds later, as I continued ranting at the bartender, Gary and Leo yanked me out of the door, and we jumped in the 'bird. As I calmly drove west on Southern Avenue, the blowing police car siren rounded east towards the bar. Yes, Gary bailed me out that time, but I would bail *him* out many times that winter!

March 1st, I returned to the Silk Mill. I needed something to keep me busy after my wild party life the past three months. However, I quickly found the old job did not challenge me, and I knew I would not make a career of weaving acetate rayon for women's undergarments.

As I attempted to acclimate myself to civilian life, I realized that the war was never far off. My dreams were like flashing television pictures of Khe Sanh, where 6,000 Marines in trenches and bunkers like those used in the First World War fought 40,000 NVA troops. Local men were coming home wounded or in bags. Many others were departing for Vietnam, including my cousin, Gary Steinbacher. "It didn't mean nothing!"

That spring, a pleasant surprise appeared back in my life—Diane! I would come in from my carousing around town and find Diane sitting at the kitchen table talking to Mom. She had broken off her engagement when, ironically, her fiancé joined the Marines! Just when I thought I was getting over her, there she sat, damned attractive and alluring as always. Often, as the moon shined down on the mountain, we would go out on the porch and kiss before I watched her walk back across the field to her home.

That fall I walked away from the Silk Mill and began construction training at Williamsport Community College. Construction was a good fit for me, because growing up I was constantly building something. Looking back, I was still traveling warp speed ahead—serving as an officer at a newly formed Veterans' club at the College in addition to the VFW, completing college studies, and doing chores around the homestead.

Diane and I finally married on a beautiful fall day. You're damn right—I still feared commitment; however, Diane was a rock solid woman—bright, pretty, and a perfect body. Furthermore, what kind of a man would hesitate proposing marriage to a woman capable of writing a love poem as beautiful as this?

To the One I Love

I decided to write these few lines to you
And believe it that they're all very true.
You see, you fool, I'm in love with you;
So deeply, there's nothing that I can do!

Although, occasionally we have a fight,
I still love you with all of my might.
And nothing on earth, 'tween day and night,
Will ever change this wonderful plight!

For I love you and you alone
And all I want is you for my own.
I want to be happy with a family and home,
so you and I will ne'er again be alone!

So you see, my love, I'll not change my mind,
For you are so loving, considerate, and kind!
And for all of your love I'd be run through a grind,
But still, I'd hang on regardless of time.

Well, about time to end all of this,
And since I can't seal it with a kiss,
I'll just have to end it right like this:
I'll always love you, "W.T.S."!!

-Diane Weston

Walter and Diane's wedding, October 4, 1969

After a honeymoon to Niagara Falls, New York, we moved into Diane's parents' home, because they had moved to York, Pennsylvania, to open a restaurant. I left school to work for a local contractor; however, the deep snow and cold weather came early that year and I was laid off in early February 1970. I tended bar at the VFW for some income, but it was not enough. Hell, I was still figuring out how to proceed with my life after the bush.

Walter and Diane

The next life changing event for me happened with the birth of our first baby girl, Jodi. While holding our helpless little life, I felt the humanity seeping back into my life, and that feeling cemented my bond with Diane.

A few months later, I landed a job at the local C. A. Reed paper products factory, owned by Westvaco Corporation. The band leader at the VFW was also the plant manager at Westvaco. Obviously, he deserved most of the credit for giving me that opportunity.

Time passed, and in the summer of 1971, I received an enticing offer to reenlist in the Marines for one year. I would be promoted one rank, given living quarters and full medical for our family, and a prime duty station in Quantico, Virginia. Furthermore, my assignment would be a 'cake'—training second lieutenants for jungle warfare. I gave it some hard thought; however, I decided against uprooting Diane, our little girl, and myself from the mountain.

By early 1972, I held our second little bundle in my arms, Kristie Jean. We called her our 'miracle baby,' because Diane had experienced serious health issues during her pregnancy. We were overjoyed to leave the hospital with a healthy newborn.

Struggling to meet the needs of our growing family, I left Westvaco in 1974 for a job uptown—Bethlehem Steel. Bethlehem was not a 'cupcake' factory. The conditions were dirty, dangerous, noisy, and the air was downright unhealthy; however, I was locked in survival mode because our family needed more income.

Walter and Diane holding Jodi and Kristie

Vietnam remained never further away than the next dream, when I'd jerk up in bed mumbling. Diane's hand would always slide over and she'd say, "It's okay." The next year, on April 30, 1975, I happened to be seated at the bar at the VFW, when the television flashed the news: North Vietnamese tanks busted through the gates in Saigon! My God, I was horrified and felt like crawling under the bar. I quickly ordered a triple shot of scotch and soda.

By early 1981 Diane's health had improved, and we decided it was time for a new 'little angel' to enrich our lives. In early January 1982, during a heavy snow squall with a wind chill factor outside at thirty degrees below zero, our little Jenna came into this world.

Kristie, Diane, Jenna, Walter, and Jodi, Easter 1982

Christmas at the Steinbacher home

The 1980s were some of the best years for our family. We continued to have a large garden and Diane and I enjoyed canning and freezing the rich bounty. For vacations, we travelled to Canada during the annual two-week plant shutdown in July. During the autumn months we were busy attending football games and band competitions. Jodi was a majorette and Kristie played the trombone.

Walter and Diane enjoying the harvest

I was a union representative for the second shift at the Rope Mill—a fitting position for me because I cherished providing a *voice* and *hope* for people in the trenches covered with sweat and grease, day in and day out. However, at that time, the steel industry in the United States was in a sharp decline and our mill was suffering. On a cold December night in 1988, I received my layoff notice. I picked up my red tool box, lunch bucket, and punched out for the last time at 11:00 p.m. I walked alongside many other men to my truck in the massive parking lot and left behind fifteen years, many good memories, and friends.

Thus, in January 1989, I became a forty-four-year-old student, seeking to complete 64 credits in four semesters to obtain an Associate's Degree in Forestry under the Trade Readjustment Assistance program. Hell, I was not student material, but failure was not an option! While I adapted easily to hands-on work, some of the technology posed a challenge. I didn't know how to turn a computer on, much less navigate the damn thing. But I found the classes challenging, and I enjoyed working among the bright, young students surrounding me. Furthermore, I benefitted from an in-house tutor; Kristie, our second daughter, helped me with algebra and other mathematics.

Jodi, Jenna, and Kristie

In college, I also began to explore writing. Nature had been a constant companion in my life, and thus became a frequent focus of my compositions.

Early Morning Peace and Tranquility

The long dark night gives way to the first signs of early morning, as the sun peaks her shining face over the tall misty mountain. In fact, the land behind lies silent, except for a pair of morning doves singing their hearts out, while perched in the graceful white pine tree. However, the sweet music of the doves is falling on deaf ears, because the small populace in the valley are still three sheets to the wind. Yet, if the doves' music could be put into words, they might be singing:

Awake, awake, yonder multitudes,

Ye are missing the greatest show on earth,

Dawn is both fleeting in its length and elegance.

By December 1990, I had in my hand a fancy degree framed under glass; however, I needed to resume making money quickly, so I began a frantic job search. My search revealed forestry positions in Alaska, Maine, Michigan, and even in foreign nations. However, I wasn't a free twenty-two year old! Jodi was in college at Millersville University in Lancaster, Pennsylvania, and Kristie would be entering college in eight months. Also, Jenna was in grade school and Diane was working two part-time jobs. Our home was in Pennsylvania, and I needed to find a way to make things work here.

My dilemma was solved in late January 1991 when my cousin, Fred Plocinski, called and asked me if I wanted to help him with a tree job. He had a tree trimming and take-down business. We made $40 that first morning and I never looked back. Hell yes, it was dangerous work hanging out of a bucket eighty feet in the air, sometimes with the world's largest chainsaw, a 3120 Husqvarna with a thirty-six-inch bar—but, it was money, and I had a job for the first time in twenty-six months.

At the same time, Desert Storm broke out in the Middle East. I recall sitting with Jenna while the news report of the war flashed on the television. She was frightened and cuddled close to me. Now, a nine-year-old has no conception of space in the world. She thought the war would come to our neighborhood. However, I was feeling disturbed by the war, too. Like all combat veterans, I had hoped that future generations of young people would not have to endure the horrors of combat. Thankfully, although plenty of blood was spilled in Iraq, that war was short!

On June 1st, 1992, I took a position with the Bureau of Forestry as a seasonal Semi-Skilled Laborer. The wages were a humbling $7.61 an hour, but what the hell? I was in the door and working outside in the mountains I loved, not enclosed by brick walls. That June, our first daughter Jodi graduated from college with a Bachelor's Degree majoring in Commercial Art and moved back to Williamsport. The years were flying by!

Late April 1993, I returned to District 7 of the Bureau of Forestry and took a position at the district office. My new assignments were closely related to my education. For example, I surveyed timber sale boundaries and marked timber sales. However, I was still paid for job Class III wages. That summer I grew impatient because our family needed medical insurance and also because my five-year window to transfer to another Bethlehem Steel plant would end in December. I visited the nearest plant in anticipation of transferring, but there was no way I could have disrupted Jenna and Diane, and abandoned Kristie and Jodi with a move 575 miles away. So I continued to get by during the winter selling firewood and occasionally working with Fred.

The winter of 1993-94 was the most severe in my entire life. By late January the snow was four feet deep where I was cutting firewood on the camp land, thirty miles from home. In fact, I was forced to hire someone to clear the logging road with a bulldozer. After that man broke his clutch, pushing the deep snow, I rented a skid-steer to reopen that road. I built an aluminum wood-framed 'boat' and started digging wood from the deep snow and pulling the cut lumber over the deep snow to my jeep with a snatch block and a long poly rope. Now, what drove me to work under those harsh conditions for $45 a pickup load? I was convinced that the alternative, returning to the rope mill would have been worse.

Bobcat Walter used to clear the logging road, 1993-94

Walter's dependable truck and homemade firewood sled

I worked two eight-month seasons at a district forty miles away before transferring to District 12, the head office only six miles east of my home, in 1994. That May, our second daughter, Kristie, graduated from Shippensburg University and took a position in Carlisle, Pennsylvania, as a licensed social worker.

Kristie, Jodi, Walter, Diane, and Jenna

For the next three years, I continued to work eight months a year for the Bureau of Forestry; during the winter I sold firewood and completed tree work for Plocinski's tree service, when it was available. When I returned to District 12 in the spring of 1996, I was growing impatient with the seasonal employment that didn't include medical insurance for our family.

Thankfully, my fortunes changed that spring when the head Forester of the State visited the District 12 office. After he had a meeting with the District's personnel, I approached him and asked if we could talk privately. We entered a small lunch room where I expressed my concerns. First, I explained stories of technicians that were forced to quit because they felt they would never reach a salary level commensurate with their education. Second, I suggested the present time was ideal to pay the required job class five for technicians to mark the large timber sale requirements now in progress throughout the state. Third, I noted that I was considering filing a class action grievance against the state in order for two-year graduates to receive the class five pay. He appeared to be receptive to my concerns. I thanked him for listening; we shook hands and five minutes later I saw him talking in his car to the top District commander before he drove away. Now, I'll never know what was discussed in that car, but the next morning the other District technicians and I were given work assignments that would pay us the fair rate.

In January 1997, our sacrifices paid off and I finally became a full-time employee. I received the full package—health benefits, sick pay, and accelerated vacation time. It had been a long, twisty road back from the security of Bethlehem Steel, but it was worth the adventure, moving from factory to forest work.

At the same time, our family was evolving. Jodi married Jeff Myrdal that year. Kristie completed her Master of Social Work Degree in 1998, and Jenna entered Millersville University in 2000, making Diane and I empty-nesters.

Early September 2001, while driving south after a one-week vacation in Canada, the *Grim Reaper* cast a shadow over the car. I began experiencing strange chest pains. Not wishing to alarm anyone or to accept that something might be seriously wrong, I didn't tell Diane or her parents, who were riding in the back seat. Instead, I drove the remining 150 miles home. Tuesday, Wednesday, and Thursday, I marked timber in the mountains north of Williamsport—still experiencing those strange pains in the chest. On Friday morning, I decided to check into the emergency room at the Williamsport Hospital. Sure enough, after a few quick blood tests I was admitted and told that I had experienced a heart attack while driving home on Monday. Two days later, two skilled surgeons and their team inserted a stent into the blocked artery. More *angels*, huh?

My brief hospitalization was punctuated by a national tragedy. Tuesday morning, September 11, I woke to the television flashing images of hoodlums flying passenger jets into the Twin Towers of the World Trade Center in Manhattan. The world had been thrown off-kilter once again, but fortunately I made a full recovery. Two and a half weeks later, I was back in the mountains marking timber.

Thirteen years later, I was told that many Vietnam Veterans had developed Ischemic Heart Disease from exposure to Agent Orange. Who knows if my blocked artery was one of these cases? I never was one to blame everything on the War!

I soon found many new reasons to be thankful for my recovery. Our first grandchild, Evan, was born to Jodi and Jeff in 2001, quickly followed by his brother Joel in 2003. I never thought I'd be much of a grandfather, but it was a great feeling, having little ones in my life again!

Kristie married Bill Wade, a young man from the Philadelphia area in 2003. Our last daughter, Jenna, graduated from college in 2004 with a Bachelor of Arts with a major in Social Work and married her high school sweetheart, Mark Lorson, the following year. (Gary Lorson was Mark's uncle, making us now not just lifelong friends, but also family.) You look twice and your kids are gone from the nest.

I kept busy the next three years at the Bureau of Forestry. I surveyed boundaries and marked timber sales in the rugged mountains of North Central Pennsylvania—sometimes on snow-shoes and sometimes alone. I loved the work and loved getting paid to spend my days outdoors exploring nature.

Kristie and Bill Wade, 2003

Jodi's family, 2006

Another interesting duty I enjoyed was fighting fires. I can still smell sweet Sassafras smoldering at night as I watched from the fire line, hearing the loud snapping and seeing the orange flashes shooting from hollowed trees. It was strange to witness a back fire meet an oncoming blaze as a loud explosion occurred, dousing both angry flames. Afterward, the eerie burnt forest was like many carved Halloween pumpkins flickering on a cold October night.

In the middle of 2007, I retired from the Bureau of Forestry, leaving behind many great memories and workmates. I looked forward to settling into retirement, left to my own devices. I soon began rebuilding our deck, tending the garden, and selling firewood.

On a windy morning in March 2008, I lost my old Marine friend, Gary Lorson. Ironically, a month before he died, he was granted 100% disability because they determined his cancer was caused by agent orange. We had planned a glorious retirement travelling in his motor home. "It didn't mean a thing."

Jodi, Jenna, and Kristie, 2015

The loss of my lifelong friend was soon followed by the arrival of new life to love. Three sweet grandchildren, Nora, Mya, and Haven, were born to Jenna and Mark in 2009, 2013, and 2015. Diane and I became full-time babysitters a few days a week. What a joy for me to watch them grow!

Walter picking corn with granddaughters Mya and Nora

A scan in September 2016 revealed two spots of cancer in my prostate. Hell, I had enjoyed great health throughout my life—sooner or later the "boogeyman" was due for a visit! I quickly started radiation treatments under a machine that reminded me of a strange spaceship rotating around my body as I laid still for ten minutes. Two and a half months later, after forty-two treatments, I was told a blood test in March would reveal the results.

Rather than sitting at home waiting for my verdict, I became a 'beach bum' traveling to Treasure Island, Florida, where I enjoyed a week's vacation with our family in early February. We enjoyed party time, dancing, long walks, shopping, and glorious sunsets over the Gulf of Mexico. In late March, the major blood test revealed that the radiation treatments had knocked out the cancer. 'Angels' again had interceded, saving my ass. In this case, the 'angels' were the doctors, radiation technicians, and all the supporting staff simply doing an efficient job every day.

The family at Dewey Beach, Delaware, October 2019
(back row) Jodi, Kristie, Walter, Diane, Evan, Joel, Mark, Haven
(front row) Nora, Mya, Jenna

Mya, Nora, Jenna, Mark, and Haven Lorson, 2019

Joel, Jodi, and Evan Myrdal, 2019

In April and May, I was busy planting the garden and pushing to put to rest the last pages of this memoir. Then at 4:30 p.m. on June 26th, I took my pen and tablet to the wooden bench near the garden, under the yellow delicious apple tree that Diane and I had planted in 1971. Now, 4:30 p.m. was the exact time, fifty years ago, that I picked up my rifle on that rainy afternoon on the western perimeter of Khe Sanh and walked into the jungle with 39 men following my path. I did not plan to end this story sitting on the bench, near our garden in 2017. On the contrary, I would have preferred to have finished it years earlier. But as I sat there, I looked west and thought a while. I knew that Vietnam remained branded forever in my soul and spirit. I can still see the men at the end of the day, carrying a wooden plow out of the rice paddies, as the water buffalo splashed ahead. Likewise, I see the women, kids, and old men bent over, planting thousands of rice seedlings in straight rows, acre after acre, every day. I remember those more than worthy, scrappy Viet Cong and NVA fighters. And who could forget the intense bond I formed with all those Marines that I lived with each day.

Similarly, I still see the faces of the dead and wounded and remember how they walked and talked about their girlfriends, homes, and families. I recall bumping against them in those cramped, damp foxholes, night after night. Now, I am powerless to bring them back, but I can hope that those bright young eyes were peeking through the puffy white clouds, smiling as I told their story. Moreover, the bitter disappointment still lingers that we did not return triumphantly, marching down Main Street America. And yes, the occasional night dreams still occur.

After five minutes in deep thought, I heard it—a morning dove singing 'coo, coo, coo, coo' over near the spring house across the field on the old homestead land. There, perched in the wine sap apple tree planted in 1948 by Mom and Dad, a cardinal was happily singing '*purty, purty, purty, purty.*' From the bench, I glanced up at the majestic Bald Eagle Mountain, its broad shoulders still covering my back side from the south. Abundant life surrounded me, just as it had while I hand-tilled the garden soil fifty years earlier. No, there is no gloom and doom here, because I still firmly believe—I am one of the luckiest and richest men that ever walked the face of this earth!

Walter and Diane on their 35th wedding anniversary

Appendix:
Correspondence

THE CORRESPONDENCE in this memoir is limited to letters I sent stateside from Vietnam and a few letters to me from my Marine buddies after I returned stateside. The letters I sent to Diane Weston from April 1966 until April 1967 could not be located. The correspondence I received in Vietnam perished.

* * *

Figure 1: Soldiers in Vietnam were able to send letters to the 'World' for free by writing the above instead of using a stamp.

Figure 2: Even the inside flap of an envelope provided opportunities to connect with loved ones, such as this personal message from Walter to Diane Weston.

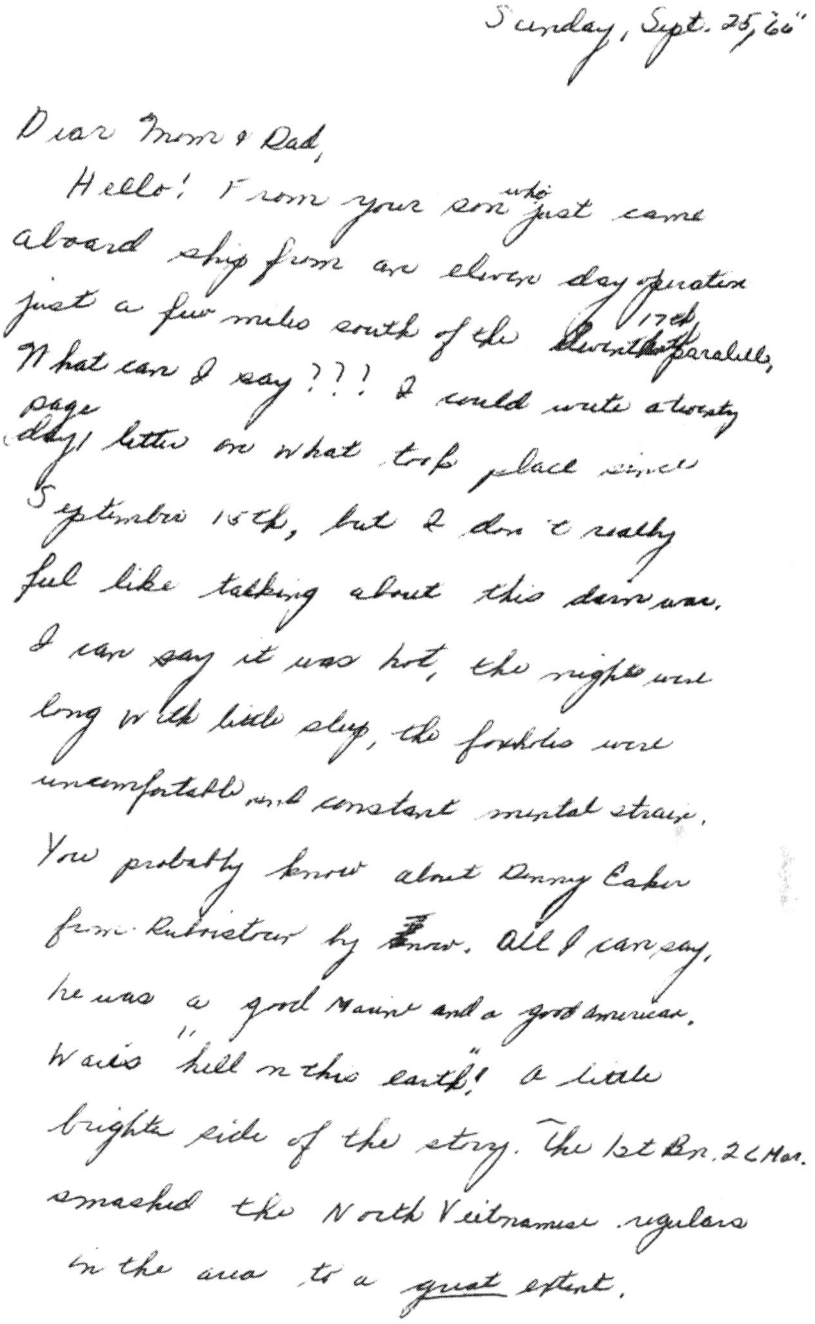

Sunday, Sept. 25, '66"

Dear Mom & Dad,

Hello! From your son who just came aboard ship from an eleven day operation just a few miles south of the seventeenth parallel, 17th. What can I say??? I could write a twenty page day! letter on what took place since September 15th, but I don't really feel like talking about this damn war.

I can say it was hot, the nights were long with little sleep, the foxholes were uncomfortable and constant mental strain.

You probably know about Danny Eaker from Ruhrstour by know. All I can say, he was a good Marine and a good American. War is "hell on this earth"! A little brighter side of the story. The 1st Bn. 26 Mar. smashed the North Vietnamese regulars in the area to a great extent.

Figure 3: Letter from Walter to his family, 25 September 1966.

Oh! Yes! I received some mail from home while in the field. It really upped my morale a lot.

How are things at home lately? I was happy to receive a letter from Theresa and Dad today. We have more mail coming today so I might get more. Thanks for the article on the Irish, Dad. It looks as if they should have a good team again. I am anxious to find out how they made out in the first game. Boy! The world series starts quite soon. The National League will go right down to the wire again, I guess.

Where I am going now? I will be stationed near Da Nang on a perimeter for 90 days or three months. Then I might go to Okinawa for awhile. I am not sure. I'll write the details when I find out the definite word.

Time to go so I'll write soon.

P.S. Thanks for all the letters & prayers.

Love always,
Wally

Best wishes how Gary made out? How is he doing?

Sunday, Feb. 12,

Dear Mom, Dad & Family,

Here it is early Sunday morning and I'am on radio watch. A radio is playing songs on Armed Forces Radio bringing back many memories. At 7:00 A.M. this morning the "truce" comes to an end.

Not much new around here except the same old day to day activities. Tomorrow our platoon moves to Hill 55 from Hill 1. Boy! We never stay anyplace very long. We even set up a shower tank while we stayed here and now it's moving time. This is being a "grunt", for you! Somehow it will all pass and I'll be able to come home to my loved ones. Truly, it will be the greatest day of my life.

Figure 4: Letter from Walter to his family, 12 February 1967, Hill 1.

So Bobby Steinbacher is coming over huh? I was hoping this mess could be ended before my friends and cousins have to come but its not the kind of war to end fast.

Things going okay at home? I guess this is the day you go in the hospital mom. I received the last sports book. Thanks! Yesterday I sent home a roll of film in a little package. The pictures were taken at the artillery Battery, & the bridge we were guarding. They are of my friends who came over with me and myself.

You asked me for the address of the two guys I went on R & R with. I can get the guys address from man Phil (the Irish guy), I am not sure about the other guy. He was wounded in the leg and went Stateside before Christmas.

Take care. and I'll write soon.

Love, Wally

Saturday Feb. 18,

Dear Pauline

Received your swell letter this morning so I'll write my youngest sister a few lines. I love to hear from you kids.

Life here is about the same. Your brother has been very busy and I am counting the days until I can see my dear family.

The snow must have been real deep. I'll bet you were out in it a lot, right? When I was your age I lived outside. Its nice to live in the country isn't it? How is school? I am glad Sister Bridget & the 5 & 6th grades liked my letter. I enjoyed writing it.

Take care and be good,

your loving brother
Walter

Figure 5: Letter from Walter to his sister Pauline, 18 February 1967.

Tuesday April 11

Dear Mom, Dad & Family,

I've received at least three letters from home the past few days but I haven't been able to answer them or anyone' else's letters.

Things around here have been going hard & crazy. The song are popping up all over and the're staying and fighting. Every day observers are spotting movement and our platoon goes out on tanks after them. Sometimes I think the only way we'll win the military war is move the people out (which has been done in areas around here) and tear everything up. I don't even want to tell you what war is like. And believe me, this is as

Figure 6: Letter from Walter to his family, 11 April 1967.

furious as any, as far as I am
concerned. I might as well forget
about getting out of a line company
and a combat zone. Maybe they'll
cut me some slack the last
month over here. I don't know
if I'll get R & R again either, all
these new guys have to go once
before I can go the 2nd time.
Oh! Well.

Yes! I received both packages.
Boy! I didn't know Dram was
75 years old. I did get the fudge
from Aunt Mary. You said Diane
has been coming to the house a
lot lately! Maybe its because I
don't write her much anymore.
Girls are the least of my problems,
all I want to do is keep my

head "wired together" and try my best to get out of here soon. War makes a guy "hard", I think. By the way, I had a mustache but I had to shave it. BN. orders for all of us. All us "old" guys wore them

I don't have much more to say so I'll end. Thanks for all the letters and prayers. I need them both.

Your loving son &
brother
Wally

Saturday April 15,
9:00A.M.

Dear Mom & Dad,

I am in the air terminal at
Da Nang waiting for transportation
North to Phu Bai. I wrote a letter
while on 55 but I forgot to mail it,
I hope someone picks it up and
mails it. You'll probably get this
letter 1st. Anyway, I've been transferred
to 3/26 and I don't know much about
them. What can I say after being
with 1/26 for a year. 1/26 will always
be my outfit in heart. I've been
through so much with them since
last April. Here it is a year after
I left home. Really something, huh!?
Just 3½ months and its so close

Figure 7: Letter from Walter to family, 15 April 1967, Da Nang airport.

yet so far away. I'll probably
land back in the gunite at 3/26.

I don't know what my address
will be, but I'll send it as soon
as I get to Phu Bai, Phu Bai is
about 40 miles south of the D.M.Z.

I hope life is okay at home.
Spring must be starting to show up
by this time!

I'll go now so I'll write soon.

Your loving son,
Wally.

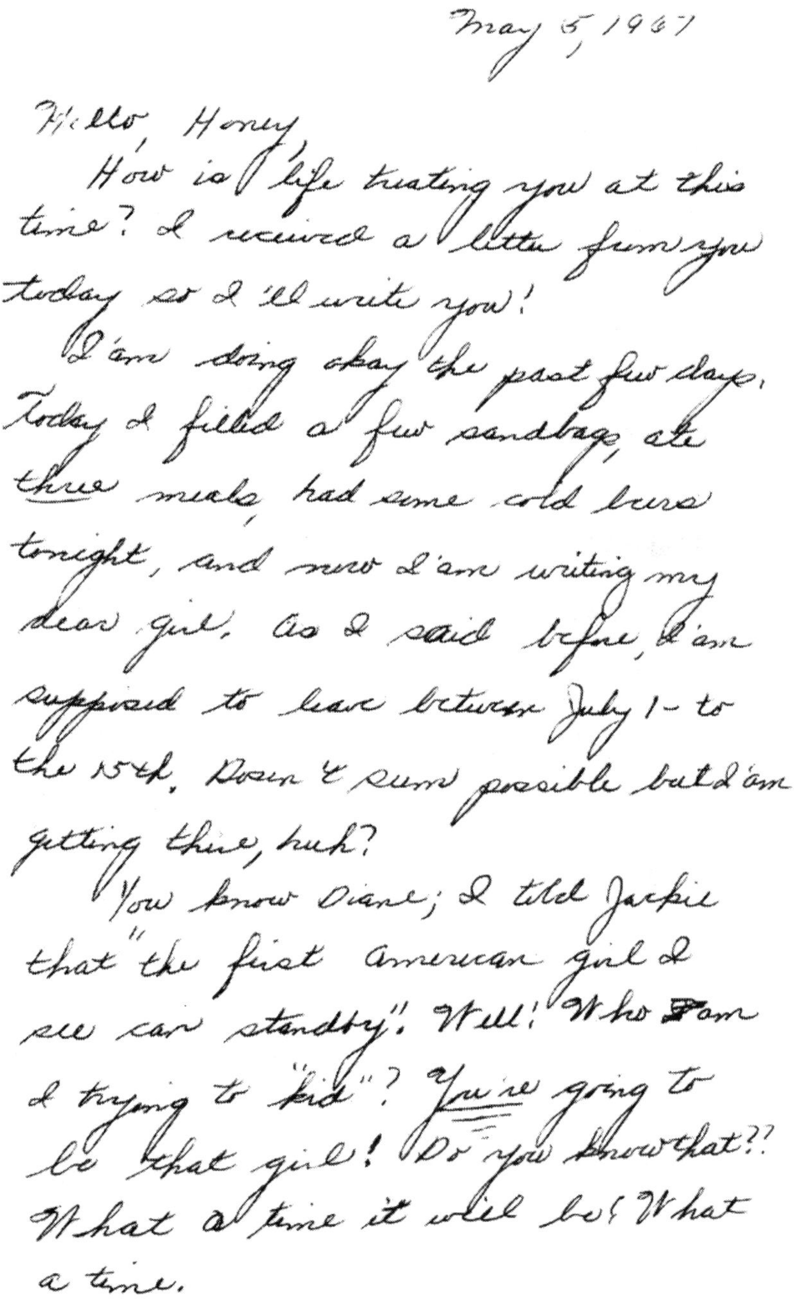

May 5, 1967

Hello, Honey,

How is life treating you at this time? I received a letter from you today so I'll write you!

I am doing okay the past few days. Today I filled a few sandbags, ate three meals, had some cold beers tonight, and now I am writing my dear girl. As I said before, I am supposed to leave between July 1 - to the 15th. Doesn't seem possible but I am getting there, huh?

You know Diane; I told Jackie that "the first American girl I see can standby". Well! Who am I trying to "kid"? You're going to be that girl! Do you know that?? What a time it will be! What a time.

Figure 8: Letter from Walter to Diane Weston, 5 May 1967.

You're going to Bloomsburg, huh?
I hope you take care of yourself!
Boy! You git around lately, right?
Don't forgit to get a swimming suit
ready! I am a big tease right?!
Will! I don't have too much
more so keep praying and so will
I.

My love to you from
many thousand miles
Always
Wally

Okay!
I'll
← Just different, that's all!
now writing
pictures from you Okay!

I miss you
very much!
left handed)

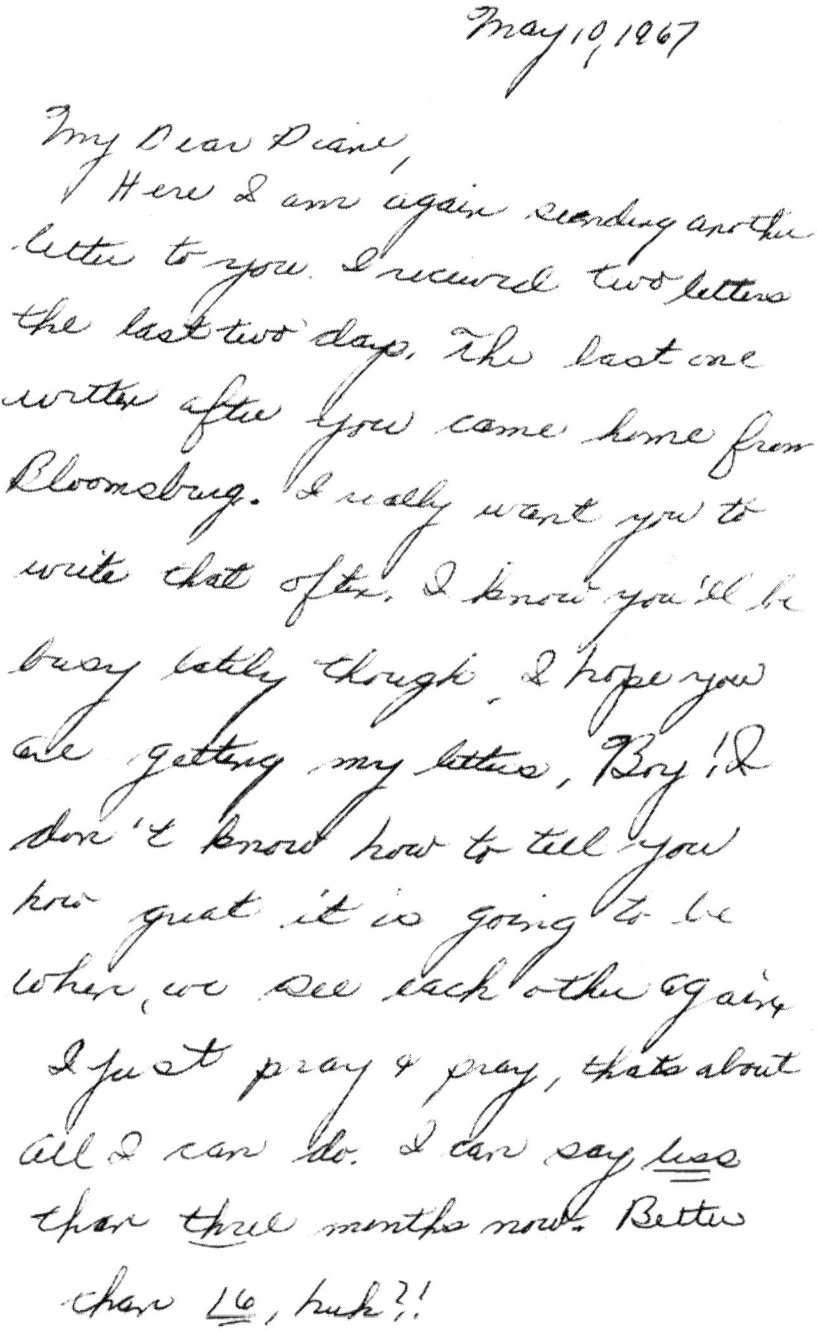

May 10 1967

My Dear Diane,

Here I am again sending another letter to you. I received two letters the last two days. The last one written after you came home from Bloomsburg. I really want you to write that often. I know you'll be busy lately though. I hope you are getting my letters. Boy I don't know how to tell you how great it is going to be when we see each other again.

I just pray & pray, that's about all I can do. I can say _less_ than _three_ months now. Better than _16_, huh?!

Figure 9: Letter from Walter to Diane Weston, 10 May 1967.

Soon I can put down this pen
& paper and come home.

Take care until then and a
certain Marine is very anxious to
to see a girl he thinks a lot of
I'll write as soon & often as
possible.

My love to you,
Wally

P.S.

I am getting so brown from the
sun you won't be able to
see me at night! Not really!

I hope you can get rid of
the throat trouble soon, Might
create some problems, you
know, like bucket seats in T. Bird
Am I unreal or what!?!?

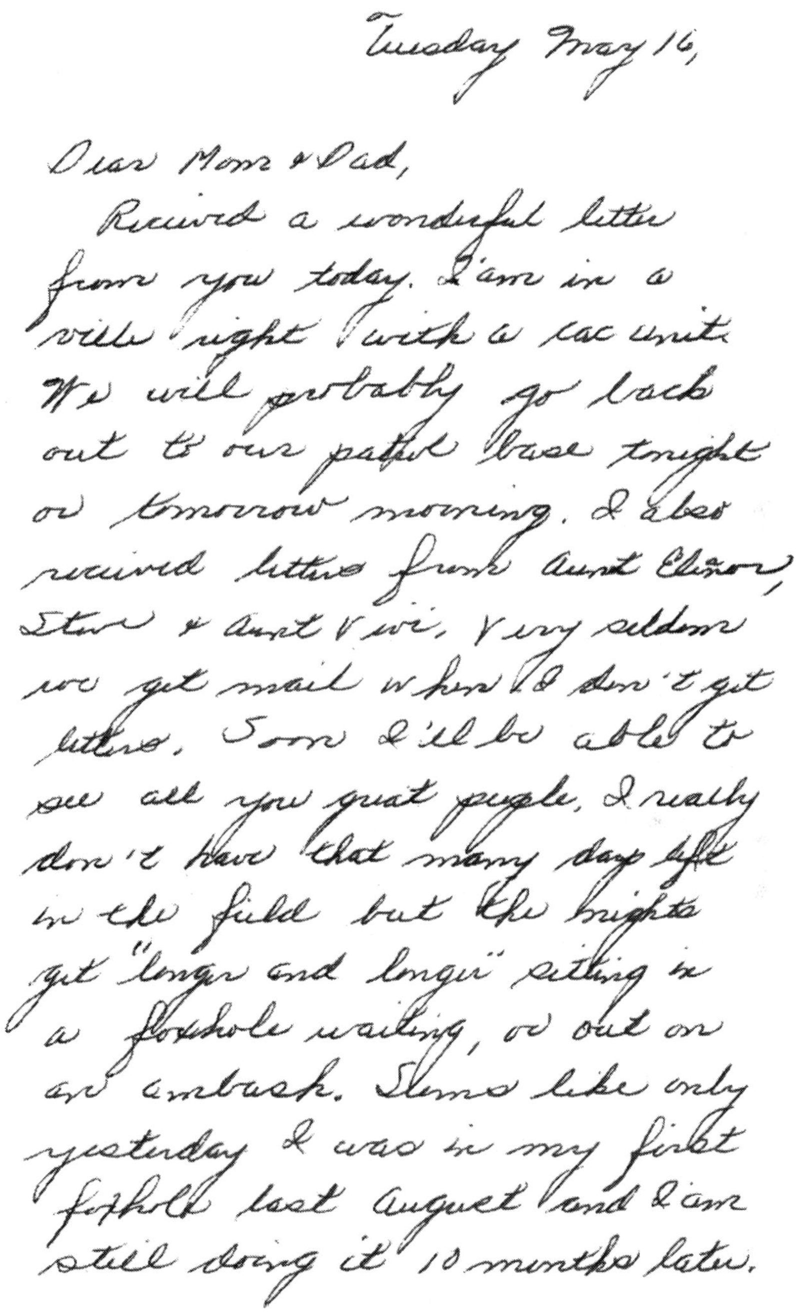

Tuesday May 16,

Dear Mom & Dad,

Received a wonderful letter from you today. I am in a ville right with a lac unit. We will probably go back out to our patrol base tonight or tomorrow morning. I also received letters from aunt Elinor, Steve & aunt Vivi. Very seldom we get mail when I don't get letters. Soon I'll be able to see all you great people, I really don't have that many days left in the field but the nights get "longer and longer" sitting in a foxhole waiting, or out on an ambush. Seems like only yesterday I was in my first foxhole last August and I am still doing it 10 months later.

Figure 10: Letter from Walter to his family, 16 May 1967.

Somehow, this "nightmare" will end soon and I'll come home. Too bad the war isn't going to end before I leave, but we Americans have still a long struggle ahead, during miracles.

How is the garden coming? Soon you'll be going to Steve's graduation. He wrote me a real nice letter.

I'll go now so as ever thanks for the many prayers & letters.

Your loving son,
Wally

3D MARINE DIVISION (REIN), FMF, VIETNAM.

May 28,

Dear Diane,

I am just lying here "rotting away" in the hot sun so I'll try to occupy myself by writing you. We have a shelter but the sun beats though. When I can't find anything to do I take out my wallet and look at your pictures and wish I could see and touch you in person. Days drag by as I get closer but really, time to take, it just works on your mind more than ever. Diane! all kinds of thoughts go through one's mind over here. I can better explain myself when I come home. We'll have plenty of things to talk about and it will be a *very* fullfilling time in my life. I find myself thinking of you and home while on a small mission and its quite a fight to get my mind on my job. Don't worry though, I do manage to "keep on my toes" just like always. Tonight our squad will have the ambush!

Figure 11: Letter from Walter to Diane Weston, 28 May 1967.

(2)

Many times it feels I've been over here for a lifetime living with the sounds and dangers of war, but I remember that once I had life great and now I am sort of paying for what I had easy in the states. Believe me, there is no place in the vast world like the U.S.A.. I am not feeling sorry for myself, I am just telling you, someone I am "close" to, how it is over in the Nam. I'll tell you a lot more in about ten weeks.

By the way; are you still planning on going to California this summer?? Probably, if you and Jackie get a job you won't be able to go, right? It takes a lot of money to go that far. I'll probably never be able to take you to a place like California but we sure can have a wonderful time around the beatiful mountains rivers, lakes and valleys of Pennsylvania. Are you going to have to buy another car? Suddenly; How does my car run any more? Mom told me you drove it to school once. I am glad you could do that,

(3)

3D MARINE DIVISION (REIN), FMF, VIETNAM.

after all, Jackie drove it already.

Boy! My brother will be home before you receive this letter. You'll get to talk to him most likely. As you know Steve and I are very close, and I can't wait to see him also. I guess Stan is quiting the Seminary this year. He's talking about coming in the Marines if he does. What can I say?! Its no glorious picnic, that for sure!

I am sure you'll do okay getting a job Diane. You might get turned down a couple of times, thats how it happens in Williamsport. Remember me?; I looked all summer and finally started to work in September. You have a good background in business courses at South Side and from what I hear South Side girls get jobs okay. You'll be working long before I drive or score. I'll pray for you as always.

Again, thanks for the pictures and remember I love and miss more than ever.

My Love to you,
Wally

P.S. → over

May 29

Hello! Honey,
I broke the letter out of the envelope because I received a letter from you, I'am back in Phu Bai; and to send those pictures.

I'am not sure if that's all of them but that's all I have. Doesn't seem like long ago we took them, over 13½ months.

Diane!, --- I'am going North!! Yes! By the time you get this I'll be about 10 miles south of the D.M.Z., at a camp called Khe Sanh. Not sure what we'll do up there but the 1st week of July I'll be getting out of a combat zone & boarding Ships. Keep praying dear one and I'll see you soon, Gods Will be done!

You mean a lot to me
Diane

I Love you,
Wally

3D MARINE DIVISION (REIN), FMF, VIETNAM.

June 22nd

Dear Mom & Dad,

Well! Time is going by but I am still waiting, hoping and praying!

Our unit is maning the outer perimiter of Khe Sanh while two companies are in the mountains. I hope they don't hit Nothing!! Another thing! My orders are in! I don't have them on me but my plt. Seargent gave me the word my next duty Station is Quanico, Virginia. Straight word, I am leary still, even though most likely we were told we won't have to go to the field anymore. I am counting on a few ambushes yet! It is a "step in the right direction" though, right? I talked to Father Bide and he said three ships are leaving! One the 3rd, 16th, & 28th. No later than the 16th Mom & Dad, because 2/26 will be on the last one. 1/26 came over three weeks before them. So much for all this scoop! I told you everything I know, maybe it will help relieve you all! Very soon I'll be taking a plane to Da Nang and a happy guy will

Figure 12: Letter from Walter to his family, 22 June 1967.

board a ship for Okinawa & the States. Everything back home okay? I sure hope so! I wrote just about everyone my last letter so please tell everyone I probably won't write again 'till I see them.

I'll end this letter in better spirits so please keep praying and the Stein be home soon.

Your loving son,
Walby

3D MARINE DIVISION (REIN), F . ... TNAM.

June 23,

My Dear Diane,

I haven't written you for awhile but really haven't had the time. We came in off a operation in the mountains just a few days ago.

Right now our unit is manning the outer perimeter of Khe Sanh. We're supposed to be here a couple of weeks. Another thing! My orders for stateside duty are in but I don't have them on me yet. My next duty station will be Quantico, Virginia. Really, I am not out of here yet so it didn't excite me that much. Two ships are leaving, one the 3rd & one the 15th of July! I think I'll be on the one the 15th. This means a very maximum of 21 days left in Nam. We were told that we might never go to the field again but I am leary of that. These fools have a lot of guys who are going home with me out in the jungles now. Tomorrow night I'll probably get an ambush so you know I'll be sweating

Figure 13: Letter from Walter to Diane Weston, 23 June 1967.

the next few days. I am praying I never have to go on another operation! I am so close now I wish I was in the far rear but they aren't going to leave us go until about 5 days before the ship leaves. So much for all this.

How is your job coming? Is the work trying or better than your job you once had? Are you getting a car? It won't be long but time is dragging worse than ever. I am in suspense wondering what will happen the next few days etc.

Well! Please write me soon Diane! Did you get that film yet? I'll bet some of the pictures are wild, huh? I've lost a lot of weight and look older I guess.

Keep praying, Okay!
Love Ya,
Wally

June 25th

Dear Mom & Dad & Family,

Just some more words home. I try to write every day while I am back near the perimeter.

Well: The summer must be rolling along back home! Everything about normal? My dream is getting closer every day. Time has went by fast since I was transferred in April but now it seems to be dragging.

Situation report! - all us guys that came over with 1/26 are still in the "field". 1/26 is short of men and these guys in 3/26 are waiting for replacements just like 1/26. Word is they will start to come in around the end of June. a maximum of 13 days & a wakeup.

Figure 14: Letter from Walter to his family, 25 June 1967.

should be boarding a plane for
Da Nang, to board the ship the 15th. Its
quite definite and I am praying.
What more can I say?!: Makes
us guys sick to see guys back in
the rear "skatting", when were two
weeks from getting out of here. Oh! Well!
Being "short" is hell also!

Can't think of much more so
I'll write soon again.

Your loving son
& brother,
Wally

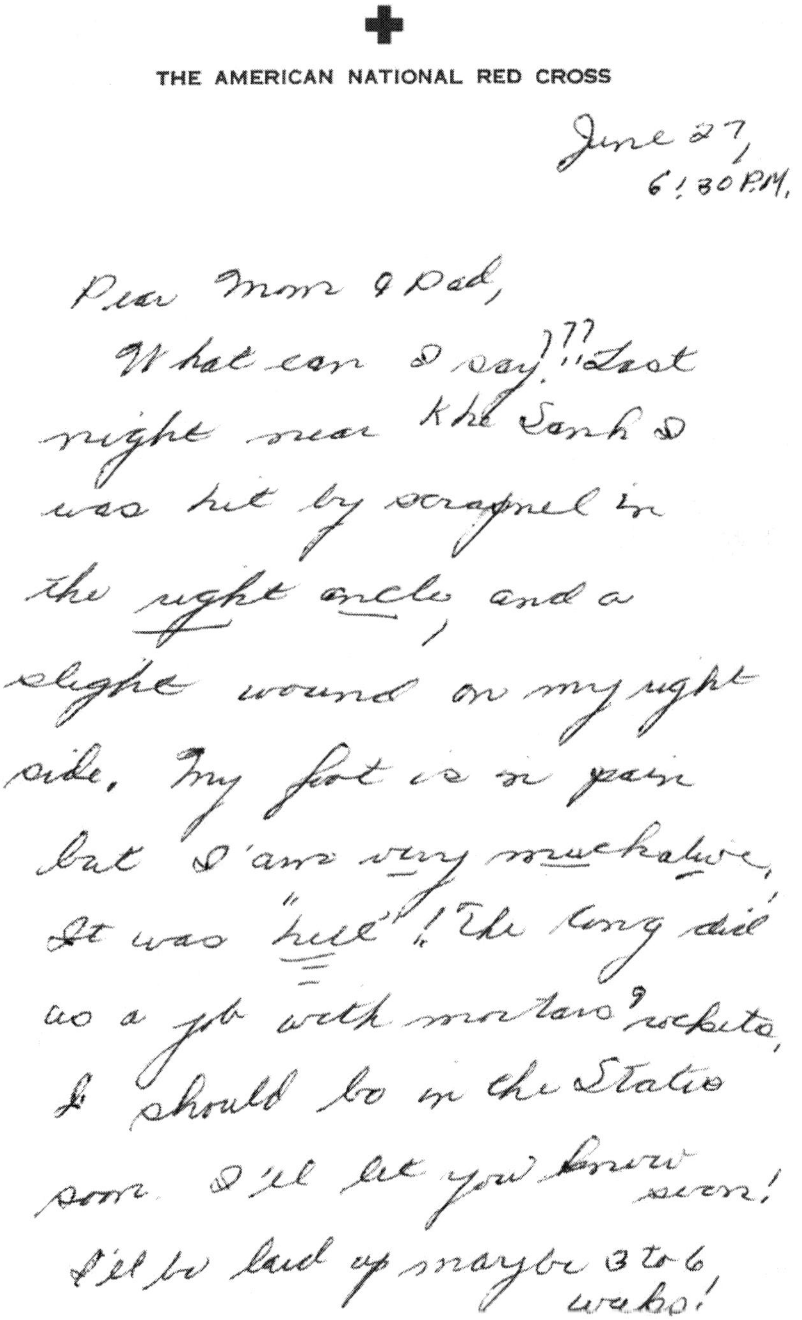

✚

THE AMERICAN NATIONAL RED CROSS

June 27,
6:30 P.M.

Dear Mom & Dad,
What can I say!!! Last night near Khe Sanh I was hit by shrapnel in the right ankle, and a slight wound on my right side. My foot is in pain but I am very much alive. It was "hell"! The long dit as a job with mortars & rockets. I should be in the States soon. I'll let you know soon!
I'll be laid up maybe 3 to 6 weeks!

Figure 15: Letter from Walter to his family, 27 June 1967.

I'll be glad when the pain goes away; I knew I was pushing my luck.

I told the Marine Corp Not to contact my next of kin. My decision so please understand.

I'll end so remember I'm a lucky guy, no loss of limbs etc. just pain.

I love you all,
gp ally.

P.S. It must all be Gods will Everything turned out like I said.

June 28th.

Dear Mom & Dad,

This may be my last letter from the Nam. Yes! I'am in D∧N ang waiting for a jet Stateside, I'am under good care so try not to worry. I hope my letter I sent yesterday got home, If not I'll repeat I was wounded by scrapnel in right ankle and right side of my chest, a Navy Doctor took pieces out of my ankle but <u>NO</u> broken bones. Probable be a couple of weeks before I can walk but I'am <u>very</u> <u>lucky</u> as I said before. "Hell" was erupting up

Figure 16: Walter to his family, 28 June 1967, Da Nang Hospital.

at Khe Sanh after I left and today also.

Please stay "cool" at home and I'll see all of you soon.

I'll go to Philly Naval Hospital!

Your loving son,
Wally

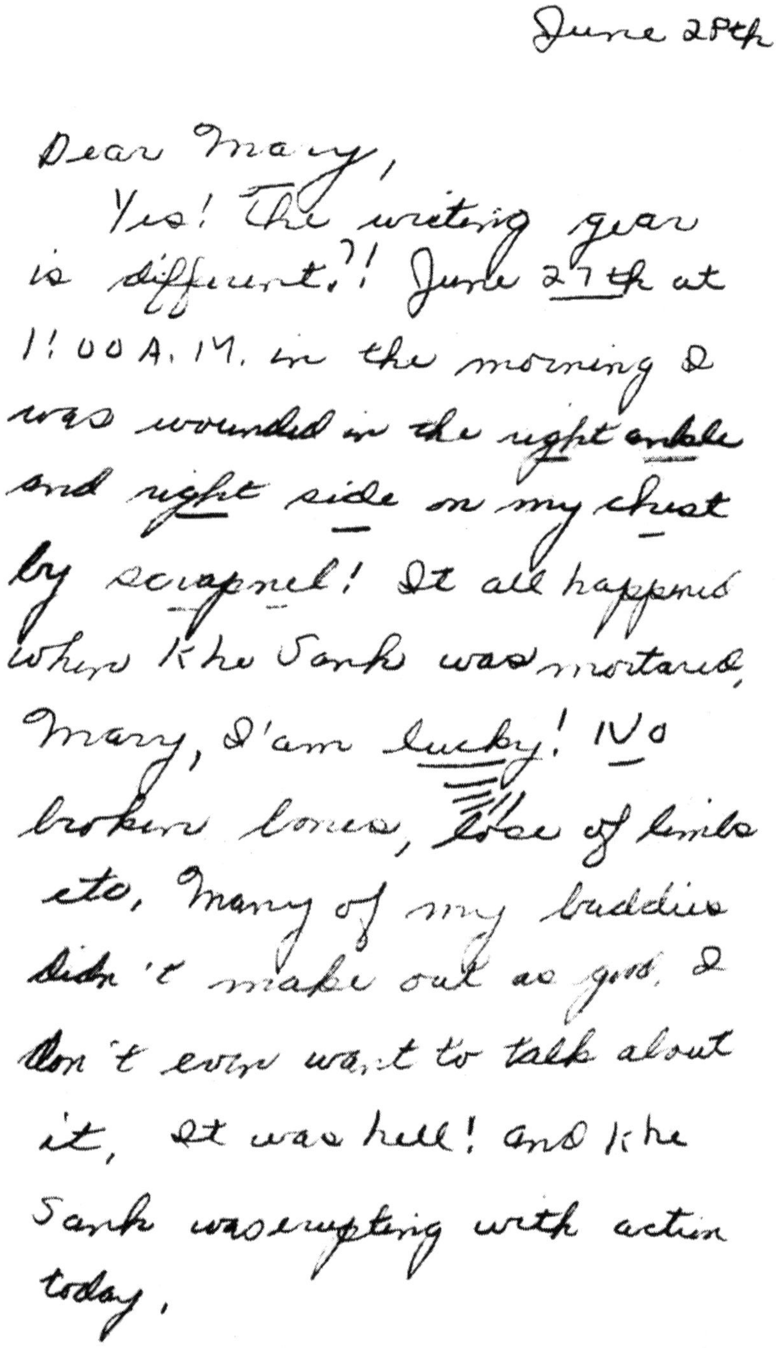

June 28th

Dear Mary,
    Yes! The writing gear
is different.!! June 27th at
11:00 A. M. in the morning I
was wounded in the right ankle
and right side on my chest
by scrapnel! It all happened
when Khe Sanh was mortared,
Mary, I'am lucky! No
broken bones, loss of limbs
etc, Many of my buddies
didn't make out as good, I
don't even want to talk about
it, It was hell! and Khe
Sanh was erupting with action
today,

Figure 17: Walter to his sister Mary, 28 June 1967, Da Nang Hospital.

I am at DA Nang in a decent hospital waiting to be sent stateside, maybe tomorrow morning. What else can I say. I won't be able to walk on my foot for a few weeks to come but God's will be done.

Oh! Yes! The 1st medivac chopper I got on crashed in the jungle at 1:30 in the morning. Yes! All this in one night plus more. Wounded and all we walked through the jungle 500 meters to our original landing zone. So much for all this. See you very soon!

Love, Wally

P.S. Mom already let your know what (it)

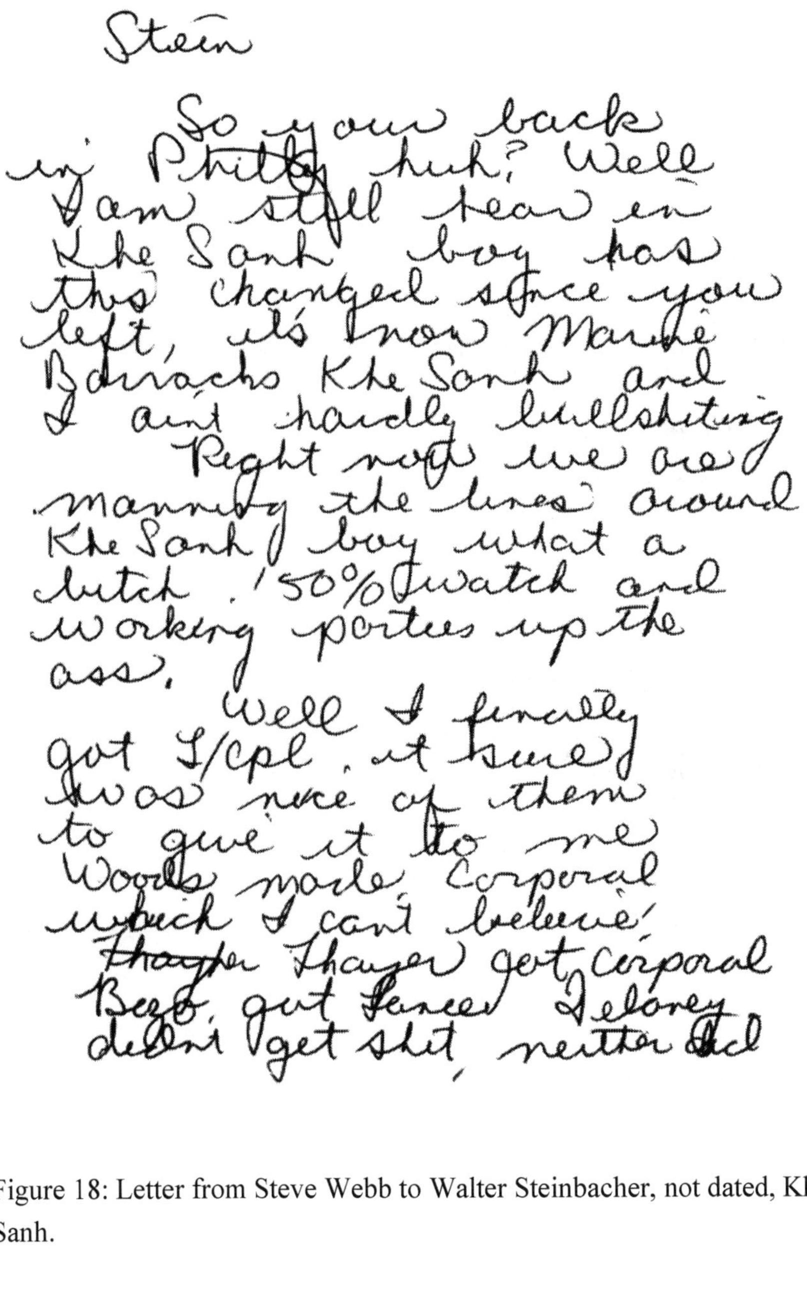

Stein

So your back in Philly huh? Well I am still hear en Khe Sanh boy has this changed since you left, it's now Marine Barracks Khe Sanh and I aint hardly bullshitting

Right now we are manning the lines around Khe Sanh boy what a bitch. 50% watch and working parties up the ass.

Well I finally got S/cpl. at least it was nice of them to give it to me Woods made Corporal which I can't believe, Thayer Thayer got Corporal Bezo got Lance Delorey didn't get shit, neither did

Figure 18: Letter from Steve Webb to Walter Steinbacher, not dated, Khe Sanh.

Vasquez, Terrell got Lance
and all kinds of good
shit. Man I tell you
Wally I can hardly
wait to get out of this
hole. Well take care
of yourself Wally and
get the hell out of that
hospital.

Steve,

3D MARINE DIVISION, FMF, VIETNAM.

1 Sept. 67.

future Ex Marine

I received your letter yesterday + all the boys say hi or at least whats left of us.

I don't know if you've heard but the day after you were hit we took hill 689. Here's who was killed — Lt. Allen, S Sgt. Hamilton, DeCeases, Mullard, David, Walker, Freddy Johnson, Gardiner, Gaddis and a few others I forgot, many were wounded. Out of 2nd sqd. Cullen, me. Nabinger + Oscar were left. O'Brien was wounded but he's back working in the rear.

It was a bad day + lucky you weren't around. Them ass holes put Me + Musgrave up for Silver Stars + Bristol + Lindsay up for Bronze stars! I got a Purple Heart for a small leg wound.

Happy to hear you a fine walking. We threw one hell of a party for Rioux + Bristol when they went home.

I went to Hawaii on R & R + I flew home + spent 4½ days there, I brought back all the booze for the party.

Figure 19: Letter from PFC Lommer to Walter Steinbacher, 1 September 1967.

3D MARINE DIVISION, FMF, VIETNAM.

We got all kinds of new replacements. They are all boots. 3/26 rotates at the end of Sept. 18 more days and they get out of the field.

We are in the same area! We built bunkers and should be here at Khe Sanh for the Monsoon. K & L Co. went to the DMZ to assist the 9th marines.

There hasn't been any action here lately so we ain't to worried.

Sorry I have to end but today we are security for engineers building a road. It was good to here from you write again

Your Automatic rifleman
Lommes

3D MARINE DIVISION (REIN), FMF, VIETNAM.

2 Sept. 67

Dear Stein,

Well I guess I had better tell you now. I am in the first platoon now. And would you believe I am a squad leader now.

In class case you don't know second platoon was wiped-out by rockets and mortors one night. Mr. Charles has given up on 60 mm.'s He is useing 120mm and 82mm mortors now.

Steve is in second platoon now an I don't see to much of him anymore.

Hell, everyone is either dead, wound or gone home an all that is left here is a mess of boots. Last night my squad got lost on an ambush, a platoon ambush the people we got can't

Figure 20: Letter from Cpl. John W. "Spenc" Spencer to Walter Steinbacher, 2 September 1967.

3D MARINE DIVISION (REIN), FMF, VIETNAM.

3 Sept. 67

even play follow the leader they are so dumb.

Oh, well enough for that, I am glad to hear you are alright now. An I am sorry to hear about your girl but don't feel bad. I think mine is already married to somother guy.

Well I guess I had better close for now

Take Care & Good Luck
Spenc.

27 Sept 1967
Wednesday

Dear Walter,

It was real good to hear from you and to know you're in good health now. Yes I knew Marine Barracks is good duty, I've spent a little time in them myself.

I too was coresponding with "Scott" and Tommes until scott got killed earlier this month, Tommes hasn't answered since I last wrote I wonder if anything has happened to him.

I have received a letter from Schaff recently and he told me about a few of the fellows getting hit. Carr Policius, Lindsay, and a few others got killed th 7th of Sept I wish I could go back and help them walter They were the best men

Figure 21: Letter from Sgt. Jim Bailey to Walter Steinbacher, 27 September 1967, US Naval Hospital.

-2-

I have ever worked with. I'm
trying to keep up with them
as much as possible but its
sort of hard to do. Have
you heard from Sgt Khondust?
I was hoping to but I haven't.
    Walter if you happen to
get orders to camp Lejeune
drop by Ward #9 at the Hospital
and see me I'm trying to
contact most of the guys that
are coming back to here so
we can get them all together
and have sort of a party.
    I'm out of bed in a
wheel chair now, I got out of
traction about 2 weeks ago. I
still can't use my leg but
its getting better all the time
I hope to get on crutches before
long so I can go home, I'm
so close yet still far away.

-3-

As you know I'm suppose
to get out of the corps the
20th of Oct. but Doc said I'd
be extended a few months. I
think he'll let me go around
the 1st of the year, hope so
anyway.

If you hear any news about
the fellows let me know. I have
all their home addresses if you
want any. just say so.

Well Walter I wish you
the very best of luck and
success. Hope to see you
again before to long. May
god richly bless you.

Jim Bailey

My address

Sgt Bailey J.D.
Ward #9 US Naval Hospital
Camp Lejeun N.C 28542

11 Nov. 67

Dear Stein,

Well it's the day after the
Marine Corps birthday and everything
is all messed up around here.

We are up on 861 now
and charlie company and the
rest of the companies really
messed up this hill.

Old charlie is on the move
again and we are getting
ready to take 918 pretty soon, I
guess I am going to have to
walk up that damn hill
before I leave here.

Well, I am down to only
38 days left in the Nam or I am
to short to walk up 918
now.

I have to tell you some-
thing decent. Well, we got all
these boots in now and
they shit canned me as a
fire team for some boot which
just made cpl. and got just
got over here a month ago.

Figure 22: Letter from Cpl. John W. "Spenc" Spencer to Walter
Steinbacher, 11 November 1967, Hill 861.

② 11 Nov. 67

This guy is so mixed and screwed up he can't even controll with use to be my mix. They still take orders from me.

I don't really care except they made me a rifleman in my own fire-team. This guy is even junior to me.

I guess this A-company is still as paued up as it was when you left.

The reason I was slit canned is that I don't know what I am doing in the field.

There is only two of us in the squad that have ben shot at. The other guy is a P.F.C. and he has ben in a one fire fight, I don't and is always talking about being shot at. Boy, I don't know what this company is coming to.

Well I guess I have better close for now

Your Buddy
Spene.

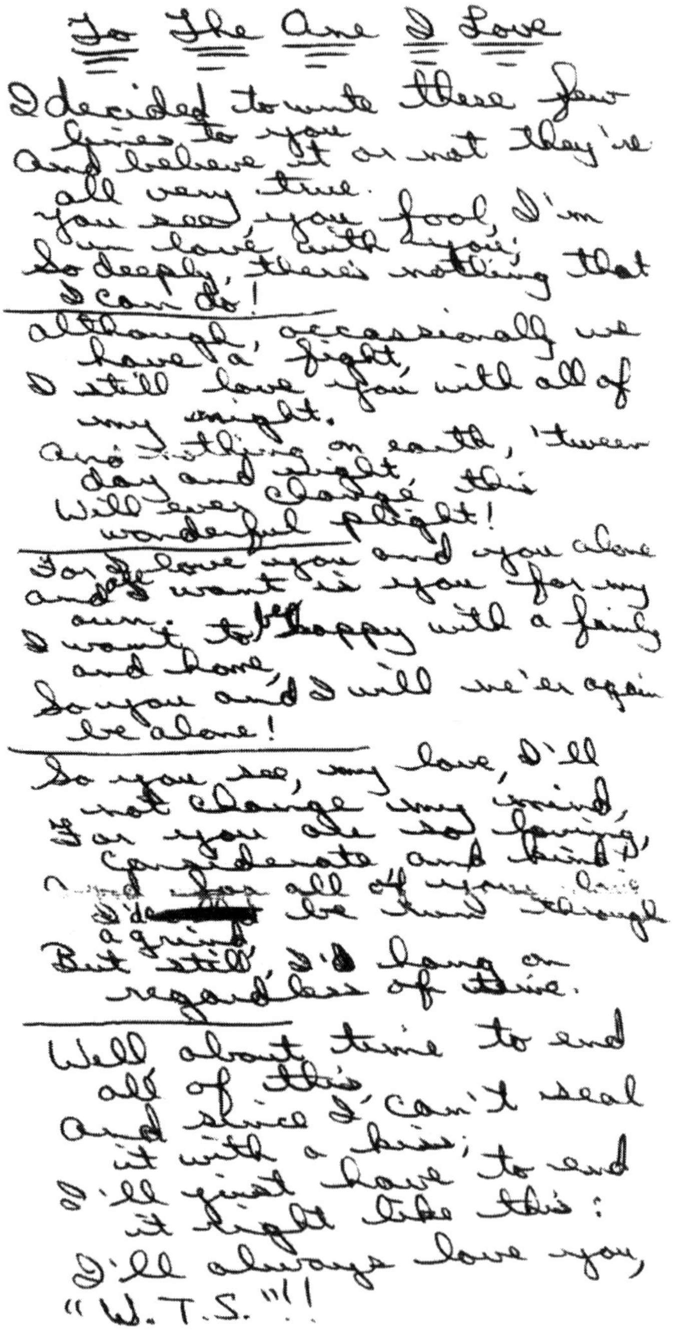

Figure 23: Love poem from Diane Weston to Walter Steinbacher.

Acknowledgements

MY LOVED ONES have supported me throughout this long journey. First and foremost, thank you to my soul-mate who watched me retire to the kitchen table countless times since late 2008. She also was my expert spell-checker. Thank you to my daughters who offered me encouragement and assistance by checking some of my chapters in the second manuscript. When I started to write the first version, I received the gift of a notebook at Christmas that I have carried with me ever since.

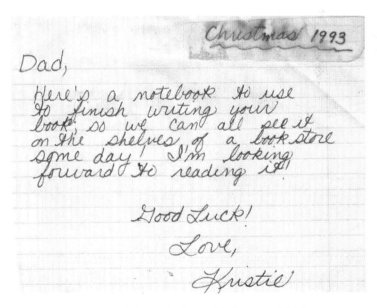

Notebook inscription, Christmas 1993

Likewise, my siblings—Mary, Bernadette, Theresa, Pauline, and Steve—urged me on to the finish line. I simply could not have completed this project without my cousin, Jackie Bland, who so brilliantly spent countless hours keyboarding and formatting my somewhat complicated manuscript into a digital document for publication.

Wally, Bernadette, Theresa, Mary, Steve and Pauline

I also owe a debt of gratitude for the encouragement of local authors. Alivia Tagliaferri inspired me to finish this memoir by her empathy for war veterans and their struggles to survive afterwards, as illustrated in her documentary films and incredible novel, *Beyond the Wall: The Journey Home*. A special thanks to Steve Hunter, author of *Sgt. Libby: 100 Years of Stories* and *From the Command Car: Untold Stories of the 628th Tank Destroyer*

Battalion, who gave me advice on moving forward with my manuscript.

Although I had a vision for the book, I needed help to bring that vision to life. The third-generation owner of Hoyer's Photo, Rob Colley, and his talented assistant laid out the back cover and scanned photos and letters I wrote from Vietnam. It was a joy to get local assistance from my old friend. And a treasured loved one—my daughter, Jodi Steinbacher Myrdal—skillfully created the front cover.

Walter, surrounded by his family

Help sometimes comes from the places you least expect it, like from, Chris Knipe, a visiting physical therapist working with Diane. When I told Chris I was seeking someone to edit and guide me through the final printing of the book, he, with the speed of light, gave me phone numbers, including one to a history professor, Dr. Sarah Silkey, who taught a course on the Vietnam War at his alma mater, Lycoming College. Less than a week after our first meeting, she found yet one more angel, Sarah Bain, a senior at Lycoming who volunteered to edit my manuscript on top of her heavy college work load! Then Dr. Silkey walked me through the difficult process of sending the final manuscript to the printer.

Words cannot describe my debt owed to all the *angels* mentioned in the acknowledgments!

References

The following resources were helpful with terminology and spelling of words that I had not used in many years. *Where We Were in Vietnam* contains maps, base camps, firebases, and a chronology of the war from 1945-1975 covering both the French and American involvement and illustrating the massive American presence. The Virtual Vietnam Archive at Texas Tech University provides access to a variety of US Marine Corps records as well as detailed maps from the Army Map Service. Battalion commanders submitted monthly Command Chronology reports, detailing everything from weather conditions and supply logistics to engagement with enemy forces and efforts to cultivate positive relations with the local population.

Combat Area Casualties Current File, 6/8/1956-1/21/1998, Record Group 330, National Archives and Records Administration.

Command Chronology, 1st Battalion 26th Marines, August 1966-April 1967, and 3rd Battalion 26th Marines, April 1967-June 1967. US Marine Corps History Division Vietnam War Documents Collection. The Vietnam Center and Archive, Texas Tech University, https://www.vietnam.ttu.edu/virtualarchive/.

Delta Company History Project. http://www.khesanhvets.org/.

Hoffman, Jon T. *USMC: A Complete History.* Fairfield, CT: Hugh Lauter Levin Associates, 2002.

Kelley, Michael P. *Where We Were in Vietnam: A Comprehensive Guide to the Firebases, Military Installations, and Naval Vessels of the Vietnam War.* Central Point, OR: Hellgate Press, 2002.

Glossary

AK-47: The standard assault rifle, developed by the Soviet Union and used by the North Vietnamese and Viet Cong.

Amtrac: Amphibious armed vehicle used to transport troops and supplies, armed with a 30-caliber machine gun.

ARVN: Army of the Republic of South Vietnam.

Bush: An infantry term for the field or the 'boonies.'

C-4: Plastic explosive; a white clay-like material.

C-141 Starlifter: Four-engine plane with a top speed of 570 kilometers per hour.

CH-34: Main work-horse helicopter used by the military. Looked like a giant grasshopper.

CH-47 Chinook: American twin-engine, tandem rotor heavy-lift helicopter. Could carry 30 fully equipped troops. Often carried external loads, artillery and supplies.

CH-53 Sea Stallion: A heavy-lift helicopter introduced in Vietnam in1967 with two engines, a six-bladed main rotor, and a four-bladed tail rotor. Developed as a transport helicopter and an assault helicopter.

Clutch belt: Cartridge belt worn by the Marines.

Combined Action Platoon (CAP): A program started by Marines in Vietnam in which troops would work with local Vietnamese militia to monitor the Viet Cong.

County Fair: Another program installed by Marines to establish trust with the villagers in which no one was permitted to enter or leave the village and residents were issued identification cards.

C-Rats/C-Rations: Contained canned and precooked meal items, generally 1 meat item, 1 canned fruit, bread or dessert (pound cake, pecan or fruit cake, etc.) Could be eaten hot or cold but were better heated. A B-unit accessory packet contained cigarettes, matches, chewing gum, toilet paper, coffee, cream, sugar and salt, and one P-38 can opener.

Dinks: Derogatory term for any Vietnamese people.

DMZ: Demilitarized zone that created a border between the Democratic Republic of Vietnam (North Vietnam) and the Republic of Vietnam (South Vietnam).

F-4 (Phantom): Fast fighter/bomber, widely used in both ground support and bombing role, with a top speed of 1,500 kilometers an hour.

FNG (Fucking New Guy): generally derisive U.S. slang denoting newly arrived replacement personnel, who were considered bad luck omens.

Get Dinged: Slang used for anyone who was shot dead.

Gook: Slang for the NVA or Viet Cong or any Vietnamese in general. While often derisive in use, we used such slang words to simply talk about the enemy.

Head: A bathroom.

Howitzer: A 105 mm standard artillery piece used by troops needing fire support.

It Don't Mean Nothin' (or any variation of that expression): It was a term used as a coping mechanism. It actually meant "it does mean something," but the troops used the expression to suppress their true feelings after witnessing a horrific event, a death, or injury to one of their fellow Marines.

Klick: A kilometer. 1.609 kilometers = 1 mile.

LST (Landing Ship, Tank): A ship designed to carry vehicles, cargo, and troops directly on shore for amphibious assaults.

M-48 Patton Tank: U.S. heavy tank (104,000 lbs, top speed of 30 mph) armed with 90 mm cannon, 7.62 mm and .50 caliber machine guns.

M-60 Machine Gun: 7.62 mm, air-cooled, belt-fed, crew-served machine gun capable of 100 rounds per minute effective rate of fire, and sustained rate of approximately 600 rounds per minute.

M-79: Breech-loaded single-shot 44 mm grenade launcher. Looked like a short sawed-off shotgun.

Mike: Radio operator lingo or code for the word 'minute.' Created by simply substituting military phonetic alphabet for first letter of whatever word it represented. As such, hotel replaced 'hour,' sierra replaced 'second' (or south), and so on.

NVA: North Vietnamese Army

Roger: Radio communication code meaning 'received and understood.'

Seabee: Nickname for U.S. Naval construction units—mobile construction battalions.

Shaking and Baking: Slang description of M-60 machine gunner firing at full capacity.

SKS: Standard issue Soviet 5-shot semi-automatic rifle. Had built-in magazine and some also had built-in folding bayonets (Russian and Chinese manufacture).

Slop chute: Any facility where beer was served.

Sparrow Hawk: An operational name given to a company for rapid reaction (shock troops).

VC: Short for Viet Cong.

Viet Cong: Derisive nickname originally given to the southern Communist element of NLF (officially The National Liberation Front).

'World': The United States.